The Riding Experience & Beyond

PERSONAL DEVELOPMENT FOR RIDERS

Authors:

Jill K. Hassler Scoop
and Kathy Kelly Ph.D.

With Linda Benedik, Tanya Boyd, Elizabeth N. Clarke,
Sophie Pirie Clifton, Janice Dulak, Cathy Frederickson,
Beth Glosten M.D., Stephan Keisewetter,
and Russell H. Scoop

Illustrators:

Susan Carlson and Franklin White

Editors:

Robin Kolb, Beth Parker, and Russell H. Scoop

2002
GOALS UNLIMITED PRESS • HUSON, MONTANA

Front Cover Art by Susan Carlson

Art by Susan Carlson: Pages 1, 25, 93, 99, 100,
109, 151, 207, 223, 224, 225, 249, 250, 251, 266

Art by Franklin White: Pages 10, 19, 65, 69, 71,
110, 118, 122, 125, 130, 172, 345, 349, 351

Published By:
Goals Unlimited Press
c/o Equestrian Education Systems
25155 Huson Road
Huson, Montana 59846

PRINTED IN THE UNITED STATES OF AMERICA

Library of Congress Cataloging-in-Publication Data

Hassler-Scoop, Jill K., 1944-
   The riding experience & beyond : personal development for riders /
authors, Jill K. Hassler Scoop and Kathy Kelly Ph.D. with Linda
Benedik . . . [et al.] ; illustrators: Susan Carlson and Franklin White ;
editors: Robin Kolb . . . [et al.].
      p. cm.
Includes bibliographical references and index.
   ISBN 0-9632562-8-9 (pbk. : alk. paper)
   1. Horsemanship. I. Title: Riding experience and beyond. II. Kelly,
Kathy, 1959- III. Benedik, Linda. IV. Kolb, Robin. V. Title.
   SF309 .H38 2002
   798.2'3—dc21
                                                          2002013817

We dedicate this book to
the horses and riders we so love.

We thank:

The horses and riders who
have taught us so much.

Those who have shared their experience
in clinics, books and articles.

The equestrians who contributed to this
unique collection of information.

And to our students, friends and families
for their patience and support.

Contents

Introduction

The Theme of This Book
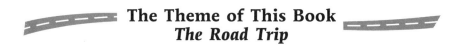
The Road Trip

Becoming an accomplished equestrian is like taking a long road trip. It is made up of long stretches where the learning is easy and progress is steady, steep hills where the going gets harder and progress is slower, and down hills where you can coast, feeling the exhilaration of accomplishment! As with all road trips, no two journeys through the riding experience are alike. Riders have their own road to choose, with all of the plateaus, highs, lows, and roadblocks that accompany such an endeavor. The process of discovery is an exciting one, and there is no set amount of time for this learning to take place. This is *your* road trip, and the road can be as long or short as is realistic given your time, talent, and resources. However, the horse—being your partner in this process—has a say about the speed in which you learn! Learning to ride, and ride well, is a lifelong challenge, and we only hope that the information contained in this book helps you avoid some of the common pitfalls along the way as well as appreciate the many side trips available to you that can deepen your knowledge and enjoyment of the learning process. Each book section is briefly described below.

We begin our journey with **Discovery Insights,** which provides an important starting point for any learning journey. This section answers many of your "why" questions. Once we have laid the discovery foundation, **Personal Insights** invites you to take a look at yourself as the driver in control of the learning process. We have included many important topics related to learning, including motivation, awareness, personality and learning styles, and human biomechanics, plus others. While some of these chapters may seem "out of the ordinary" in a riding book (they are), most riders find this information, which is geared specifically towards equestrians, to be a very valuable part of their riding journey. Self-discovery is at the heart of "knowing thyself" as the great riding masters and other masters refer to it. Socrates said it first.

Your horse is your most valued teacher, so **Horse Insights** provides a few basics about the horse's mind and biomechanics that we feel every rider needs to know. This information alone can change much about how you approach your partner as you travel the road together.

Fact Insights includes important information about the realities of rider fitness, riders' rights and responsibilities as a consumer, and the important distinctions between amateur and professional riders. Equestrians from all disciplines will benefit from knowing this information.

In **Learning Insights,** we provide our readers with information that allows them to attain what many riders consider to be the "holy grail of riding"—learning how to feel. Here you will learn about the link between such diverse abilities as awareness, training framework, goal setting, communication skills, mental practice, and the rider's ability to feel.

The main focus of our book is the section on **Technical Insights.** Here we introduce you to a systematic, logical progression through the "learning to ride" process. Based upon the classical German system of riding education, our American System of Education deals specifically with the unique situations and challenges many riders face in the United States when trying to learn how to ride well. Designed for riders, this book is the companion guide to our previous book, *Equestrian Education,* a thorough "how to teach" textbook for helping instructors take their students through the classical system. This section is intended to serve as a guideline for you, the rider, as you progress in your training program. It reveals the logical progression through the five stages of learning, and helps you identify the reasons behind each specific set of instructions.

 This book is not designed to be a replacement for regular, quality riding instruction. What it is designed to do is help you better understand and evaluate your current training program.

Last but not least is **Supplementary Learning Insights**, which includes an overview of a few of the more popular complimentary training exercises that have been found to improve riding. Riders and trainers today are experimenting with and using concepts from the Eastern traditions, such as yoga, Pilates, T'ai Chi, and the more common methods of massage and relaxation.

Threaded throughout the book are **Tales From the Trip,** stories of the experiences of a variety of riders from their journey and Travel Tips, important points to keep in mind during *your* journey.

So take this book and read what you want, take away what you will, and above all, enjoy. Being a "life-long learner" is one of life's greatest gifts, and, having picked this book up you are already on that path. Thank you for allowing us to share our experiences with you.

 The *Tales From the Trip* are based on true student experiences but the names of the students and instructors have been changed to protect their privacy.

The Riding Experience and Beyond

Philosophy

Equestrians the world over spend a lifetime trying to learn how to dance with their equine partners. Yet, how is this accomplished? Two words stand out in response: *awareness* and *feel*. Awareness refers to that special quality of being in the prsent. The good news is that awareness is a skill that riders can learn and develop just like the regular riding skills that most instructors and books teach. However, awareness is a difficult skill to learn for many riders. It cannot be controlled or forced; it must be allowed. As riders, we can open the door for awareness of the many different aspects of riding and life, and be alert to its appearance. Sometimes, the harder we look, the more elusive it is; but, other times when we are just about to give up, we realize that it has slipped in unnoticed.

Being aware of all of the aspects that go into riding helps you learn another elusive but critical factor in the art of riding, the quality of *feel*. It is through learning to feel that you develop the proper muscle memory to sit correctly on a horse so that someday you can become one with your partner. The mind plays a large role in helping the body create muscle memory and learn to feel. Gifted riders have this awareness and feel naturally. A well-qualified riding instructor, and an appropriate school horse, will allow you the ability to develop the proper muscle memory that leads to a good sense of feel. Muscle memory takes time and patience to develop, and there are no short-cuts to the end goal of becoming a sensitive and feeling rider.

The Riding Experience and Beyond takes you on a personal de-velopment journey based on awareness and feel. We believe all riders deserve the unbridled sense of joy and satisfaction that comes from tuning in to our equine friends, and learning how to listen to what they are telling us. Being able to communicate with the horse on such a level not only serves you well in your riding education and career, but in life as well. It is our goal, as writers, riders, and instructors, to bring to you many of the experiences we have learned as we have made our own unique journeys down the road of equestrian sport. It is our hope that you can learn from us so that your journey can be equally rewarding and successful.

DISCOVERY INSIGHTS

*Discovery is the result of an inquisitive mind
in constant pursuit of information.*

The journey to become an accomplished rider who can enjoy the sport and create a fuller life experience is more rewarding as you pursue personal development. To grow as a person, you must expand your knowledge and work toward a more balanced life.

When you work on personal development you will discover that the process of integration will help you combine new information with existing information, whether within the sport or between the sport and the rest of life. Integration allows you to use what you know about yourself and your horse, and to learn more about both by using the fundamental learning skills. These skills will put the technical knowledge of the stages into action. The better student you are, the more you will get out of your journey. The "right" instructor and training plan plays a major role in the process.

Why Personal Development?—by Jill K. Hassler-Scoop

Why Integration?—by Jill K. Hassler-Scoop

The Characteristics of A Good Student?—by Jill K. Hassler-Scoop

Finding the Right Instruction Plan—by Elizabeth N. Clarke

WHY PERSONAL DEVELOPMENT?
by Jill K. Hassler-Scoop

*Your senses define the edge of consciousness, and because
you are born explorers and questors after the unknown, you
spend a lot of your lives pacing that windswept perimeter.*

–Diane Ackerman,
A Natural History of the Senses

Our senses define a large part of our journey through life. The
more we acknowledge the role of our senses, free them to give us
information, and listen to what they are telling us, the more resources we will have for our equestrian expedition. Whether we
know it or not, we are in constant pursuit of learning. Tools and
knowledge open the doors to balance. The search for balance is a
never-ending process, whether in the horse world or in the rest of
life. Like a half-halt, balance is a word with endless meanings and
combinations. Each of us is unique and has distinctive factors that
influence the development of our personal balance.

Movement towards balance is a process that is influenced by
the stage of life you are in and your environment *(See Chapter—
Life Philosophy—Personal Insights)*. As a horse lover you add the
challenges of balancing your time with horses with your personal
life and of balancing your horses when you ride them, to the regular
challenges of balance in everyday life. You have chosen to interact
with horses for one reason or another (from recreation and pleasure
to competition). Seeking pleasure and satisfaction is part of being
human. One of the many circular truisms of life begins here:
you need to know enough about yourself to know what gives you
pleasure, and whatever gives you pleasure will help you better know
yourself.

The link between personal development and riding is very important for
riders. Feel and muscle memory are
two very difficult skills to acquire. There
are many factors that mask, confuse,
clutter, and interfere with the ability to
feel. Openness to recognizing and accepting as much as possible about who
you are is an important key to freeing your

*Equestrian art, perhaps
more than any other,
is closely related to the
wisdom of life. Many
of the same principles
may be applied as a
line of conduct to follow*
–Alois Podhajsky

You will discover that the more you understand yourself, the more you will get out of riding; and the more you get out of riding, the more you will understand yourself— and the more you will get out of life in general.

body, mind, and spirit, creating the most ideal learning environment.

In riding, we know when we are ready to learn a new skill, and we take the necessary steps to continue the learning process. In life there are also steps that ensure growth. In our lives with horses we take the time to learn new skills with care, but we do not always take the time to nurture our development toward more balance in our everyday lives. In many cases it takes a trauma in life to initiate the necessary look inward. You will discover that the more you understand yourself, the more you will get out of riding; and the more you get out of riding, the more you will understand yourself, and the more you will get out of life in general.

Tales From the Trip

Tina

Tina, a nineteen-year-old college student, discovered the interrelationship between horses and life at a young age. She quit college after her sophomore year to get married. As a young mother and wife, she quickly learned that many of the skills she had developed during her years in Pony Club carried through to her new role in life. Many of the same principles she applied to training young horses worked with the two young children that had become her responsibility. One of the most important principles she often expressed was the role of tough love, very much like a strong half-halt. Since she consistently followed each "half-halt" with forgiveness, the children began to respond to her "half-halts" quickly and with no resistance. Seeing the effects of this one principle of *riding* on other aspects of life inspired her to become aware of other *life* principles, and how they, perhaps, would help improve her riding and teaching.

Anna

Anna began riding at age forty-five. She had always loved horses but never had the time or money to ride. Anna raised five children, two of them disabled. In pursuit of helping her own children develop as fully as possible, Anna invested considerable time in her own growth and development as a person. Anna had a deep love for her children and developed her love and knowledge into a profession in which she helped families facing similar challenges. When Anna started to ride, she realized that she had a clear perception of what she wanted to do with her riding. Her time with the horses recharged her. She loved the immediate feedback she received from the horses. While talking to the other women in her riding class, she realized how lucky she was to be able to feel so much and thus progress quickly. She realized that she had developed this inner balance in order to cope with her disabled children and to work professionally with challenged families.

Cindy

Cindy, twenty-five, was shocked when her instructor asked her, "Why are you riding?" Cindy sat on her horse speechless for at least two minutes before she answered, "I have no idea! No one ever asked me that question before. I have always ridden." Her instructor than asked, "What is your dream related to riding?" This was followed with another pause. Cindy's assignment was to return to her lesson the following week with an answer. She had to write down her riding dream no matter what it was. She also had to write down what she wanted to achieve by the end of the year, eight months in the future. Her third assignment was to look at this list and then decide why she was riding.

When Cindy returned to her next lesson, she had her lists. She told her instructor that this had been a very *big* task for her, and that she realized how interwoven her riding was with her day-to-day life. In order to figure it out, she had to imagine what her life would be like without riding. When she did this she realized that her motivator was her need to be with horses. She asked herself "Why?" Her answer revealed a lot to her: "I love horses, they are in my blood, I need to be with them." Once she understood this, she was able to figure out her dream: "I want to always be with horses and learn as much about them as possible. I want to have the most harmony I can with them, as this gives me energy to deal with the rest of my life." Her instructor now had all he needed to make the most out of their lesson time. This exercise helped Cindy realize the role horses played in her personal development.

WHY INTEGRATION?
by Jill K. Hassler-Scoop

Combining parts to make a whole

Recently a rider said to me, "I really don't understand integration; what do you mean by it?" This is a powerful question. Integration leads to *discovery,* and it is one of life's natural processes. Combining what we know with what we want to learn or are learning, and turning all of that into a useful asset in our banks of knowledge is a constant life process. It is even *fun* if we remain open and do not limit ourselves or put on blinders. Each discovery you make either confirms what you know or gives you information to add to or alter what you already know.

Integration is a process that allows information to be interactive, bringing parts together to create a whole. It is vital to the learning process. The fundamental learning skills—awareness, communication, and goal setting—provide the tools to put the project into action. A curious mind opens the pathways for learning.

Integration can happen as a result of what you learn within an activity, but it also comes from the most unexpected places. Sources of information can include your daily rides, taking part in or watching clinics, reading, and activities of your day-to-day lives outside of the horse world. An inquisitive mind will discover the similarities between life skills and riding skills.

SUGGESTIONS FOR INTEGRATION

Know yourself and your goals

Let your curiosity run free

Listen with an open mind to gather
information from each and every experience

If you have questions, ask them

Evaluate new information related to
what you already know, compare it

Expand your learning process

***Many roads lead to Rome—
choose the road you want to take!***

Tales From the Trip

Mary

Mary had been working on her soft, consistent leg contact for years. One day she came into the arena and announced, "I finally figured something out." "What is that?" I asked. "If I keep my legs softly on Bell's side, she stays quiet." "Cool, what made you put them there?" was my next question. "I read an article in *Dressage Today*, and it made sense, so I tried it." To myself I wondered if I had said this 200 or 500 times! Mary had to hear it from another source so that when the "right" moment came she was able to own the "feel."

Tim

Tim struggled with the same concept. He came to his lesson with his leg correctly placed on Swordfish. I asked, "Wow, your leg looks terrific! What happened?" "I went to the circus with my kids over the weekend, and as I watched, I realized that in order for the performers to do their thing, they had to have independent use of their bodies. I watched the twirlers and high wire performers with great interest. It must have been meant for me, as the riders came in last. I watched as they did their tricks and rode normally, and saw that the horses never changed rhythm and that the riders' legs and bodies were soft, supple, and connected," Tim replied. "Great, Tim, it was fantastic to learn while having fun at the circus! Great job integrating."

Integration allows skills and information to be interactive, filling in gaps and bringing parts together. Using integration broadens your learning base of opportunities. Some people automatically integrate, while others need to make a conscious effort to do so. In all cases integration improves your balance in riding and in life, and gives you more learning opportunities.

Everyday life and the activities you pursue give you opportunities to learn in many areas. It is exciting to make discoveries that expand and develop your solid foundation, and that promote independent thinking and decision-making, resulting in successful horsemen and horsewomen.

THE CHARACTERISTICS OF
A GOOD STUDENT
by Jill K. Hassler-Scoop

*The object of training for the rider is to give him
the physical and mental proficiency to be able to understand
his partner, to execute with him all movements, to be able
to follow them with skill and power, and to be
able to resist them if necessary.*
—Alois Podhajsky

Learning is a discovery process. The more we know about the characteristics of a good student, the more we will reap the benefits of this life long process. As you read *The Riding Experience and Beyond* you will have the opportunity to learn more about these qualities and use them as you wish.

KNOW YOURSELF

It is important to know what you want to do with your riding so that you can make a plan. To make this plan there are many things that you first need to know about yourself. You may discover that in some areas you are very clear, while in other areas you have work to do to fill in the gaps. The more you know about yourself, your interests, your motivators, and your emotional responses, the more success you will experience on this journey toward your long-term riding goals. *(See Chapters—Personal Insights)*

SEEK AND ACCEPT A REALISTIC APPRAISAL

Accept a realistic appraisal of your and your horse's skills. Once you know what you want to do and why, it is important to collect some factual information that will give you a starting point for your journey. It is always good to have several sources of information so that you can compare your self-appraisal, your instructor/trainer's appraisal, and a qualified third party's appraisal. It is also a great idea to get periodic appraisals at regular intervals to maintain a realistic view of where you are in relationship to your destination. Perhaps you accidentally went off route, or perhaps you need a detour to put in something you missed along the way.

SEEK QUALITY TECHNICAL KNOWLEDGE

Seek the technical knowledge needed to attain your goal. There is a lot of information available to you through instructors, clinics,

---

10 Qualities of
a Good Student

1. Know yourself, what you want to do and why
2. Seek and accept a realistic appraisal
3. Seek quality technical knowledge
4. Find a well educated, like minded instructor
5. Commit to a system
6. Practice -give yourself time to practice one skill at a time until committed to muscle memory
7. Define what success means to you
8. Keep a journal
9. Keep an open mind
10. Integrate

---

magazines, books, and the Internet. Be certain to be an educated consumer and sort through the new information. Correct training remains the standard of learning. History has proven that classical training is central to all riding disciplines as the base of a safe seat for riders and comfortable and fair for horses. To gain an understanding about the correct technical knowledge we suggest reading some of the books listed in our suggested reading at the end of this book. All new information must fit into the classically correct system of training and learning. Compare all new information with what you understand to be classically correct, and with your current level of performance. *(See Chapters—Technical Insights)*

FIND QUALIFIED INSTRUCTION

Find an instructor who understands your personality, and your learning and communication styles. Research and investigate until you find an instructor who is classically correct and right for you. *(See Chapter—Finding The Right Instruction Plan—Fact Insights.)*

COMMIT TO A SYSTEM

Submit with commitment and loyalty to the instructor and to his/her system. Once you have found the "right" instructor and instruction program, listen with an open and clear mind. Commit to practice what your instructor tells you. Seek to understand your instructor's system and remain aware that you are staying on the system. Hold your instructor to the system as well. This does not mean simply doing whatever your instructor tells you, no matter what; but it does mean being committed enough to think through what you are told and process it yourself, and ask questions about things that do not seem to fit into the system as you understand it. A good instructor will seek to help students develop a degree of independence within the system, rather than teach them in a way that encourages lifelong dependence upon that certain instructor.

PRACTICE

Give yourself time to practice until the skill is committed to muscle memory. The heart and soul of this book is wrapped around feel and muscle memory. They are the basis of learning to ride. Since you are unable to watch your performance in the mirror all the time, you need to rely on feel to decide what to do, and then do it. Feel is dependent upon muscle memory. You must remember that you can learn only one thing at a time, so it is important to learn it and then practice the *one* skill until you can do it without consciously thinking about it.

DEFINE WHAT SUCCESS MEANS TO *YOU*

Develop a clear understanding of what success will feel like, so that when you have achieved it you will recognize it *(See Chapter— Motivation—Personal Insights)*

KEEP A JOURNAL

Progress is often hard to notice on a day-to-day basis, and sometimes in your busy life you may find it difficult to keep a mental record of what has happened from ride to ride. Journal keeping is a quick and effective way to help you remember each training session with less mental effort. A journal can be a simple account recording what you worked on, the results of the day, and what your plan is for your next training session, or it can be detailed and complex, including what you think, feel, and observe.

A well-kept journal is simple but as detailed as possible regarding points you feel are important. At the beginning of your journal, write down your long-term goal and the steps you need to achieve this goal. As with getting an appraisal, seek support from your instructor to create a plan. The basic outline of your plan with the steps needed to achieve your long-term goal is very good to keep in your journal. Periodically review this section.

The following items are suggested for your journal:
- Date of lesson or riding experience
- Instructor's name, or note that you rode on your own
- Plan/goal for the day
- What the warm-up told you
- Comparison to yesterday's warm-up
- Comparison to end of yesterday's ride
- What you worked on before you began working on your training goal—result of your warm-up information
- What you accomplished at the end of the ride
- What you want to work on tomorrow
- Remember the three main points from this ride to take to your next day's ride
- Document any difficulties or successes and what went into them
- How you *felt* about the ride

You may discover that after keeping a written journal for awhile, you will automatically record the facts and feelings in your mind and thus eliminate the need to maintain a written journal.

KEEP AN OPEN MIND

The more you learn, the more you will realize there is to learn. A learning attitude with an open, curious mind creates the opportunity for a fulfilling journey. When you allow your curiosity to run free, you will discover many opportunities for integration.

INTEGRATE

Integrate new information with trusted experience. When new information is introduced, you must understand its relationship to your goal and how it will help you move from where you are to where you want to be. As an educated consumer you need to examine what is new, evaluate it with an open but critical mind, and then practice what "feels right"

Why do you need a journal?

Journals help you to express your thoughts and feelings.

A journal can serve as a review when you hit a roadblock and discover that you are getting discouraged. A review of your journal will enable you to check your progress and compare it to your current state of progress and state of mind.

The act of writing makes it easier to remember what you experience and learn.

Journaling helps you track your progress towards achieving your goals.

after this process. The results will let you know whether to keep it or discard it.

QUALITIES OF A SUCCESSFUL STUDENT

This list will help you look at your qualities as a student. Rate the following qualities from 1(weak) to 5(strong).

_____ I clearly and specifically identify my goals.

_____ I have a clear understanding of my skills.

_____ I have a clear understanding of my motivation.

_____ I take responsibility for my own learning.

_____ I enter the barn and arena with an uncluttered mind.

_____ I respect my horse and my instructor.

_____ I understand and use integration.

_____ I am open-minded.

_____ I am eager to learn.

_____ I have a desire to expand my communication abilities.

_____ I have a desire to develop keen awareness and observation skills.

_____ I have realistic expectations of each day's ride.

_____ I seek to understand the overall picture: horse, rider, and sport.

_____ I commit to practice.

_____ I seek to learn skills that I can practice productively without an instructor present.

_____ I am eager to continue character development and growth, so I get to know myself better.

FINDING THE RIGHT INSTRUCTION PLAN
by Elizabeth N. Clarke

*Seek an instruction plan that matches your goals
and a realistic assessment of your life situation,
and then stick to it!*

FINDING THE RIGHT INSTRUCTION PLAN FOR YOU AND YOUR HORSE DEPENDS ON MANY, MANY FACTORS.

Among them:

- how dedicated you are to improve and progress in your riding and your horse's training;
- the educational resources available to you either where your horse lives or within a reasonable distance;
- the horse transportation options you have available;
- the horses you have available to you to ride and their physical and mental talents;
- the financial resources you have to devote to improving your riding;
- the time you have to devote to your riding;
- your own self-discipline and willpower; and
- the climate and riding facilities where you live.

THE FIRST STEP TO DESIGNING AN INSTRUCTION PLAN FOR YOU AND YOUR HORSE IS AN HONEST SELF-EVALUATION.

- Where are you now?
- What skills have you mastered already and where do you want to be in one year, two years, four years? What do you and your horse need to master in order to get there?
- Assuming that you have acquired enough skills to safely handle a horse on your own (if not, you need to ride with an instructor present until you reach that point!), are you the kind of person who can take occasional instruction and constructively work on your own to master the things you worked on in your last lesson, or do you need more frequent feedback?
- How aware are you of your own body, and how well can you feel what your horse is doing under you? Are you generally making progress in your riding or frequently frustrated?
- How much can you comfortably commit in terms of time and money without sacrificing other important aspects of your life?

Regardless of where you live and what resources may or may not be at your doorstep, it is important to recognize that you are the person responsible for your progress or lack thereof.

Once you have made an honest assessment of yourself, look around at the options. In the United States instructional resources can vary a good deal depending upon where you live. In some areas if you are looking for a riding instructor you can take your pick from among multiple Olympic medallists. In other areas, there may be nobody for many miles who has ever ridden at the top level of your chosen discipline. It is also important to recognize that the person with the most recognized name may not necessarily be the best instructor for you at the moment. Regardless of where you live and what resources may or may not be at your doorstep, it is important to recognize that you are the person responsible for your progress or lack thereof. While even the best riders depend on good help from someone on the ground who can watch, they did not get to be the best by abdicating responsibility for the quality of their riding to someone else.

I know people who have uprooted their families, changed jobs, and moved literally across the country to ride with a particular trainer. I also know people who have done a remarkable job and made it to the top ranks of their discipline by taking advantage of occasional clinics and enlisting a friend or family member to serve as "eyes on the ground." Both are rare: Most riders fall somewhere in between, trying to strike a balance. On one side are lesson situations where an instructor can help with habits and issues that may be creeping in without your being aware of them, as well as providing exercises and techniques to help you move to the next level. On the other side is the need for "digestion time" to work on your own, figuring out what works best, how much to push, why something isn't working, or how to do it just a little more smoothly. What mix of these is right for you is something only you can determine.

Whatever program you pick and whatever the elements are, make sure they are consistent with each other. Pick a system that seems to be appropriate for your goals and your horse's temperament and stick with it long enough to evaluate whether it is a system that works for you.

Trying something new often brings some frustration and maybe even a little confusion. Some skills take longer to master than others. Overall, however, the program should make logical sense, and you should feel like you are moving toward your goals on a monthly or even weekly basis, even if it is in very small steps. Stop once in awhile to ask yourself whether the things you already know are better than they were three months ago. Can you and your horse do something you were not able to do before? Is your horse happy and relaxed in his work, or becoming increasingly tense or resistant? Forgive the occasional "bad day," but if it seems as though the two of you are having a bad month you should reassess whether the "system" you are trying really works for you and your particular horse.

While many sophisticated riders integrate elements from different training philosophies into a system of their own, this is best done after a fair bit of experience. Inconsistency is very difficult for horses. They thrive on routine. Doing something one way one day, a different way the next, and changing it yet again the next time you ride is more likely to result in confusion and resistance from your horse rather than progress. Listen to what your horse is telling you and make small adjustments as needed, but avoid major changes in method unless what you have been doing is very clearly not working. Within the system you pick get as much education in as many different formats as you can. People learn differently. Some people are visual learners, others learn by hearing, still others are experiential learners. If you know the way you absorb information the best, use that to your advantage. If you are a visual learner, watching someone else do what you want to do before you try it the first time may be a good idea. If you are an experiential learner, doing it yourself with a knowledgeable instructor talking you through the first few times may be more productive. Knowing what works for you, and figuring out what works for your horse, is a big and important step in developing your instruction plan because it enables you to seek instruction that is the most productive for you and your horse. *(See Chapter—Learning Styles—Personal Insights.)*

⬡**TT** All people learn differently

I do not know of any successful riders who do not at least occasionally have someone on the ground watching and providing feedback. If you are one of those individuals who is lucky enough to have the gift of "feel" and are very aware of everything the horse is doing under you and the effect of every aid you give, both intentionally and sometimes unintentionally, you are very lucky indeed. Even if you are, you may develop occasional undesirable habits of which you are unaware. All of you need help from the ground at least occasionally to optimize your riding. Having established that, let's start formulating a riding plan with formal instruction on the ground and finding the format that works for you.

The most common form of training help is regular lessons with an instructor. There are several elements to building the best instructional plan for you, and most of them revolve around the choices made about a regular lesson program. The first thing you have to do is find an instructor with whom you want to work. Remember that the best riders are not always the best teachers. In fact the very best riders ride very much on instinct and feel in a process that is sometimes subconscious if not unconscious. The best teachers are analytical and able to verbalize what is going on. If you are lucky enough to find someone who is an instinctive and feeling rider, but who can also explain how she does what she does, that's great. An important thing to remember is that while not all people who ride well teach riding well, very few people who do not ride well can teach riding well. Start with finding instructors whose riding and horsemanship you would like to emulate. It is worth doing some shopping. It may not be the person with the most ribbons on the wall or the medal around their neck. Look for the person you want to emulate because you love the way their horses go and you like their approach to training. Then watch their students ride to see if they can pass on what they practice. I have watched trainers ride, and admired what they do, only to realize later that their students do not ever seem to progress beyond the lower levels. When I recently moved to a new area I decided to use a different approach. I went to a horse show and watched everyone. I picked out what I thought were the best, most polished riders at various levels and then watched to see who was helping them. Sure enough, several of the best riders at the lower and middle levels were being coached by an upper-level rider I admired. It was a good way to find a good teacher. I had already spotted him as the best rider around. It became apparent that he could also teach, because his students were riding well.

Once you have identified those who ride well and whose students ride well, it is time to pick the instructor whose teaching style best fits you. If you have the luxury of having a list of instructors from whom to choose, watch them each teach. Their teaching styles may vary a great deal. Some instructors "ride through" the student, giving each aid verbally as the student is to carry it out. Others set up exercises for the student to ride and figure out more on their own. Others use some combination. Mentally ride the lesson you are watching as you stand there, and make sure it works for you. Better if you can watch each instructor teach a few different riders and see how well the instructor adapts to each student's needs. If all of this watching has taken place at shows or clinics, which are great places to see a variety of trainers work with a variety of students usually for free or for a very low admission price, be sure to visit the home stables of the trainers in whom you are interested. Watching the horses with which they work regularly can be very telling. Look for happy, relaxed horses, and friendly, relaxed people. A stable full of horses with vices or sullen horses that will not come to the front of the stalls will tell you much about the trainer as a horseman. Watch also to see if the training methods change at home. Are all the horses ridden in restrictive devices that were not in evidence at the show? Do they appear happy in their work? In short, is the instructor's overall horse management something you also want to emulate? Good horsemanship is as important in an instructor as good riding. It is often the case that the trainers who are humane, meticulous, and ethical in the treatment of their horses are also the most ethical and honest in the treatment of their clients. The reverse is also often true. As with every generalization, this one has its exceptions, but for the most part it does seem to hold. Observing and chatting with clients can also be very telling. It is normal for riders to be a bit tense at shows, but at the home stable there should not be a lot of tension and unhappiness. Your experience will probably be similar to that of the trainer's other clients, so pay attention to their demeanor around the barn. Are they focused and concentrating when they are on a horse? Relaxed and happy when they finish? Does the trainer's demeanor with students change when she is at home rather than at a show where potential clients and competitors are watching?

 While watching look for happy, relaxed horses, and friendly, relaxed people.

If you are in an area where there is not good instruction regularly available, but can transport your horse, or can hire someone else to, you can still probably find occasional clinics that will fit in with the riding system you choose in most parts of the country. Clinics are best used as a supplement to a regular lesson program. It can be incredibly helpful to occasionally get input that is consistent in method, but maybe slightly different in emphasis or focus. For example, I ride with a very talented trainer who is very good at helping me with the training of my horse, and my position is basically sufficient. He will tell me when I need to correct something about my position, but the emphasis in the sessions is clearly on my horse. I recently rode in a clinic with another trainer of similar background, but who places enormous emphasis on the rider's position. She was basically happy with where my horse's training was for his age, experience, and fitness level, so she focused on my position. My sessions with her were absolutely consistent with what I hear from my regular trainer, but the emphasis on my position helped to "polish" things that may get less emphasis when the focus of a lesson is more on my horse. My horse and I both benefited tremendously.

There is a limit to how much truly new work one can or should try to do in a one or two day clinic, but sometimes hearing the same thing one has been hearing in regular lessons, expressed in slightly different terms or with a slightly different emphasis, can provide a breakthrough. A clinician may provide a different approach, a new exercise, or a different vocabulary that can reinforce work one is already doing, or may open the next door for progress. Just like any other people, riding teachers and students can get in ruts. You carry with you the history of the horse and the training progress to date. The clinician comes with fresh eyes to evaluate the horse and rider and what they are ready to do. A good clinician will not ask you to try anything that is a big stretch. It is very often the case, though, that a clinician can show you that you are in fact

ready for more than you thought you were. The general rule of thumb for a clinic is that if you leave with one good new bit of progress, however small or simple, and you can achieve it again yourself when the clinician has gone home, the clinic has been a success. If the clinician leaves you or your horse confused or stressed, go back to what you know works, think about it for awhile, and as the person responsible for your own and your horse's progress, make the best decision you can about whether to try to incorporate the clinician's feedback into your riding program. If you do work with a regular instructor, discuss the clinic session with your instructor. Maybe she can help put the confusing parts in perspective. If your regular instructor is resistant to the idea of your occasionally riding with a clinician, try to ascertain whether it is that your instructor has doubts about the particular clinician, or is simply not open to your getting feedback from other people. If your instructor is resistant to your riding with anyone else, no matter how good they are, it is legitimate to question whether she is putting her business interests ahead of your riding progress. Trying to save you and your horse from the confusion of riding with someone whose methods your trainer questions may be valid. Trying to protect herself from the possibility that you might learn something valuable from someone else is not.

At the opposite end of the spectrum from occasional clinics are total immersion situations such as working student positions and riding camps. Not just for kids anymore, many organizations are providing opportunities for interested adults to spend a week or two, sometimes more, in a horse focused learning program. Riding programs for adults usually assume some level of riding competence, though they do not usually require a high level of accomplishment. They often combine one or two riding lessons a day with lectures and workshops on issues related to horse management and rider body awareness. If you have to travel to get to good instruction, getting it in a relatively intense format can be an efficient way to use both your financial and time resources. Provided that the instructors are qualified, riding camps can be a wonderful supplement to a regular lesson program and they can be a great source of inspiration and camaraderie, especially if you spend much of your riding time working on your own.

Working student positions require a much greater time commitment, usually six months to a year, and generally a very high energy level, but they can also provide intensive education in a relatively short period. The expectation is that the working student works in a trainer's stable in exchange for instruction, and sometimes lodging or board for a horse. For anyone considering a career as a horse trainer or riding instructor, a working student position can be an incredibly valuable look at how a training business works. Being a working student provides an overall view of horse and horse-business management that simply showing up for lessons, no matter how frequent, cannot even come close to providing. Generally filled by riders just out of high school or college, working student positions need not be limited to the young. I have known more mature individuals, serious about improving their riding and horse management, who have had wonderful experiences as working students, either during a career transition or during a sabbatical or other "break" from the normal demands of adult life. For riders who began as adults or who did not have the benefit of Pony Club or 4-H as children, and who may have learned to ride, but not necessarily had the benefit of horse management education, riding camps and working student positions are wonderful sources of more rounded equestrian education than lessons and books can provide. For younger riders, they can be an intensive overall look at riding and the horse business. Programs vary greatly from trainer to trainer, so be sure to understand thoroughly what is expected and what is provided before signing on as a working student.

Another option for riding education is through the many organizations that exist for just that purpose. The United States Pony Club is legendary for providing excellent horse management skills and well-rounded riding education in the English disciplines in a framework that provides a logical system of progression. For more information, or to find the closest Pony Club, contact the U.S.P.C. national office at www.ponyclub.org, or by phone at 859-254-7669.

Unfortunately U.S.P.C. limits its programs to riders 21 and under. There is now a loose network of local groups providing a similar experience for adult riders who want to ride safely and have fun in the U.S.P.C. tradition, but who are too old to be eligible for the U.S.P.C. programs. You can find a list of them at www.oldpeoplesridingclub.org. While 4-H is not a totally horse centered organization, some 4-H clubs provide horse management instruction as well as some riding instruction and competition opportunities. You can find your local 4-H club through your state agricultural extension service. Many national discipline organizations have regional or local chapters that host competitions and sponsor clinics and seminars. You can usually find the local chapters through the national offices of these discipline organizations. There are also many local riding clubs that sponsor clinics and educational opportunities in various riding disciplines. Look for contact information in regional equestrian publications, and on the bulletin boards at local feed and tack stores.

Whether or not you have access to a regular lesson program, there are many other ways to enhance your equestrian education. Supplementing lessons will help you make the most of your lessons, especially if they are less than regular. Even if you do ride regularly with an instructor, you can enhance your riding education by working outside of your lessons to improve your riding knowledge.

- Be a sponge! Absorb everything you can when there is riding and training going on around you. Watch the best trainers you can. Listen to the instructors and clinicians with whom you ride teach other people. Sometimes it is easier to absorb the "big picture" when you are not on the horse actually trying to do it yourself. Go to clinics even if you cannot ride. They are a great place to learn new exercises and techniques. Go to competitions where you are not riding. Pick the highest level ones within reach. Watch show ring technique, and watch the warm-up areas to see how the very best prepare for the competition arena.

- Read theory books. For most disciplines there are texts that are considered the classic expressions of the theory for that kind of riding. If you understand the theory and the overall framework of your disciplines it is much easier to carry out the execution of specific parts of it. It gives you a perspective within which to fit your more specific lessons.

- Watch yourself on videotape, especially if you cannot have regular lessons, but also even if you do. If you do not have a video camera, a friend or relative probably does, and they would probably be willing to tape you in exchange for some return favor. Sometimes seeing what you look like enables you to understand and correct training and riding issues much more quickly. This is especially helpful during a lesson when you can combine your observations with your instructor's feedback, and enables you to understand and correct training and riding issues much more quickly.

- Watch others on videotape. You can now see the very best riders in the world in your own TV room, both in videos of the top competitions and training tapes made by some of the very best riders. Watch the best and see how they ride. Pick riders who are particularly good at something you are trying to master.

- Take any opportunities to ride other horses. If you are a one-horse owner, it is very easy to develop habits to which your horse becomes accustomed. Trade horses with a friend. Exercise horses for people who cannot ride often enough. Horses are the best teachers, and they tend to be pretty consistent in their teaching methods. Correctly applied aids get correct responses. If you ride with an instructor who has school horses, make sure you ride a variety of them. If you usually ride your own horse in your lessons, ask your instructor if you can occasionally ride a school horse instead.

All of these methods are great supplements to regular riding. They are also productive alternatives to keep advancing your skills when you cannot ride. When the weather is too bad, or your horse is lame, or life is simply not allowing the time, 15 minutes of a video or a chapter of a riding book can keep your education going.

Once you have found an instructor and maybe clinicians you enjoy working with, established a lesson or clinic schedule that balances help from the ground with time to work things out for yourself, and rounded it out with supplemental learning that allows you to keep your lessons in perspective in terms of long-term goals, one of the most challenging jobs you will have is to periodically re-evaluate your program. The instructor who is perfect for you at one phase of your riding may not be the person who is right for you two years later. The instructor who taught you your posting diagonals and how to hop over cross rails may or may not be the person who can help you pursue your dream of completing a three-day event. The person helping you from the ground ideally has knowledge and experience several levels above that at which you are working. When you start approaching your instructor's level of knowledge, it may be time to find someone who can take you further.

Limitations imposed by your horse may mean you reach the day when it is time to either find another horse who is capable of taking you to the next step, or resetting your goals to accommodate the horse you love and to which you are committed. My favorite horse developed arthritis in her spine, and it was clear that she was no longer happy doing upper-level dressage. She had always loved riding out on the trails and was comfortable moving in a longer frame without weight on her back, so after what could have been the end of her career with me we spent several happy years doing low-level combined driving. She always won the dressage phase, and soon learned how to manage her way through hazards and cones as though she enjoyed the puzzles. It was a new challenge that kept me happy at levels that were well within her physical ability. The choice to find a new job for my old friend rather than moving on to another horse added much to both of our lives, but it is not the right choice for everyone. Pressing horses beyond their comfort or ability levels is not kind to the horse and is not going to improve your horsemanship. Assessment of your riding program must include an honest assessment of how much your horse is enjoying the process. The decisions can be tough, but there does often come a time when your riding goals and the abilities of your very best teacher are no longer compatible. At that point you owe it to the horse to find a different way, whether by changing what you are pursuing together or with new partners for each of you.

As the old saying goes, "Nothing is constant except change." Set a date for annual re-evaluation of your riding program. Keep a training journal; even if it is a simple notebook you keep in your car in which you jot a few notes before you head home from the barn. *(See Chapter—The Characteristics of a Good Student—Personal Insights)* Review it every six months or year. If you are seeing repetitive resistances from your horse or frustrations for yourself you need to reassess the way you are doing things. Patience is critical in training horses. They need time to build the physical fitness and mental skills necessary to advance in their training. Sometimes it seems as though they are making progress every day. At other times it seems as though the two of you are getting nowhere. A journal will help you assess your progress more objectively. If you are working on the same thing you were working on a year ago, and having the same frustrations, you need to restructure your program. On the other hand, if it seems that you are not progressing fast enough, or you are feeling frustrated, it can be reassuring to look back and realize that you have come further than you thought, or be reminded of the training time lost when your horse had an abscess and the other weeks you could not ride because of weather or some other obstacle. Even though progress takes time, you should still see progress over the longer periods of time, and problems should be solved so that if you are facing issues they are new ones and not the same old ones. Knowing when it is time to change your program can be difficult. Actually moving on from an instructor with whom you have a good personal relationship can be very difficult for both of you. If you have an enlightened instructor and are ready to move on, it may be your instructor who sees and mentions it first. Once again, do your "shopping" carefully, and take care not to unnecessarily hurt feelings or burn bridges, but remember that your riding and your horse's well being are ultimately your responsibility.

 Keeping a journal allows you to assess your progress more objectively

PERSONAL INSIGHTS

*The big personal picture that stimulates
and oversees your journey.*

Getting to know yourself is a lifelong process of discovery. The more you learn, the more you realize there is more to learn. You may seek a starting point or a review. Personal Insights is designed to help you with whatever path you need to discover or review.

Philosophy—by Jill K. Hassler-Scoop

Motivation—by Kathy Kelly, Ph.D.

Perception of Self—by Jill K. Hassler-Scoop

Experience the Moment—by Jill K. Hassler-Scoop

Feel and Motion—by Jill K. Hassler-Scoop

Personality Styles—by Kathy Kelly, Ph.D.

Learning Styles—by Kathy Kelly, Ph.D.

Insights from Our Horse—by Jill K. Hassler-Scoop

Worry, Anxiety and Fear for the Equestrian—by Kathy Kelly, Ph.D.

Basic Human Anatomy for Riders—
        by Beth Gloston, M.D., Illustrated by Sandy Johnson

PHILOSOPHY
by Jill K. Hassler-Scoop

Awareness of unitary reality expands consciousness, facilitates human perception into the immaterial realms.
—Sherry L. Ackerman, dressage instructor and philosophy professor, Dressage in the Fourth Dimension

Your riding is influenced by both your riding and life philosophies, which set the framework for your decisions related to how you organize your life, the decisions you make, the money you spend, and the values you place on the activities of life. Ideally, at the core of your philosophy is a balance that meets your life's needs. Philosophy changes as you travel through life, so a periodic review can be a valuable exercise. Often you make your voyage through life paying no attention to defining your philosophy, but taking the time to identify it can play a valuable role in your success and happiness.

LIFE PHILOSOPHY

Your philosophy of life influences every decision and action taken, whether consciously or unconsciously. Your philosophy can be thought of as your sense of purpose; your beliefs about why you are here and what kind of legacy you want to leave behind. Philosophy of life becomes apparent in the decisions you make in the main categories of life; love, money, relationships, religion/spirituality, career, duty to country, and use

There is no part of life that does not contain lessons. If you are alive, there are lessons to be learned.
—Cherie Carter Scott

Stages of Life		
Stage	**Age**	**General Characteristics**
Child	6 – 10	Play, experimentation, fantasy and exploration
Preteen	10 – 13	Develop finer foundation skills of life: consistency, responsibility and discipline
Teenager	14 – 17	Challenges authority, with major emphasis on peer pressure and social acceptance
Young adult	18 – 21	Personal and professional uncertainty, society and family pressures often result in insecurity
Early adult	22 – 42	Career development, nurturing partnerships and raising a family
Middle age	43 – 65	Reflection, knowing yourself, challenge is accepting the aging process
Late middle age	Over 65	Wisdom, honesty, awareness, and self acceptance

26

of time. Often you have trouble knowing and stating the priority you give each of these life factors. Yet your philosophy and attitude towards these factors will influence your decisions, set the standard for long and short-term success, and provide a framework for continued personal development. Each time you are faced with a crossroad in your life, it is a solid understanding of your life philosophy that allows you to make the best possible choice. This understanding comes from examining your past decisions, their consequences, and your attitudes in each of these areas.

Your belief system influences/controls the big picture in your life journey.

If you already have a clear understanding of your life philosophy and can state it in a paragraph, write it down. If not, go to a quiet place and review your philosophy by rating the important points in the Value Rating Scale 1 and 2 following. Once you have done this, write out your philosophy as you understand it now. Life

Values Rating Scale 1	
Importance in your life	Rate 1 (least important) – 10 (most important)
Love	1 2 3 4 5 6 7 8 9 10
Money	1 2 3 4 5 6 7 8 9 10
Time	1 2 3 4 5 6 7 8 9 10
Relationship to peers	1 2 3 4 5 6 7 8 9 10
Relationship to family	1 2 3 4 5 6 7 8 9 10
Religion/spirituality development	1 2 3 4 5 6 7 8 9 10
Career	1 2 3 4 5 6 7 8 9 10
Duty to country	1 2 3 4 5 6 7 8 9 10
Understanding and acceptance of death	1 2 3 4 5 6 7 8 9 10

Values Rating Scale 2	
List in order of importance	1 (least important) - 10 (most important)
Love	
Good Life	
Money	
Time	
Relationship to Peers	
Relationship to Family	
Religion/Spirituality	
Career	
Duty to Country	
Understand & Accept Death	

Values Rating Scale 3										
Importance in your life	Rate 1(least important) – 10(most important)									
Love of horses	1	2	3	4	5	6	7	8	9	10
Love of your horse	1	2	3	4	5	6	7	8	9	10
Mental well-being	1	2	3	4	5	6	7	8	9	10
Exercise	1	2	3	4	5	6	7	8	9	10
Challenge	1	2	3	4	5	6	7	8	9	10
Companionship	1	2	3	4	5	6	7	8	9	10
Competition	1	2	3	4	5	6	7	8	9	10
Recreation	1	2	3	4	5	6	7	8	9	10

philosophy can change depending upon life experiences and stages in life, so what you write is not binding. Change is normal and good; as you progress through life, you will uncover the common thread (the core of your life philosophy) that is included in each of the stages of your life. It is important to know that there is no "right" or "wrong" answer; the key point is to know yourself. Knowing will equip you to integrate your experiences much more clearly.

Tales From the Trip

Lisa

Lisa struggled with an important decision. At twenty she knew she loved horses and wanted very much to be involved with them but did not know how. She did not have much money, and worked hard to maintain a horse and take lessons. Between her family ties and her job she had little time for social life. Her mother kept reminding her that she needed to meet people and have a social life. Lisa decided to spend one year in her job, riding and learning as much as she could afford, live at home (to save money and have family time) and not worry about her social life.

As the end of Lisa's year approached, and she reviewed her year and her goals, she decided that it was time to add some social life. She decided that she would take a few courses at a local university and begin attending church again. The prior year she had given up church because her church insisted that its members attend regularly, and there were many horse activities on Sunday. Her compromise was to attend when she could and continue her riding. In the meantime she saved money to attend college full time, and took an equine science course.

Ten years later, Lisa is married and has two small children and a job as an assistant in a local veterinary practice. She is riding, but during her years of experimentation she discovered that she did not want to become a trainer, but rather to have her own horse, ride, train and attend local shows. She organized her life so that she can show six times a year, enough to satisfy her but still allowing her enough time with her family. Lisa was very busy, but enjoyed each aspect of her life and feels good about it.

Inga

On her fortieth birthday Inga decided that she wanted to reclaim the time with horses she had given up when she went to college twenty-two years earlier. The big question was, "How?" Her children were teenagers, and she wanted to be home when they came home from school. Inga earned her living as a receptionist in a dental office. She and her husband decided that they could do without Inga's income if the riding did not cost any money. After they agreed, they had a family meeting and the children decided that they would help to save money by cutting their eating out down to one day a week. The entire family invested in the family change. Inga researched stables in her local community and was lucky to uncover one that needed some help in the barn were she worked from nine to three. This gave her time at home to take care of the house and to be there when the children were home. The sacrifice was that she had to work on either Saturday or Sunday, but her husband agreed to spend that day with the children. In exchange for her work, Inga was able to ride two days a week.

Six months into the new routine, Inga and her husband reviewed how the change was affecting their family life, and both agreed that Inga was happier and they had more quality time, which meant much more to them than the extra money that Inga had been earning.

RIDING PHILOSOPHY

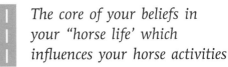

The core of your beliefs in your "horse life' which influences your horse activities

Adding horses and horse activities to your life is a choice that is intimately related to your life philosophy. A horse requires large amounts of money, time, and emotional investment; thus the choice to include horses in

Values Rating Scale 4	
List in order of importance	1 (least important) – 10 (most important)
Love of horses	
Love of your horse	
Mental well-being	
Exercise	
Challenge	
Companionship	
Competition	
Recreation	

your life influences and is influenced by your overall philosophy of life. In order to make sure that your horse involvement continues to fit into your life philosophy, you need to gain an understanding of your overall philosophy of riding.

Tales From the Trip

Mary and Ann

Mary and Ann are examples of people with different riding philosophies. Both women had ridden as teenagers, and decided to start riding again when their children were school age. Mary felt that her time with horses recharged her and gave her energy. Competing with her horse fulfilled the desire present in both her life philosophy and her riding philosophy to continually better herself. Competition was a vital report card of her growth and success. Ann shared the belief that horses recharged her and described the role of horses in her life as giving her peace and freedom. While Ann had competed as a child, she did not feel this was important now. She now considered an improved performance at home with her horse as fulfilling. For Ann competition added stress in demands for time and money, while for Mary competition provided a sense of achievement. Both had horses stabled in the same barn, where most of the riders were competitive and there was pressure to join the group to show. Ann did not question her decision to stay at home as this fit into her philosophies of life and riding. Since she felt secure in her decision and was clear about the role of horses and competition in her life, she was not swayed to make decisions that were not in keeping with her personal philosophy.

Sandy

Sandy was a teenager who didn't need to think much about the role of horses in her life, they were so much a part of her life. Her challenge came when she had to balance her riding with her school life, as few of her friends understood the importance of riding in her life. This conflict of interests with her peers prompted her to reflect: "Why am I so different?" "What is wrong with me?" Horses were a vital part of Sandy's life, so her decision to put them aside for a few months while she played basketball in school was very difficult. However, she wanted to know what it felt like to participate in activities with her peers. While she enjoyed it, she discovered that it interfered too much with her riding activities, which she loved and was willing to give up. The experience gave her the opportunity to know first hand what she wanted to do.

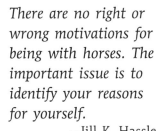

There are no right or wrong motivations for being with horses. The important issue is to identify your reasons for yourself.
—Jill K. Hassler,
In Search of Your Image

MOTIVATION
by Kathy Kelly Ph.D.

Why do you ride? Look honestly at your motivation, why is it important to you?
—Jill K. Hassler-Scoop, *In Search of Your Image*

WHY ARE YOU INVOLVED IN HORSES?

Why you choose to become involved in horses and what you expect to gain from your time with horses plays a major role in your experience of enjoyment and success in what you are doing. Understanding your motivation also gives you the stamina to survive the roadblocks and enjoy the new sights of your journey with horses.

What do you think are your motivators?

Values Rating Scale 5	
Motivator	Rate 1 (least important) – 10 (most important)
Love of horse	1 2 3 4 5 6 7 8 9 10
Excitement	1 2 3 4 5 6 7 8 9 10
Mental well-being	1 2 3 4 5 6 7 8 9 10
Social pressure (peers and/or parents)	1 2 3 4 5 6 7 8 9 10
Exercise	1 2 3 4 5 6 7 8 9 10
Challenge	
Mental	1 2 3 4 5 6 7 8 9 10
Physical	1 2 3 4 5 6 7 8 9 10
Companionship	1 2 3 4 5 6 7 8 9 10
Competition	1 2 3 4 5 6 7 8 9 10

What is your number one motivator?

Values Rating Scale 6	
What I hope to Gain	Rate 1 (least important) – 10 (most important)
Ribbons	1 2 3 4 5 6 7 8 9 10
Excitement	1 2 3 4 5 6 7 8 9 10
Mental well-being	1 2 3 4 5 6 7 8 9 10
Recognition	1 2 3 4 5 6 7 8 9 10
Exercise	1 2 3 4 5 6 7 8 9 10
Companionship	1 2 3 4 5 6 7 8 9 10
Results- Improved skills	1 2 3 4 5 6 7 8 9 10
Harmony with my horse	1 2 3 4 5 6 7 8 9 10
Financial gain	1 2 3 4 5 6 7 8 9 10

WHAT IS *SUCCESS* ANYWAY?

Our pursuit of success is part of our motivator, how do we define success? *Webster's New World Dictionary* describes "success" as "the achievement of something desired or attempted."

In order to feel successful, riders need to achieve something they desire or to accomplish something they have attempted to do. It sounds simple, but people often differ in what they desire. That is, athletes do not always define success in the same way. Despite finishing a competition with the same result, different riders are likely to have different feelings about it. What may feel like success for one rider may feel like a disappointment for another.

Tales From the Trip
Sally and Nancy

Sally and Nancy are good friends who train at the same barn. Getting ready to go to show, they both prepare by riding often. However, while Sally prepares by taking additional lessons, Nancy focuses on practicing what she and her horse are good at. The day of the show arrives and both Sally and Nancy enter the first class. They both feel that their performance was one of their better rides to date. The results show Nancy to be in third place, while Sally finishes in the middle of the pack. While Sally is thrilled with her performance, Nancy is clearly disappointed and unhappy. What is going on?

Well, it seems that Sally and Nancy define success differently. Sport research tells us that there are two major ways of defining success: which are called *task goals and ego goals*. And, depending on whether you are mostly a task rider or ego rider, different things will make you feel successful when competing. Let's learn more about task and ego goals and see if they can help you better understand the difference between Sally and Nancy's reactions:

Task and Ego Goals

Both task and ego definitions of success are valid and legitimate ways to approach any achievement situation. Actually, most of us identify a bit with both! However, riders differ in the importance they give to these two goal orientations.

Whether you are predominately task-oriented or ego-oriented can tell a lot about:

- what motivates you for competition
- how you will prepare for the competition
- how you will respond to competition

Task Goals	Ego Goals
Riders who hold task goals feel successful when learning, improving, and mastering challenges. They participate in sports because they enjoy the activity (or task) in and of itself. These riders concentrate on their own performance, paying little attention to the performance of others. In a word, task riders are "self–focused."	Riders who hold ego goals feel successful when demonstrating their ability to others. They participate in sports because they want to show off their talent and skills. These riders concentrate on comparing their ability with others, and focus on "beating" their opponents, being the best, and finishing first. In other words, ego riders are "other-focused".
Task Goal = personal progress	**Ego Goal = superior ability**

How do Task and Ego Goals Motivate riders for competition?

Motivate for Competition	
Task Riders	**Ego Riders**
Riders high in *task* goals are motivated to compete in order to *learn*. They may want to see how their training program is working, challenge themselves or their horses to move up a step in their training, or get more exposure. These riders like to win, and when they do, their "thrill" comes from knowing that they rode a "personal best" and/or their horse has performed well.	Riders high in *ego* goals are motivated to compete in order to *prove* something—to themselves or others. They often want people to notice their own or their horse's talent and ability. These riders like to win, and when they do, their thrill comes from knowing that they were superior to their competitors that day.

How do task and ego riders respond to competition?

Response to Competition	
Task Riders	**Ego Riders**
Task riders respond to competition with a laid back attitude. They tend to minimize the competitive aspects of the horse show, and focus on accomplishing a personal goal, whatever it may be. They are often the last ones to go up to the scoreboard, and they don't tend to watch other riders competing. When asked, "how are you doing?" task riders reply with information about their ride - "Oh, my horse was so good today! He stayed relaxed and he didn't even try to buck me off!"	Ego riders get pumped up in response to competitions. Their adrenaline gets running, and they feel excited and motivated by seeing all the other competitors. Ego riders are usually the first ones at the scoreboard, and often watch the other riders in order to contrast and compare these performances with their own. When asked, "How are you doing?" ego riders reply with information about their placing, such as "I am in 2nd place so far - I hope I can move up!"

How do task goals and ego goals influence how riders prepare for competition?

Prepare for Competition	
Task Riders	**Ego Riders**
Task riders enjoy the preparation for competition. Their goal is personal progress, so task riders see any chance to learn something new, master a new challenge, or improve upon a past performance as a way to become successful. As a result, these riders prepare for competition by training hard, putting in a lot of effort, and taking lessons when given the opportunity. It can be said that task riders enjoy the journey as much as, if not more than, the destination. Their instructors often call these riders "natural students."	Ego riders look at preparation as a necessary evil. Because ego riders have a goal to demonstrate superior ability, they want to perform correctly right away and have little tolerance or value for gradual improvement. They tend to practice only as much as they have to, and they work on what they are good at, avoiding the difficult or weak areas in their riding. In fact, the learning process, because it tends to expose one's "holes" or weaknesses, frustrates ego riders. Under conditions of repeated difficulties, ego riders may even begin to demean the activity, withdraw effort, or even quit. However, ego riders will work hard if they can see how what they are practicing can help them perform better at the show, or give them a better chance of winning. Ego riders will work hard if they feel that they are doing better than the other learners around them. Instructors often call these riders "naturally competitive."

LEVELS OF MOTIVATION

Highest Level of Motivation

High task combined with high/average ego: These are our "elite athletes." These individuals have a strong desire to succeed and a love of competing, combined with a strong drive to practice and improve. As a result, these athletes can feel satisfaction no matter what the outcome. If they succeed, they feel *great*! If they fail, they can fall back on their task orientation. They learn from the experience and work hard to improve next time. They like the challenge. Learning for these athletes is a lifelong requirement for enjoyment.

Lowest Level of Motivation

High ego combined with average/low task: These are the athletes most at risk for frustration, tears, anger, and "dropping out." These athletes get "high" on success, and crash in defeat. When all is going well, they appear committed and work hard. However, under conditions of repeated difficulties or failures, their self-esteem takes a big hit, and they tend to withdraw, or demean the effort to try. They do not feel a sense of accomplishment with "a job well done";

rather, they need external vali-
dation of success. Learning
holds no personal interest to
them. Indeed, early unskilled
efforts often leave them feeling demoralized, inadequate,
and inferior.

So, let's go back to Sally and
Nancy. Can you guess what
combination of task and ego
each one holds?

*The most confident and
happy competitors are those
with high task goals. The
level of ego goals appears
to be less relevant. Raise
the task levels and let the
individuals be as ego as they
want. High ego folks with
low task are most at risk!*

High task goal, low ego goal—Sally:

Sally prepared by taking additional lessons, and was pleased
with the outcome of her performance, despite that fact that she
didn't place. Why? Sally took extra lessons to help her learn something new so that she could "try it out" at the competition. She
then entered the competition with a personal goal of working on
whatever she learned in her lessons. When she accomplished this
personal goal, she was thrilled. Sally felt successful because she
was comparing her performance to her own previous performances
and she felt that she had improved on some aspect of her riding.
And, because Sally has a low ego goal, she doesn't get too excited
about the "thrill of victory," therefore she doesn't really experience
the "agony of defeat."

Low task goal, high ego goal—Nancy:

Nancy did not seek out extra instruction when preparing for
the competition, and despite finishing third, Nancy was disappointed with the results. Why? Nancy entered the competition with
the goal of winning the class. She did not want to take more lessons
in case it confused her or her horse, hurting her chances of winning. At the competition, Nancy watched the other riders and felt
that she and her horse were "better," and thus expected to win the
class. When this didn't happen, Nancy felt bad about her riding
and her horse, thinking that others must be more talented because
they scored better. Nancy's all-out effort made her feel even worse.
Because she tried hard and put out her best effort, Nancy feels that
her best was not good enough. By holding a low task/high ego goal,
Nancy's only way to feel good about herself is to be better than

others. She does not have a strong task goal to fall back on when the going gets rough. In her mind, having talent and ability is the only way she can feel successful, so they become very important to her sense of confidence and enjoyment of the competition.

Luckily, research has shown that a person's level of task can change. Low task athletes can learn to be higher task, which acts as a risk protector in sport. Very few athletes can win all the time, or show superiority at every competition. We win some, we lose some. What keeps athletes coming back again and again is their level of *task goal*—their love of the journey.

Much of an athlete's task goal is shaped by early socialization experiences with parents, peers, and coaches. If winning, being the best, and conquering the opponent is what is taught, rewarded, and encouraged, then high ego goals will result. If improvement, learning, and mastering increasingly difficult goals are the focus, then task goals will result. Ideally, children will be exposed to *both* forms of motivation, with task goals being highly emphasized during the learning process. High ego goals can actually enhance the sport experience by providing that great feeling from being "number one." However, high ego goals need to be balanced with high task goals. As kids mature and get older, their goals are harder to change. A good instructor or coach can help an athlete develop their task goals by teaching an appreciation for the learning process. By paying attention to what is rewarded, focused on, and encouraged, in-structors can help low task/high ego athletes feel good about personal progress and individual accomplishments.

Bottom line—The most confident and happy competitors are those with high task goals. The level of ego goals appears to be less relevant. Raise the task levels and let the individuals be as ego oriented as they want. High ego folks with *low task* are most at risk!

Final Point

Sport researchers have found that people tend to be "born" with a temperament that is either competitive or not. If someone finds the thrill of head-to-head competition exciting, they probably al-ways will. On the other hand, if someone is not drawn to the excitement of competition, this probably will not change. Impor-tantly, both task-oriented and ego-oriented riders may enjoy com-peting. What differs between them is the reason they compete.

Task-oriented athletes seek out competition in order to evaluate their learning progress, or to see if they have mastered a particular skill. Ego-oriented athletes compete to demonstrate their ability, to show superior skills, and to prove to themselves and others that they are good at what they do.

All people have a little of both types of goal orientation—Task *and* Ego. It is the specific combination of task and ego that is important when trying to understand one's motivation.

PERCEPTION OF SELF
by Jill K. Hassler-Scoop

The "self-image" sets the boundaries of individual accomplishment. It defines what you can and cannot do. Expand the self-image and you expand the "area of the possible." The development of an adequate, realistic self-image will seem to imbue the individual with new capabilities, new talents and literally turn failure into success. —Maxwell Maltz, Psycho-Cybernetics

Our attitude towards our body and mind plays an important role in our ability to create, recognize and enjoy success as well as deal with the roadblocks in our journey. A positive, realistic attitude maps out progressive development while a negative or unrealistic attitude will create roadblocks.

BODY IMAGE

Our physical bodies are a gift in life. Each body is different with some things we can change and others we cannot

An honest evaluation of our physical makeup

change. In order to make the most out of what we have, we must accept what we cannot change, and change the things that we do not like that are possible to change. It is important for us to match our conformation and goals with the horses we ride and the activities we choose to participate in. Waldemar Seunig refers to our body as a tool: "This tool (our body) should be made a precision instrument; it should have an appropriate shape and be highly polished so as to achieve the maximum effect without expenditure of excessive energy." Very few riders are gifted with the perfect body. You can study the qualities of a perfect body and then compare your body to those qualities.
(See Chapter—Basic Anatomy for Riders—Personal Insights)

Ideal Body Conformation

* Slender figure of medium build— similar to a runner or dancer

    Legs that are too short make it more difficult for riders to keep their balance, especially if the upper body is tall.

Your body is your vehicle for life. As long as you are here, live in it. Love, honor, respect and cherish it, treat it well and it will serve you in kind.
—Suzy Prudden

Legs that are too long for the size of the horse, will make it difficult for riders to keep their leg properly attached to the horse.

- Low and narrow pelvis—creates a low, stable center of gravity

  Buttocks that are too fleshy prevent the use of the pushing forward motion of the buttocks

- Thigh that is long and flat that allows the leg to fall in correct position and be useful as an aid

- Naturally straight spine allows for maximum motion between each vertabre

Carrying the ideal weight and maintaining appropriate physical fitness *(See Chapter—Fitness for the Rider—Fact Insights)* are responsibilities you have to your body and to your horse.

Each rider is an individual, and for every rider on every horse there is an individual ideal that puts that person in the best balance and place to influence that horse in that discipline. *(See Chapter—Basic Anatomy for Riders)*

What are your weaknesses and strengths? What adjustments can you make for them?

Tales From the Trip

Mary

Mary is 5'5" tall with a natural tendency toward an average weight for her height. While Mary was well proportioned, she discovered that she felt much more comfortable on horses who were not well-sprung and were 15.3 hands or less. However, after having three children she had gained some excess weight. Since Mary realized that this was the result of having children and not her normal, healthy weight range, she committed to losing 20 pounds so that her body would function better and she could purchase a thoroughbred or Arabian, one of her two favorite breeds. She realized she could keep her weight as it was and buy a horse with a sturdier build to carry her, but she wanted the hotter temperament of the hotbloods, which also came with a more refined body structure and the need for a rider with quick reflexes. She also preferred the way she looked with less weight, and took on the challenge to change her body. Big horses were popular in her barn, but Mary realized that it was difficult for her 5'5" frame to ride a horse over 16 hands. Mary had seen several of her shorter friends struggle to ride big horses and decided she would prefer to be less fashionable and have more ride ability. Since competition was important to Mary, she had to consider the role of horse size for competition as well. Small riders on large horses tend to catch the judge's eye, more quickly in large classes. Mary's philosophy of using competition to test her knowledge made it easy for her to decide on the horse that fits her best even if it does not immediately catch the judge's eye since she wanted her awards based on merit and performance, not looks!

VIEW OF INNER SELF

The inner self is made up of intelligence (mind), emotion (heart), and spirit (intuition). Each influences the others. Each *Our inner self is the makeup of who we are* is an important part of who you are; upon examination you may realize that one of these aspects may play a stronger role in your life than the other two. Some people are very logical, making decisions based on information gathered and processed in their heads. Other people are intuitive, making decisions and responding to situations based on their feelings, or what their emotions tell them. Still other people rely on a sense of connection to their spirit, or possibly to a "greater being" (God, Spirit, the Universe, etc.) or intuition, to guide their decisions. It is important to realize the roles of all three, and to develop a balance that is right for you. If you rely more heavily on one than another of these aspects of yourself, you may have to deal with various challenges that arise from the dominance of one over the others. A realistic view of your personal inner strengths and weaknesses can play a very powerful role in your joy and ultimately in your success in reaching your goals. Since your mind plays a key role as the central clearinghouse for your actions, you must understand the basic role of the mind in your learning process. It will help to transfer information to muscle memory.

Tales From the Trip

Tim, Ann, and Sandy

One Saturday, Tim, Ann, and Sandy were planning to train. The ring was very muddy due to the heavy rains of the previous night. Ann quickly decided that she could not risk hurting Misty—a decision from her heart. Sandy, on the other hand, wrestled about what to do. She wanted to train since she had not ridden for four days. It took her several minutes to make the decision with a combination of her logic and her intuition. Logically it was dangerous, but she "felt" safe for some reason, so she rode. Tim gave it some thought and decided that if he were scheduled to compete, he would ride. Logic controlled his decision to ride. All three riders made a decision based on their governing inner influence: Ann from her heart, Sandy from her intuition and Tim from his logical thinking.

The thinking rider reinforces practical ability with theoretical knowledge.

Mind of the Rider

The mind is a complex mental operating system. It is the control center for all our life functions. Information from all the senses is processed in our mind. Luckily we have some control over this process.

One important challenge to riders is the need to develop muscle memory. Even though most of us will process each new skill through the mind (a few people will feel it first—these are natural riders), we need to commit the new skill to muscle memory or feel. This book is written to give you information on how to use your mind to train your muscles.

"The better we understand our mind, develop it, discipline it, learn to give it freedom, and learn to use it, the more our body and spirit can be included in creating better total balance."

—In Search of Your Image

Ideally, you have identified your dominant learning style (*See Chapter—Learning Styles—Personal Insights*). It is through this style that you will gather the information needed to learn the new skill. Your first challenge presents itself when you try the new skill on a moving and thinking animal. You soon discover that the more you think, the slower you respond.

So how do you make this transfer from mind to muscle memory effectual? First you must recognize the need to transfer the information from your brain to the part of our body that can direct the action. Second you must commit to practice each skill repeatedly until it is committed to muscle memory. Third, when you encounter roadblocks you return to a previous step and reconfirm the prior skill. *(See Chapters—Technical Insights)*

One of the key factors that enables the transfer from mind to muscle memory is our ability to be in the "now," free of clutter about the past or the future *(See Chapter—Experiencing the Present—Personal Insights)* This in itself takes mental training. A variety of methods to help you develop this skill are included in Supplementary Learning Insights. It is important to accept that you can learn only one new skill at a time. Keeping it simple speeds up the learning process.

Tales From the Trip

John and Rainman

John and Rainman were learning how to correctly ride ground poles. John's instructor, Sue, spent twenty minutes explaining the theory, including the function of John's and Rainman's bodies, keeping in mind John's thinking learning style. The first time John presented Rainman to the poles, John lost his balance and Rainman sped up. Sue tried to talk them through the process. After three failed attempts it became apparent that John was frustrated. Sue had John walk and asked him, "What is on your mind as you prepare for the exercise?" John began a list of things he was thinking about. Sue said, "Let's just think about one thing—maintaining your half-seat position." They tried again, and again John lost his balance. Sue asked, "What were you thinking this time?" "I was afraid that Rainman was going to speed up, since you told me not to use my hands." Sue then asked him to get into the half-seat position and go wherever he wanted, and when John felt comfortable; he was to represent Rainman to the ground poles. The only rules were that John had to maintain his half-seat position and maintain a steady speed in the trot, and bug off! It took John five minutes to get his mind under control. He was finally able to process what Sue asked him to do—thinking of only the three things—and to successfully go over the ground poles. Sue explained that this was only the first step. John needed to practice this exercise until he could do it without thinking at all. Four weeks later they met their goal!

As readers of *Beyond the Mirrors* know, a horse provides an excellent mirror for the inner self of the rider. While informal feedback, tests, and professional evaluations can help give you a view of yourself from other perspectives, horses give quick, honest and nonjudgmental information. The key is to know how to listen. While horses are used specifically for this in the new field of Equine Assisted Psychotherapy, anyone can benefit from listening to what horses reflect about them. If you want to perform satisfactorily you must constantly work to allow your mind, emotion and spirit to communicate effectively so that information can flow freely as we need it to complete the tasks before us. Meditation is one of the methods used to train this connection and balance. When you are performing successfully with your horse you are in harmony, honestly and instinctively responding to one another. An outside viewer then sees the dance of two creatures in perfect partnership. *(See Chapter—Insights from Our Horse—Personal Insights)*

EXPERIENCING THE PRESENT
by Jill K. Hassler-Scoop

Gives us the freedom to feel

Being aware in the present moment is vital for your safety and optimum performance, and shows respect for your horse's natural state of living in the present. People who can live completely in the present experience a wonderful sense of mental freedom. Most people, however, struggle with lingering issues from the past, or worry about upcoming events in the future. Issues of fear and anxiety are tied into this aspect of self-awareness—fear about repeating events from the past (such as getting bucked off, or always getting the wrong lead in a certain corner), or anxiety about what is still to come (how will you ever make it over that *hugh* jump, or complete your first dressage test without embarrassing yourself?) *(See Chapter—Worry, Anxiety and Fear—Personal Insights)* While the past and future do influence you, the only thing you can truly affect, work with and make a change in is the present. If you are wrapped up in the past or the future you often miss many opportunities in the present. Being in the present will eliminate the fear about the past or anxiety about the future.

Horses live in the present; and this can be a challenge as well as a good thing. If you take a horse away from his friend, it doesn't matter that you have taken him away and brought them back a thousand times before; he will still miss his friend at that moment, and will not be afraid to let you know about it! By the same token, many horses immerse themselves fully in what they are doing, whether it is trying to understand your aids and do the correct thing, or enjoying each morsel of fresh spring grass, or soaking in the sun on a winter day. Their minds are employed in

A rider's ultimate goal is to learn a skill, practice it until it is natural (committed to muscle memory), and engage it when needed without thought; to do this we must be in the moment.

45

just *being,* not thinking about what happened yesterday or what might happen tomorrow.

If you watch and observe your horse's ability to be in the present all of the time, you can see the powerful effect it has on his peace of mind. When a horse is tuned in to you, his responses are immediate, without thought, there is no delay. Many riders spend so much of their time thinking about what they want to do, what they forgot to do or did incorrectly, or what might go wrong that they lose many of the precious moments connected to their horse. Also lost is the ability to make corrections that are timely.

The most effective way to learn to be in the moment at will is to find out enough about yourself to know how to eliminate fear, worry, or anxiety about the past or future. Some form of meditation is usually central to learning this skill. It is not easy and takes considerable practice to empty your mind at will. You need to learn to put any issues at rest or "on hold" to return to in the future. Though difficult at first, meditation practice will increase your ability to deal calmly with issues and to experience life in the present moment.

ARE YOU IN THE MOMENT?

The following rating scale will help you recognize if you are distracted and under what circumstances. It will enable you to recognize whether or not you are "in the present" while working with your horse, and thus are getting the most out of your time. You may discover that it is beneficial to ask yourself these questions several days a week to discover if you are distracted more on certain days and, if so, what is distracting you.

In the Moment Rating Scale	
Are you in the moment?	Rate 1(least true)—10(most true)
As I enter the barn I feel excitement to see my horse.	1 2 3 4 5 6 7 8 9 10
As I enter the barn I think about what I need to do after my ride.	1 2 3 4 5 6 7 8 9 10
As I groom my horse I enjoy his responses.	1 2 3 4 5 6 7 8 9 10
As I groom my horse I think about what I am going to do when I ride.	1 2 3 4 5 6 7 8 9 10
As I groom my horse I talk to my friends.	1 2 3 4 5 6 7 8 9 10
While riding I discover I am distracted.	1 2 3 4 5 6 7 8 9 10
While riding I enjoy my horse's movements.	1 2 3 4 5 6 7 8 9 10
While putting my horse away I review my ride.	1 2 3 4 5 6 7 8 9 10
While putting my horse away I enjoy his response to returning to his home environment.	1 2 3 4 5 6 7 8 9 10
While putting my horse away I begin thinking about what I am going to do next.	1 2 3 4 5 6 7 8 9 10

Tales From the Trip

Kelly

Kelly had a very busy life. She discovered that distracting thoughts were always barging in while she was riding. If it was not, "What do I need to get in the grocery store for dinner?" it was, "I am so angry that I did not get my spots right yesterday while schooling the course." After years of not making progress in her riding, she read a book about positive self-talk. The book was an eye-opener; she discovered that she had two major interferences besides thinking too much about what she was doing while riding; she was either reviewing what went wrong on previous rides or thinking about what she had to do when she finished riding. She committed to researching more about the experience of being in the moment. She discovered that she needed to write down all the things on her mind that she was trying to remember, put the list in a safe place, and trust that she could return to it after her ride. She also learned that yesterday's ride was valuable only for comparison—thinking of the details or being irritated about it interfered with progress. It was not easy for Kelly to change her habits, so she asked her instructor to help her. Six months later Kelly realized that she was getting her spots and was much more energized after her riding. Upon reflection she realized it was the mental training she had practiced, as her mounted instruction remained the same.

Ann

Ann mixed her training time in the ring with conditioning time riding in the country. One day she realized that she was so consumed with the outcome of her fitness training that she was missing the joys of the process. On this day, as Ann waited for Misty to finish her drink, the birds singing in the trees interrupted her thoughts about her next set. Then, to her surprise, Misty, once finished, stood quietly and took in the cool breeze, the shinning sun, the soft white clouds, and the singing of the birds on the branches overlooking the stream. Ann wondered why she had never noticed this beauty around her before. She decided to make the effort to bring herself to the present more often so she and Misty could share the total experience of living and "being" together.

FEEL AND MOTION
by Jill K. Hassler-Scoop

*Besides knowledge of the physiology and psychology
of the horse, the rider must have a clear notion of
the theory of movement and balance.*
—Alois Podhajsky

FEELING INDIVIDUAL AREAS OF YOUR BODY.
*Provides the foundation of an independent seat
and effective communications*

It takes time to learn how to feel and use each body part independently, and it takes even more time to practice it. While riding, you don't have time to think about what part of your body needs to do what; the feeling must come from your muscle memory. Before your muscles can learn what to do, you need to take the time to train them. The first step in this training is to be able to become aware of each part separately. Once you can do this, you can train your muscles to remain relaxed with the appropriate tone or to be useful with appropriate driving controls.

When we are children, we learn to coordinate the different parts of our bodies in many different ways to do many different things. As children, we run, play, crawl, climb trees, and roll down hills. All these activities build neurological pathways that determine what kinds of movements each of our individual body parts can do and what they can do in combination with other body parts. The creativity of childhood allows for many possibilities. But we mature, we fall into habits of doing things a certain way, and we develop muscle memories to go along with these habits. It is these distinctions that allow people who know you to recognize you in a crowd or across a long distance.

You have certain ways of standing up, walking, talking, and laughing; these become habitual and the multiple pathways that were formed in childhood begin to be covered up from disuse. When you begin to ride, especially if you learn as an adult, it may be hard to learn to move your body in ways that you have not used since childhood. Riding requires

Each individual part must work alone so that it can come together as part of the whole and move with the horse in motion creating harmony.

48

cross-coordination in which you often have to use or think about diagonal leg/arm pairs, or shoulder/hip pairs, or even eye/ heel pairs. This challenges your brain as well as your muscle memories, and often the brain needs retraining as well as the muscles. It is possible to rediscover these pathways with exercise training programs.

Can you feel each of your joints and your main muscle groups with ease?

Tales From the Trip

Mim

Mim discovered that she rode from her thoughts, and could not feel the individual parts of her body. The first time Mr. Jones asked her to soften her eyes and think less, she thought this was a strange request. The second time, Mr. Jones stopped her and explained that because she was thinking so much her body tightened up. Mim remained doubtful, she thought she needed to think the details through that she was taught. Mr. Jones then began a conversation with Mim about the opera, and before she knew it her horse was moving forward happily. Mr. Jones then drew Mim's attention to her wonderful, forward, happy horse; it was at that moment that Mim discovered the powerful role her mind was playing.

Concerned about how to make the shift Mim asked Mr. Jones for suggestions. They discussed several ways to approach this: yoga, t'ai chi, meditation, or general exercises focusing on one part of her body at a time. Mim explored the different ideas given to her by Mr. Jones and decided to begin by reading Sally Swift's book, *Centered Riding*, as it had many exercises to increase awareness of different body parts. Now Mim realized that she was becoming even more consumed with thought to get each part of her body. Toby, her horse, was not going forward as nicely as before. She began to get discouraged and discussed this with Mr. Jones, who helped her understand that this was a phase of learning she had to go through—"temporary reduced performance for long term results." Mr. Jones spent time during the lessons teaching Mim how to use small parts of what she was learning and recognize the effect on her rides with Toby. One exercise that really helped Mim was related to the "soft eyes" exercise: Mim would do a posting trot, and think very intently with her eyes and mind on doing a circle. Mim then rated the trot on a scale of one to ten. She practiced

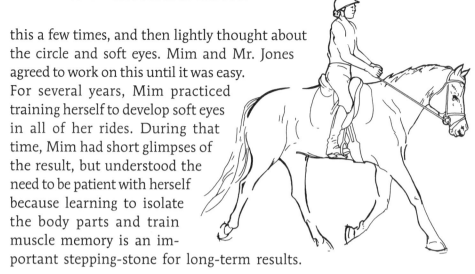

this a few times, and then lightly thought about the circle and soft eyes. Mim and Mr. Jones agreed to work on this until it was easy.

For several years, Mim practiced training herself to develop soft eyes in all of her rides. During that time, Mim had short glimpses of the result, but understood the need to be patient with herself because learning to isolate the body parts and train muscle memory is an important stepping-stone for long-term results.

AWARENESS OF MOVEMENT AND HARMONY

The basis of giving our self up to our horse's movement and understanding movement

Each part of your body moves differently. One goal in riding is to look as though you are sitting still; but, since the horse is moving, in order for you to appear still you must move. Some instructors tell their students again and again to "sit still" or to keep their legs, hips, hands, head "still." This is a deceiving term because still is a relative term on a moving horse. Your movements must follow the motion of the horse's movements to create a harmonious performance. Feeling motion is an advanced form of feeling your individual body parts. First you need to feel centered, with your body motion going from your head through your center, and then down equally through the inner sides of your legs and out the inside of your heels. This movement is the foundation of a "deep seat" and results from elastic joints and a feeling of being centered and deep. While your body weight moves down through your hips, your hips must have the flexibility and freedom to follow the horse's movement and power from back to front. So your hips have two motions going on at the same time, while your hands remain still. In order for your hands to be still your shoulder joints must be relaxed with the appropriate tone and separate from your spine.

Before you can work on all of this, you need to be aware of your anatomy *(See Chapter—Basic Anatomy for Riders)* and that of the horse (Susan Harris has some good books on the anatomy of the horse.) Developing the appropriate movement in your body takes a long time because it involves balance, elasticity and well-trained muscle memory. You must first develop a deep seat with our weight going down your center out the inside of your heels. Second you must develop flexibility and tone in your muscles to maintain your position while you follow the motion of the horse. Third, you must develop the coordination and flexibility to use your aids to influence the horse without losing your position, elasticity, and relaxation. Ideally, this is learned on a lunge line so that you can focus on the feel of your body and the horse without trying to influence the horse. However, this is often not possible, so the learning time is even longer. This is an essential step in the learning process that cannot be missed if you want to have a safe, harmonious, and successful performance. *(See Chapters—Technical Insights)*

Tales From the Trip
Ann

As Ann developed her awareness of her body parts, her instructor, Angela, helped her identify the motion of the horse at the same time *(See Chapter—Awareness Leads to Feel—Learning Insights.)* Angela helped Ann with both skills when Ann demonstrated her advanced body awareness. The movement of Monty was discussed but was not the main priority in each lesson. Angela explained the importance of following Monty's forward body movement as they did exercises to practice using one leg at a time. As long as Ann and Monty were staying on a circle or going around the ring without making any changes, the ride went well. The trouble slipped in when she began doing more figures and transitions with Monty. When she used her aids together her body would cease to insist that he continue forward with the same motion, thus they got stuck. Three things were added to Ann's education. She began t'ai chi lessons to improve her coordination in motion; she simplified her ring figures so she could move forward as she used her aids; and she rode another horse who was more experienced and responsive than her green Monty. Ann has no idea which of the three helped her the most, but she was very happy that within a month she and Monty had developed forward rhythm and relaxation as they did several ring figures.

PERSONALITY STYLES
by Kathy Kelly, Ph.D.

*Everything that irritates us about others can
lead us to an understanding of ourselves.*
—Carl Jung

WHAT EXACTLY IS PERSONALITY?

*Personality is considered to be your characteristic way of responding
to your environment.*

Both nature and nurture have an influence on your personality. Nature refers to your genetic makeup, while nurture involves your learned behavior. As a child, you try out different behaviors to get what you need. When a behavior works, you get reinforced, so you are likely to use this behavior again and again. Actions that do not work for you are cast aside. Imagine two young children. One is naturally outgoing, and finds that being funny and loud works well for her. Another is more reserved and finds being patient and a hard worker to be key to his success. Whatever your particular strategy, the more you rely on a set of behaviors, the more they become familiar and comfortable to you. Over time, these successful behaviors become like habits, which you use automatically. We call these automatic behaviors your 'personality'.

Personality Styles are sets of behavioral traits that tend to cluster together into distinct groups. There are four basic personality styles, although as many as sixteen styles have been defined by various personality researchers. For the purposes of this book, the four main personality styles will be described.

As you read through these personality styles, you may find yourself relating to one style most easily. This is your "primary" style—the style you adopt most often, especially under stress. Most people also have one or two secondary styles, which are those behaviors you have learned in life to be valuable under particular circumstances, such as in a job or social situation.

Each of these styles has positive traits that can be a source of real personal strength. Each style also has negative traits than can be a source of interpersonal difficulty, as they undermine your relationships with others. Ideally, you want to develop a sense of comfort with all four styles. This is considered a *balanced personality.* A balanced personality finds it easy to relate to people from any style, as they can understand from where the person is coming from—personality-wise.

LEADER STYLE

Leaders are fast moving, high energy, take-charge-type folks. They want to be "the best" and are willing to work hard to achieve that goal. They are doers, and thrive on action. They have many wonderful ideas, and are often accurate in their business intuition. They have no trouble articulating their ideas to others, and they expect others to agree and follow their plan. In the extreme, Leaders can get so wrapped up in achieving their goals that they forget the human element. They are not always sensitive to the feelings of others, and may find themselves with all the material success they desire, but with no real friends because of their single-minded push toward the top. It helps leaders to adopt some of the traits of the *Nurturer style* to balance out their personality.

Leader Style	
Do you like to . . .	*Are you . . .*
■ Take charge of activities? ■ Make decisions? ■ Get to the point in conversations? ■ Be the best? ■ Take on the leadership role in groups?	■ High in energy? ■ Direct, even blunt, with people? ■ Concerned about getting things done? ■ Someone who inspires confidence? ■ Focused on the "bottom line"?

Leader Traits	
Positive Traits	In the Extreme
■ Excellent business intuition ■ Level head in crisis situations ■ Creative ■ Takes action ■ Passionate ■ Inspires others ■ Not afraid to make decisions ■ Does not dwell on what is in the past ■ Good problem solver	■ Demanding ■ Offensive (too blunt) ■ Aggressive (rather than assertive) ■ Struggles with authority issues (wants to be the authority!) ■ Finds it hard to say "I'm sorry"

THE MOTIVATOR STYLE

Motivators love people. They thrive on activity, excitement, and the energy of connecting with others. They seem to know instinctively what makes people tick, and they like to succeed by bringing out the best in others. Their outgoing, high-energy style can land them in leadership positions, but they often lack the focus on detail and follow-through to really enjoy or be successful in this role, unless they have a significant degree of the Organizer style. Motivators enjoy having fun, and will search out the newest and most exciting activities. In the extreme, this style can become restless, inattentive, and unable to see projects through to completion. Their enthusiasm can cause them to take risks that are not well thought out, and therefore on the dangerous side. Motivators also can be perceived as overbearing due to their exuberance and talkative nature. It helps Motivators to adopt some of the traits of the *Organizer style* to balance out their personality.

Motivator Style	
Do you like to . . .	*Are you. . .*
▪ Have fun?	▪ A fast talker?
▪ Be around a lot of people?	▪ Warm and friendly?
▪ Motivate people?	▪ Charismatic?
▪ Work in groups?	▪ Very verbal?
▪ Generate new ideas?	▪ Focused on people and relationships?

Motivator Traits	
Positive Traits	In the Extreme
▪ Playful	▪ Lacks follow-through
▪ Creative	▪ Too much of a risk taker
▪ Enthusiastic	▪ Gets bored quickly
▪ Can pump people up	▪ Moves from one project to another before finishing up final details
▪ Good people skills	▪ Inattentive
▪ Likes to dream *big*	
▪ Has vision	
▪ Can talk others into following them anywhere	
▪ Open and honest	

THE NURTURER STYLE

Nurturers are sensitive, emotional, and compassionate. They feel deeply, and can tune in remarkably well to what others are going through. They listen with their hearts, and act with empathy. People are their focus, and they will drop any task to repair a relationship that is in trouble. Nurturers pride themselves on being excellent caregivers, and will often bring you something before you even knew you needed it! In the extreme, nurturers can over-extend themselves, taking on too many roles that leave them emotionally (and physically) depleted. They can struggle to find their identity outside of being a caregiver. Nurturers are often very competent, but do not seek out leadership positions because they do not want to make decisions. They can see everyone's point of view! It helps Nurturers to adopt some of the traits of the *Leader* style to balance their personality.

Nurturer Style	
Do you like to . . .	*Are you . . .*
<ul><li>Work with people one-on-one?</li><li>Be needed?</li><li>Help others solve their problem?</li><li>Be the one others depend on?</li><li>Follow someone else's orders rather than be the boss?</li></ul>	<ul><li>A good listener?</li><li>In tune to other people's feelings?</li><li>Someone others can trust with their deepest secrets?</li><li>Always there when your friends need you?</li><li>Highly emotional?</li></ul>

Nurturer Traits	
Positive Traits	In the Extreme
<ul><li>Nurturing</li><li>Loyal friend and employee</li><li>A comforting presence</li><li>Able to feel deeply</li><li>Compassion for others</li><li>Dependable</li><li>Finds it easy to encourage others</li><li>Likes to be needed</li><li>Never gives up</li></ul>	<ul><li>Struggles to say *no*</li><li>Can become burned out</li><li>Takes on too much responsibility</li><li>Is indecisive</li><li>Takes problems personally</li></ul>

THE ORGANIZER STYLE

Organizers are analytical, careful, detail-oriented folks. They usually have an eye for quality, and insist on doing things the "right way," which in their mind is the only way. They tend to be unhurried in action and speech, and unwilling to change their minds once they have made a decision. They are ethical and hard working, but prefer to work alone, as they get frustrated by what they see as a lack of quality in other people's work. Organizers have an amazing eye for detail and yet can see the big picture at a glance. They like to have order and routine in their life. In the extreme, Organizers can become rather rigid and controlling. They can suffer from perfectionism, and because they hold themselves (and others) to such high standards, can be harsh critics when things go wrong. It helps Organizers to adopt some of the traits of the Motivator style to balance their personality.

As riders, we all approach the learning process through the lens of our particular personality style. Sometimes the conflicts we experience with our horses, instructors, and other riders are due to differences in personality styles. As you read through the above personality styles, can you guess which styles get along the best? Worst? The following section outlines how each style tends to relate to other styles. This is just a general introduction to some of the issues that crop up between styles, and is not meant to be descriptive of every human interaction. Remember that few people are dominant in only one style; most have characteristics of other styles so that they can adapt to some degree.

Organizer Style	
Do you like to . . .	*Are you. . . .*
<ul><li>Get things right the first time?</li><li>Have things work out perfectly?</li><li>Buy the best quality?</li><li>Work alone?</li><li>Be accurate in what you do?</li></ul>	<ul><li>Good at what you do?</li><li>Someone who likes to analyze things?</li><li>Unemotional?</li><li>Someone who likes to follow (and enforce) the rules?</li><li>Attentive to details?</li></ul>

Organizer Traits	
Positive Traits	In the Extreme
<ul><li>Eye for quality</li><li>Excellent taste</li><li>Attention to detail</li><li>Hard worker</li><li>Persistent</li><li>Conscientious</li><li>Dependable</li><li>High integrity</li><li>Honest</li></ul>	<ul><li>Can be viewed as controlling</li><li>Obsessive nature</li><li>Too cautious</li><li>Too serious, can lack fun in life</li><li>Tough on others</li></ul>

STYLE COMBINATIONS

Leader and Leader: Leaders don't typically get along with each other—only one can be the boss and take charge. Arguments can be ugly, as typically neither one will back down. Only if one leader type is willing to adopt a follower role does this match work out.

Motivator and Motivator: This combination works, as Motivators tend to like other Motivators. Neither one feels the need to be the boss, but both are willing to play and have fun. They feed off each other's energy and enthusiasm, but neither one will be the detail or "reality check" person that this combination can use. This combination can be unfocused and unproductive, unless one of the members adopts a more organizer style to balance the combination out.

Nurturer and Nurturer: This combination creates a lot of frustration in each member, as they both want to serve and be needed. This is a bit like the "After you". . . "No, after you!" scenario. They will both be sensitive to each other's feelings and needs, but will recognize in each other a desire to take care of the other. Neither one will want to stand up and take charge, unless one member of the combination has some Leader or Motivator characteristics as well.

Organizer and Organizer: This is a difficult combination as both have strong ideas about what is "right." If the two members of this combination agree on the goal and the plan to attain the goal, then this can work. They will admire each other's performance and work ethic, but will not spend a lot of time talking or communicating. Problems won't be brought up, just ignored if possible, or the combination will split up because of "creative differences."

Leader and Motivator: This combination can work out very well. Both are action-oriented, fast workers, and passionate. The Motivator isn't intimidated or hurt easily by the Leader's blunt style. The Motivator's lack of follow-through may frustrate the Leader.

Motivator and Nurturer: This combination works well. The Motivator can lead the Nurturer, and also be sensitive to the relationship. As well, the Motivator will enjoy having someone take care of him/her, and do some of the unglamorous work, which the Nurturer will be willing to do to keep the relationship working. If the Nurturer stops trusting the Motivator's leadership, he/she will be frustrated and unhappy, but may not do anything until he/she is truly miserable.

Motivator and Organizer: This combination is made up of opposites, and can work really well if the Organizer can tolerate the Motivator's energy level and degree of chaos. Behind every successful Motivator lies a good Organizer. However, the traits of the other, which make this team so successful, will start to wear on each one after awhile.

Leader and Nurturer: This combination is also composed of opposites. However, it can work, as the Nurturer likes the confidence of the Leader and will be a loyal follower. The Nurturer does not mind the Leader hogging the limelight, but can be easily hurt by the Leader's lack of sensitivity to feelings, and intimidated by their verbal directness.

Nurturer and Organizer: This combination struggles to understand each other. The Nurturer values feelings and relationships, the Organizer values tasks and a lack of emotion. The Nurturer will feel rebuffed, while the Organizer will feel suffocated. A difficult combination.

Leader and Organizer: This combination can be oil and water. If these two types agree on the vision and the plan, the Organizer will follow the Leader and be respected by the Leader for quality of work and effort. They will disagree on speed of pace, and Organizer can be frustrated by Leader's willingness to go forward before everything is "perfect." If they disagree, these two types will agree to part company, as neither one is willing to compromise.

Final Point: There are three important efforts you can make by understanding your personality: seek to balance it, understand how you relate to others, and understand the problems of your dominant personality. With this information you will discover that you can interact with other people with more understanding. No matter what personality style you discover is your strongest, make an effort to balance it as much as you can.

LEARNING STYLES
By Kathy Kelly, Ph.D.

*One of life's greatest gifts is the joy
that comes from life-long learning.*

Learning to ride is a complex and time-consuming endeavor. So, it follows that we would all want our lessons to help us learn with the minimal amount of confusion and frustration. However, a lesson that makes sense to one rider may seem like a waste of time to another. This is because all riders don't learn in the same way! Each of us tend to have a "preferred learning style," which is the style that tends to help us "get it" most easily. Read each of the following scenarios, and see if one of them best describes how you approach your lessons:

You ask a lot of questions. You find it really helpful if your instructor can explain the "why" behind what he or she is asking you to do. If you understand exactly what is supposed to happen, and what the steps are to get there, you learn pretty quickly. What you dislike most is to have the instructor tell you to "just ride," and then stay silent while you work things out on your own. You prefer to be told what is going on underneath you, and like it when you are allowed to ask questions when you don't understand. At the end of the lesson, you like to summarize what you did, and plan out your "homework" for the next week so you can come ready and prepared for the next step.

You are pretty quiet in your lessons. You find it really helpful when your instructor can get on your horse and show you what it is that you are supposed to be doing. Any chance you can, you like to watch yourself in the mirror, especially when your instructor says, "good, that's it!" If you have your lesson video taped, you love to go home and play it back over and over, which helps you match what you are doing with what you are feeling. What you dislike the most is being asked to do something when you don't know how to do it. You prefer it when your instructor tells you what to do and when, and when she tells you something is correct or incorrect. You spend time between lessons watching other riders, trying to learn from what the instructor is saying to them, and imagining what it is that the rider is doing and feeling.

You are very sensitive to the mood of your horse and your instructor. You can sense immediately if someone is mad, irritable, happy, or sad. If your horse is having a bad day, you don't want to push him, and if your instructor is stressed out, you try to make things go easy in your lesson. You learn best when it feels like you and your horse are "in sync" and you feel that your instructor is happy with you and your riding. What you dislike the most is riding with instructors who are aloof or hard to read, who keep their emotional distance from you when you are in the ring. You also dislike riding horses that you haven't had a chance to bond with or get to know. You prefer to have a more personal relationship with your instructor and your horse.

You like lessons that keep you moving and active. You like to "get to it" right away, and don't like to spend time talking everything to death. You find it most helpful when your instructor lets you try things after only the briefest of explanations. If problems come up, you like the opportunity to try and figure them out on your own. You speak with a lot of "feeling words," like "This feels great," or "This feels awkward, not quite right." What you dislike the most is analyzing your ride, or listening to the theory behind what it is you are doing. You like having fun, tend to be spontaneous, and can even be a risk-taker at times. You do it first, ask questions later.

WHAT ARE THE FOUR LEARNING STYLES?

A learning style is a mode of instruction that emphasizes a particular type of action: thinking, observing, feeling, or doing. While each of us will use all four of these learning styles in our life, we tend to resort to one or two of the styles more than the others. And, when under stress, we tend to fall back on our "preferred" style, which is usually the one that we have had the most success with. Which one are you?

Thinkers

This type of rider relates best to scenario #1. If you are a thinker, you tend to rely on your intellect under stress, like to solve problems, are orderly and logical in your approach to new learning situations, and can get very wrapped up in the details. It can be difficult for you to take a step back and see the "big picture," and you can mistrust what your body is telling you, preferring instead to analyze what is going on intellectually.

Thinker	
Learning strengths	Learning weaknesses
▪ Good grasp of theory ▪ Technically proficient riders ▪ Loves to learn	▪ Loses touch with the feeling aspects of riding ▪ Has trouble tuning into what their body or the horse is doing

Observers

This type of rider relates best to scenario #2. If you are an observer, you learn best by seeing what is going on, and then matching this to what you feel. You are cautious by nature and like to stand back and watch before you jump into anything new. It can be difficult for you to have the focus of a lesson be totally on you, and may find the presence of other riders, such as in a group lesson, a big stress reliever.

Observer	
Learning strengths	Learning weaknesses
▪ Often develops an excellent "eye," and is often good at using visual imagery ▪ Can carry over into their own riding what they watch and understand	▪ Often struggles to trust what they feel ▪ Relies too heavily on what other people think and say

Feelers

This type of rider relates best to scenario #3. If you are a feeling kind of rider, you learn best by tapping into emotion. Good experiences open your heart and mind, and tend to make you want to work very hard. Even negative emotion can help you learn if you have a bad experience that you absolutely don't want to repeat. More often than not, however,, you close down under negative emotion, especially if those negative feelings are between you and your horse or instructor.

Feeler	
Learning strengths	Learning weaknesses
▪ Can bring out the best in your horse because you are so in tune with him on a feeling level ▪ Tends to be a sensitive and tactful rider who instructors find a pleasure to teach	▪ Can become too focused on meeting the horse's or instructors needs instead of what you need to make progress in your riding. ▪ Struggles to pay attention to what their own body is doing as one part of the team.

Doers

This type of rider relates best to scenario #4. If you are a doer, you learn best by trying things out for yourself. Repetition bores you silly, and you don't always like to spend time practicing. You tend to be comfortable in your body, and trust what it is telling you, sometimes even more than what your instructor is saying! You find it hard to spend mental energy learning the technical side of riding, and seek out the more social aspects of your sport. If teaching others, you can get frustrated if you have to explain things too much.

Doer	
Learning strengths	Learning weaknesses
▪ Can have a great sense of "feel," along with a natural softness ▪ Tends to be brave and willing to try new things	▪ Can be impatient, impulsive ▪ If you have natural talent, you may lack sophistication and polish if instructors don't insist on you mastering the basics before progressing

Most of us use two or three of these learning styles. The danger is when you rely too heavily on only one of these styles. When this happens, you may find that you are missing out on a lot of good learning experiences. A truly balanced learner will use all four learning styles when learning to ride. Each has their strengths and weaknesses, but all four have something important to offer.

So, how can you teach yourself to learn using the other styles? First, be aware of the style or styles you are most comfortable with when learning. Second, try to figure out what style is being used in the learning situation. Third, try to relate what is being taught to what you already know through your preferred learning style. Fourth, ask questions, using your preferred learning style that will help make the material make sense to you.

Strategy to learn to use other styles

First, be aware of the style or styles you are most comfortable with when learning.

Second, try to figure out what style is being used in the learning situation.

Third, try to relate what is being taught to what you already know through your preferred learning style.

Fourth, ask questions, using your preferred learning style that will help make the material make sense to you.

Tales From the Trip

Sam

Sam is a *thinker* rider. He is taking a clinic with an instructor who is using an Observer learning style. The instructor keeps asking Sam to watch the other horses, so he can "see" what it means when a horse is traveling truly "through." Sam is frustrated, as he isn't sure what he is seeing. He first realizes that his instructor is using the observing style of learning. He then realizes that he is wanting the same information, but from a theory standpoint. So, he thinks back to what he knows about throughness. He starts asking questions about what he is seeing, relating his intellectual knowledge to the sight of the horses in front of him. The instructor begins to point out specific qualities, such as the way the muscles are moving in the hindquarters, across the loins, and up through the neck. Sam mentally puts together what he is seeing with what he is hearing and learning intellectually. Over time, Sam finds that his eye for a "through" horse is getting better and better as he integrates the visual learning with the theory.

What do you do if you are taking lessons from a wonderful instructor who relies too much on only one style?

This is a fairly common scenario. Much depends on how flexible the instructor is willing to become. To step out of one's comfort zone when learning or teaching is an anxiety-producing experience, and some instructors are unwilling to stretch in this way. Therefore, as the student, you are limited in what you can do. However, one of the best ways you can encourage your instructor to teach more according to your style is by *asking questions. Thinkers* need to find a way to have the theory explained. Some instructors will compromise and discuss theory at the end of the lesson. Others don't really know the theory, so you are on your own. Read lots of books (this one is a good start). Ask other riders and take lessons with other clinicians if possible. Just keep asking questions until someone knowledgeable answers them! *Observers* can help themselves greatly by video taping their lessons, as well as watching other people ride. Take lots of pictures of yourself riding, and study pictures of other riders as well. If possible, ask questions about how your instructor sees what they are seeing. "What is it that you are looking at exactly?" is a good question for observer learners.

Feelers have the best questions—What would that *feel* like?" Feeler riders can also ask their instructors for some quiet time, so that they can ride and pay attention to what they are feeling underneath them: "Would you mind if I took a few minutes here to really feel what it is that you are telling me?" *Doers* like to go out and try things on their own. Again, a polite question, such as "Can I go out and try what it is that you are telling me?" might be all that is needed.

The more you know about your own preferred style, the better prepared you will be to ask directly for help in *that style*. Many instructors are happy to be flexible, and will try hard to get the concepts across in different ways. However, putting the effort into learning from another style, while initially more work, can greatly enhance your learning progress. When you can tap into the insights from the thinker, the observer, the feeler, and the doer, you will find yourself riding with all of your senses, which can only serve to make the riding experience all the more enjoyable!

INSIGHTS FROM OUR HORSES
by Jill K. Hassler-Scoop

*The horse teaches us self-control, constancy and the
ability to understand what goes on in the mind and
the feelings of another creature, qualities that
are important throughout our lives."*
— Alois Podhajsky, *Horse and Rider*

Discovering your strengths and weaknesses as a rider is an easy
process if you listen to your horse who is often a mirror of your
own balance of body, mind and spirit.

First let us recognize a happy horse. A happy horse under saddle
will have his ears relaxed, looking forward but listening to his rider.
His tail will be swinging in his rhythm and he will be relaxed. An
unhappy horse will curl his lips, flair his nostrils, pin his ears back,
grind his teeth and swish his tail. An angry or fearful horse will
run, bite, kick, bolt, or rear. These expressions are very easy to
recognize and straightforward. This is acceptable communication
behavior for a horse. People, on the other hand, lean first toward
verbal expression, talking, which combined with a controlled mind
often leaves many thoughts unexpressed. The first thing we can do
when we witness a horses expressed complaint is examine what we
might be doing to cause his behavior. Whether mounted or unmounted, we can learn a lot about ourselves by observing our horse's
reaction to life with us.

Your riding skills are the easiest
to assess if you listen to your horse's
response to your aids. After each
half-halt or exercise you can get
immediate feedback if you ask, "Is
this result the same, better, or
worse?" The answer tells you
whether to do more of the same or
to make a change. Most of the
changes can be associated with your
position—alignment, elasticity,
spring and/or knowledge or your
horse's response to your aids. *(See
Chapters—Technical Insights)*

Lack of results from your change in position or reinstating the horse's response will suggest that you return to the "mirror" and look at your mental state. The better you know yourself the quicker you will be able to detect the cause; be it lack of clear mind, distraction, or uncomfortable mood. Ask yourself a few questions:

- Can you clear your mind and be in the present?
- Do you recognize when you are distracted or too focused?
- Do you recognize when your mood might interfere with your ride?

Tales From the Trip

Ali

Ali is normally a very proficient rider, but at a clinic she found herself riding below her standard—tight, distracted, and out of rhythm. The clinician was a "big name" professional with whom Ali wanted to develop a long-term training relationship. Midway through the lesson, the clinician stopped her and asked, "Why are you so uptight, Ali? Your basic skills suggest this is unusual." Ali took this opportunity to explain her wishes and that she was worried about losing an opportunity if she did not ride well enough. With the mental tightness (anxiety) released, Ali rode like her normal self for the remainder of the lesson. (See Chapter—Worry, Anxiety and Fear for the Equestrian—Personal Insights)

Often our progress and success with our horse is related to "inner" issues that thread through our lives. If you are not making progress, take an inward look and see if you can uncover a roadblock.

Your horse's development of muscle tone and education is directly affected by your *commitment, discipline* and *patience.* If you are not making progress in your training you need to examine these three areas. A regular training program is necessary to progress. It takes *commitment* to follow a regular training program no matter what else is going on in life. Within the daily riding program it takes *discipline* to follow the structure. As one rider explained, "It is easy to get into "la la land" and not follow a system." *Patience* is needed within the big picture and the day-to-day training to give each step the time required so that it can be committed to muscle memory. It also takes considerable patience to go back to a previous step to reestablish a skill that became confused or not accessible during the ride.

- Are you committed to ride regardless of what else is going on in life?
- Do you have the discipline to follow a daily training program?
- Are you patient with yourself and your horse when you need to confirm or reestablish a skill?

Perhaps the greatest gifts of learning you receive from your horse are *positive attitude, forgiveness* and *trust*. Few people can boast about their skills in these areas, but horses give these to us freely: it is part of their nature. Most horses are happy and positive, focused on what is happening, not what they don't have. You have likely experienced your horse's enthusiasm at feeding time; he is eager to eat, not angry because he is waiting. In addition, if you are a few minutes late with his meal, or if your half halt is too strong, he will forgive you and forget it. You can even make this mistake repeatedly and, unless he is in pain, he holds no grudges.

"Making a commitment is the foundation for self-discipline that we must use to start, practice, and complete the tasks to meet a goal."

Horses are much more forgiving than people. To learn to forgive, start by observing how often a horse forgives!

—In Search of Your Image

- Can you say the same about yourself?
- How often do you give the wrong aids because your body refuses to cooperate with your mind?
- Does your horse hold this against you or forget it and let you try again?
- Trust, one of the most difficult parts of life, is another gift of the horse. He wants to trust you.
- Do you trust him?
- Do you give a full release as part of your half halt, or do you hang in there waiting for him to make a mistake again?

The more you trust him and let him own his performance, the better he will perform.

Your horse gives you many opportunities to become better educated in body, mind, and spirit as well as in the balance of these elements. Discover who you are by watching your reflection in the "mirror" of your horse's actions.

WORRY, ANXIETY, AND FEAR IN EQUESTRIAN SPORT

by Kathy Kelly, Ph.D.

Life is either a daring adventure or nothing at all.
—Helen Keller

WHAT IS THE DIFFERENCE BETWEEN WORRY, ANXIETY AND FEAR?

Which of the following statements indicate fear?

- "I don't want to fall off."
- "What if I forget my course in the middle of my ride?"
- "I don't think I can jump that high."
- "Everyone is going to be looking at me!"
- "I don't want to canter on this horse, he goes too fast."
- "Just thinking about it gives me butterflies in my stomach!"

Statements 1, 3, and 5 indicate fear. Statement 2 is worry, and statements 4 and 6 are anxiety. Although the three are frequently confused, they are distinct. Fear is an acute, short-term response to a clear threat of real or perceived bodily harm. Anxiety is a diffuse, generalized response to stress, imagined concerns, and vague threats. Worry is one form of anxiety, and tends to carry with it a sense of "what ifs." That is, worry tends to focus on problems that may happen in the *future*, but do not have a present threat of physical harm. The following statements are examples of a worried rider:

- "What if my horse jumps out of the dressage ring"?
- "What if I forget my course?"
- "What if I go out there in front of everyone and goof up?"
- "What if my horse shies?"

Your Body's Fight or Flight Response

Whether you are anxious, worried, or fearful, your fight or flight mechanisms get turned on. When anxious, this mechanism is turned on only slightly. When fearful, this mechanism gets turned on full-blown. That is, the main difference people feel between being anxious and being afraid is in the degree of the body's flight or flight response. However, the reasons for feeling anxious and fearful differ—fear is a response to a clear danger, while anxiety is generated by your thoughts. Typically, anxiety responses leave you with the feeling of butterflies in your stomach and a slight increase in breathing and heart rate. Your palms might get a bit sweaty, and you might find yourself taking deep breaths to relax. Fear, with its full-blown flight or flight response, gets your adrenaline kicking into gear, getting the body ready for *action*. Your heart beats wildly, you cannot think clearly, you may become nauseous, and sometimes you may even freeze with fright. In anxiety disorders, the body's mild response to anxiety triggers a full-blown fear response. This is a complex disorder with multiple causes and we won't be going into all of that in this chapter. Suffice it to say that, when anxious, people are uncomfortable, and they can feel like they are afraid. As a matter of fact, it is not unusual for people to talk about being scared or afraid when, in fact, they are only anxious, such as the phrases "I am scared to . . .", or "I am afraid to . . ." In some ways, anxiety can be seen as a "fake fear." It can *feel* like true fear, but unless the flight or flight response is being triggered because of a true physical threat to the body, it is anxiety. Some of the most common "fake fears" include:

- Fear of criticism
- Fear of rejection
- Fear of failure
- Fear of change
- Fear of fear (yes this happens—panic attacks and agoraphobia are extreme examples)
- Fear of death (without a definite danger present)

Sport psychologists are specifically trained to help athletes handle the damaging effects of anxiety. Mental skills are as important as the technical skills you have spent so many years developing, and are they are teachable. Seeking out professional help can help you maximize your technical abilities and help increase your level of enjoyment in your sport.

The main point is that true fear brings with it a distinct threat of bodily harm, even if it is in the person's imagination. Anxiety and worry deal with perceived fears without the threat of immediate physical harm. For example, a rider is considered afraid if he or she is thinking, "This horse is going to kill me!" even when it is an old school horse who is struggling to stay awake. For that rider, the experience of threat is real, unlike for rider thinking, "I am going to be so embarrassed if I fall off this old horse!" This latter statement is a form of performance anxiety, a fear of being judged.

WORRY AND ANXIETY

Because anxiety and worry trigger the body's stress response without a clear reason to act, it is rarely helpful to riders to become anxious or worried. The physical consequences of triggering the flight or fight response just gets in the way of riding—making it harder to accomplish whatever it is that the rider is trying to do. In addition, horses are sensitive to our reactions and they feel our anxiety, which just makes them nervous—not a good thing! The good news about anxiety is that because it is generated by our own thinking, we can reduce it by changing what we think, thereby minimizing the negative effects of anxiety on our performance. Elite athletes often learn how to deal with anxiety through mental training. This includes learning how to use a variety of psychological techniques, exercises, and skills that can help athletes keep the "fake fears" at bay. These fake fears are there out of habit and are learned—are not hard-wired into you, like the true fear response is. You know the saying, "Feed a cold, starve a fever"? Well, to modify this for athletes, we can say, "Deal with fears, ignore anxiety." So, how does one learn to "ignore" anxiety?

Fear and anxiety are *not* the same thing!

Fear: *An acute, short-term response to a clear threat of real or perceived bodily harm.*

Anxiety and Worry: *Diffuse, generalized responses to stress, imagined concerns, or vague threats.*

Tips for Handling Worry and Anxiety

- Try not to say to yourself, "don't," as in "don't be nervous." The body only hears the word "nervous."

- Give your mind something productive to think about as a sort of distraction. If you are worried about something, concentrate instead on what you are doing, such as how you are riding, and what your horse is doing moment to moment. Staying focused on the "here and now" can really help keep your negative thoughts at bay. Your horse provides a wonderful focus for your attention.

- If you find that you cannot stop the anxiety from creeping in, try to use it to your advantage. Some riders learn to equate the butterfly feeling with a sign that they are mentally "gearing up" and are on high alert, ready for split-second reactions. This can be seen as positive, in that you may become acutely sensitive to your horse, and your feel and timing of the aids may become just that much better than when you are not on alert.

- Give yourself permission to feel anxious or worried for a particular predetermined period of time. Some riders allow themselves quiet time alone to think about all of their worst fears, and then they slowly replace them with what they have done in terms of training and preparation to minimize the risks of the worst-case scenario. Then when the old fears crop up while riding you can mentally tell yourself that you have already addressed these fears in detail, and that you are comfortable with moving on. Sometimes our fears keep cropping up, because we have not given them enough honest, real consideration.

- Try taking up a more formal method of relaxing your mind, such as yoga, t'ai chi, Pilates, relaxation tapes, massage, or meditation. Relaxation is a learned response, and the more you can train yourself to relax, the less anxiety can take hold.

FEAR

True fear does not just "go away," much to the dismay of many riders. Fear is hardwired as your body's internal warning signal; it lets you know that something is wrong and that you are in danger, in unknown territory, and/or out of your comfort zone. Two reasons we can't wish fear away.

- Humans have the capacity to store vivid memories of fearful experiences—this ability probably contributed to early survival, but it sure makes it hard to forget!

- Humans have the ability to reason and to think. Thus, we tend to think ahead, imagine the worst, and anticipate the consequences of having a bad experience.

Why does fear come up so often in equestrian sports?

- Riding is known to be a high-risk sport. Serious injury is a potential reality.

- Unlike other high-risk sports such as downhill skiing or car racing, equestrian sports involve an animal—thus we have to deal with the unpredictable nature of the horse.
- Riding attracts people because of the relationship with the horse. Therefore, many people that typically are unfamiliar with and not attracted to high-risk endeavors, including toddlers, and older adults enter equestrian sports.

Tales From the Trip
Charlie

Some common misconceptions about dealing with fear are explained in the following Tales From the Trip. Imagine this scenario:

Charlie is at his first horse show. During the warm-up, he makes a mistake and crashes over an oxer. He is clearly shaken by this experience, and the instructor insists that he goes right back over the fence. After a few refusals, the instructor really starts putting on the pressure. Charlie finally jumps the fence and the instructor sends him into the ring, hoping that the bad fall was forgotten.

When reading this, did you think of Charlie as a rider or horse? For many of you, your initial sense will be that Charlie is a rider. Why? Because riders and instructors typically don't push a frightened horse. Yet pushing a frightened rider is often encouraged. Riders and instructors might suggest various methods to bring back the horse's confidence after the fall, such as lowering the fence, following another horse over, even pulling out of the class and entering one at a lower level. However, riders are not always given the same consideration. There is a strong myth in the horse world that riders must overcome their fears and get right back on, or they will never ride again. While it is true that riders should not be encouraged to give up when afraid, pushing straight ahead when fear is present is not a good idea. Some reasons for this are:

- Fear is one sign that you may be overfaced, unprepared, or overwhelmed.
- Continuing on when you are afraid can be *dangerous*. You do not think or react in the same way when you are scared.
- Ignoring your feelings can leave you feeling disconnected from yourself and is a form of self-denial. If you do this too often that you lose touch with your ability to trust your own judgments and opinions.

How to deal with your fear

Just as physical injuries, such as a broken arm or twisted ankle require a period of recovery, so do "mental injuries" such as fear reactions. That is, the few seconds it takes to fall off can cause a rider to go through a psychological process (similar to grieving) that can take days, weeks, months, or even years. Fear usually robs a rider of self-confidence and a treasured sense of control. Dealing honestly and directly with your fear is often the best way back to regaining your trust in, and enjoyment of, your equestrian pursuits.

Here are some tips for dealing with your fear:

- Think of recovery from your fear as a psychological process. You will go through a series of stages, similar to Dr. Kubler-Ross's five stages of grief. The following comments provide examples of riders in each stage:

  Denial: "That fall wasn't so bad," or "I'm not scared."

  Bargaining: "Maybe if I never ride that horse again,"or "I just won't jump anymore."

  Anger: "If only that idiotic horse. . .," or "How could I have been so stupid?"

  Depression: "It is no use, I can't get over this," or "I'll never enjoy riding again."

  Acceptance: "I did fall off, but I wasn't ready to jump that high. I can work to become better prepared before I try that again," or "All horses spook occasionally, but that fact doesn't mean that I will fall off every time it happens!"

- Allow yourself permission to be fearful! Being scared is not something to be embarrassed about—it is a *normal* reaction to a real or perceived threat.

- Accept the fact that you will progress through the stages at your own pace. You may even go back and forth between stages. The key is to be patient and forgiving of yourself no matter what stage you are in.

- Express your fear to yourself and to others. Talking helps! Sharing how you really feel with others can be powerful medicine.

- Try to use the same methods you have used to overcome your fear in other situations. You most likely have personal resources that you don't give yourself credit for.

- Trust your own instincts regarding when you are ready to move ahead. We often know deep inside of ourselves when we are unprepared, overfaced, or just plain not ready. Listen to this internal wisdom! If you let yourself be talked into something you are not really ready for, then when a problem happens you may not be mentally prepared to deal with it.

- Seek professional help if you find yourself unable to make progress on your own. Techniques such as systematic desensitization can help some riders overcome paralyzing fears.

BASIC HUMAN ANATOMY FOR RIDERS
By Beth Glosten, M.D.
Illustrations by Sandy Johnson

Understand the tools you have to work with—your bones and muscles—to achieve a balanced, supple position.

Does your body present a hindrance to your riding? Do you strive for a position that keeps you moving *with* rather than *against* the horse? Perhaps one piece of the puzzle to help accomplish this goal is an understanding of the tools—the bones and muscles—within your body that can help you achieve a balanced and supple position on horseback.

This chapter will cover some basics of the anatomy of the bones and muscles of the human trunk, hips and shoulders that are important to riding. Movement problems common in riders will be described in terms of this anatomy. For reference, some terms used are defined in Table 1, at the end of this chapter. Additional reading materials that contain more detailed information are listed in the *Suggested Reading List* at the end of this book.

To be effective as a rider you must have control over your body. Such a rider is not unbalanced by the horse's sometimes, unpredictable movement, but is able to influence the horse. This takes a certain degree of body awareness, strength, and coordination. Like ballet dancing, this educated use of the body is free, graceful, and while it might look easy, takes physical effort. Time off the horse committed to enhancing body awareness and function is time well spent toward the goal of dancing with your horse

THE TRUNK

Understanding the function of the bones and muscles of the trunk is vital to effective riding. The trunk is important because it contains your center of gravity when you are upright, which is usually located in the middle of the body just below your belly button. This is also the location of the "center" referred to in martial arts and dance. The muscles around this area are designed to preserve balance; hence awareness of one's center facilitates balanced movement and riding. Unfortunately, current lifestyles make this difficult—working at a desk or computer and work that focuses on the hands draw your perception of your center higher up in the body than the real center of gravity. As a result, movement tends to be initiated and controlled by muscles around the shoulders rather than the trunk. The resulting movement is inefficient and looks stiff.

The bones of the trunk include the vertebral column, rib cage, and pelvis (Figure 1). The muscles described include those that stabilize the vertebral column in an upright posture, and connect the ribcage and the pelvis.

The bones of the trunk

The vertebral column, or spine, consists of a series of stacked bones called the vertebral bones or vertebrae. It begins below the skull and ends in the sacrum in the pelvis (Figure 2). These bones have two important jobs: 1) to provide a framework for the upright posture, and 2) to provide protection for the spinal cord which conveys neurological (sensory and movement) messages to and from the brain and the rest of the body. Between each vertebral bone (except those of the sacrum) is a disc (somewhat like a gel pad) that forms a semimobile intervertebral joint. As such, there can be a small amount of movement at each intervertebral joint.

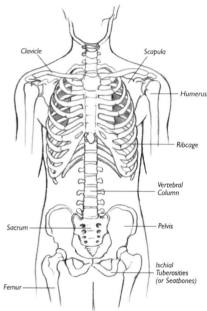

Figure 1: The bones of the trunk, hip and shoulder, front view.

The vertebral bones are not stacked in a straight line, but create several curves (Figure 2). "Neutral alignment" is the term used to describe this natural position of the vertebral bones. Good posture is that position in which the vertebral bones are in neutral alignment. With this in mind, it becomes clear that use of the phrase "sit up straight" can be confusing. Usually it is not true straightness that is desired, but rather this proper alignment of the spine. Not only is good posture attractive, it is also the posture that is healthy for the back and body; improper posture contributes to back pain and injuries.

The rib cage is formed by the ribs attached to the vertebrae in the top portion of the spine. The rib cage has the important role of housing vital organs such as the heart and lungs, as well as

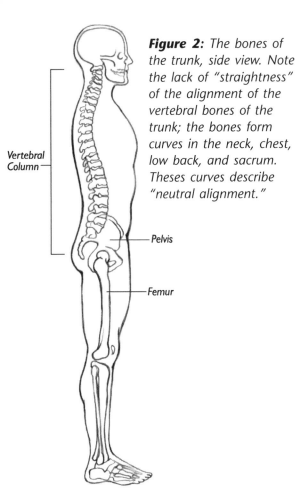

Figure 2: *The bones of the trunk, side view. Note the lack of "straightness" of the alignment of the vertebral bones of the trunk; the bones form curves in the neck, chest, low back, and sacrum. Theses curves describe "neutral alignment."*

Vertebral Column

Pelvis

Femur

providing an attachment for the diaphragm, which is a large sheet-like muscle that controls air movement in and out of the lungs. The rib cage also provides part of the framework for the shoulders to connect to the trunk, and the attachment points for several important muscles of the trunk.

The pelvis attaches to the bottom of the vertebral column at the sacrum. It is an essentially immobile ring of bone (Figure 1). This structure supports and houses the pelvic organs, transmits the weight of the upper body onto the hip joints, and disperses the concussion from the legs "pounding the pavement." The seat bones (an important reference point for riders!) are formed from the bones of the pelvis (ischial tuberosities) (Figure 1). The pelvis serves as an attachment point for several muscles of the trunk, as well as the many muscles that operate the hip joint.

The muscles of the trunk

Several deep sheet-like muscles of the abdomen, along with the deep muscles of the back, provide the means to stabilize the trunk of the body (Figures 3-5). Gaining awareness of and access to these muscles is a necessary skill for preserving balance and posture. In fact, awareness of neutral vertebral alignment, and access to and control of the muscles that affect this alignment, are the most important skills for a rider to master. With control of the muscles

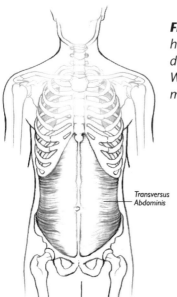

Figure 3: *Abdominal Muscles. Note the horizontal orientation of the fibers of this deepest muscle, the transversus abdominis. When these muscles contract (shorten), the muscles pull the abdomen flat.*

Transversus
Abdominis

Figure 4: *Abdominal Muscles. This shows the three layers of muscles that lie over the transversus abdominis: the internal oblique (shown on the right side of the figure); the external oblique (shown on the left side of the figure) lies over the internal oblique; and the rectus abdominis. The rectus abdominis lies in the midline of the body.*

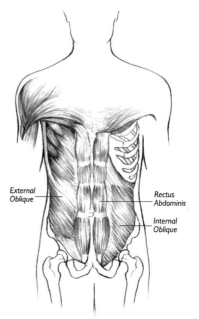

External
Oblique

Rectus
Abdominis

Internal
Oblique

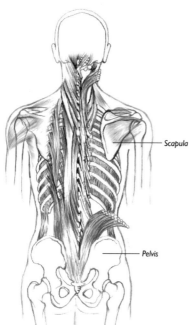

Scapula

Pelvis

Figure 5: *Back Muscles. The muscles of the back consist of many layers of muscles that connect the vertebrae to each other and to adjacent bones. The deepest muscles are the smallest and span few segments.*

of the trunk, the rider is empowered with the tools to preserve posture and balance in any activity. With strength and coordination, these muscles support the rider in neutral alignment during the various movements of the horse.

There are four layers of abdominal muscles. The deepest abdominal muscles, the transversus abdominis and the internal oblique muscles (Figure 3 & 4), play an important role in stabilizing the vertebral column in neutral alignment. When these muscle fibers contract, the fibers move closer together and squeeze the internal organs. This same action supports the vertebral column. Therefore, learning to use these muscles helps support posture. It takes some practice to engage these muscles without causing tension elsewhere, but engaging them should feel as though you put on a snug corset or back support. There should be a scooping-in effect of the abdomen without changing the alignment of the spine to a rounded or arched position (which is what often happens when one first learns to use these muscles).

The other abdominal muscles are the external oblique and the rectus abdominis, which you might know as the body builder's "six-pack" muscle (Figure 4). These muscles, along with the deeper abdominal muscles, facilitate movement of the trunk bending forward and to the side.

The deep muscles of the back (Figure 5) are also important for trunk stability. These muscles are in several layers and connect the vertebrae to each other. Some muscles connect one vertebra to its neighbor, while others might span several segments. The deeper, shorter muscles are important for stabilizing the vertebral column in neutral alignment. There are also muscles that connect the pelvis to the rib cage. These muscles move the trunk into an arch (extension) or side bending.

It is easy to allow the vertebral column to come out of neutral alignment. Especially when fatigued, it is easy to slouch and stop using muscles to support the spine. One way to check if you are in neutral alignment is to assess the relationship of the ribcage to the pelvis. In neutral alignment, the rib cage is balanced over the pelvis (Figure 6A). When lack of awareness or support causes the vertebral column to come out of neutral alignment, the front of the rib cage either moves closer to the pelvis (such as when one slouches forward, Figure 6B), or moves away from the pelvis (as when one

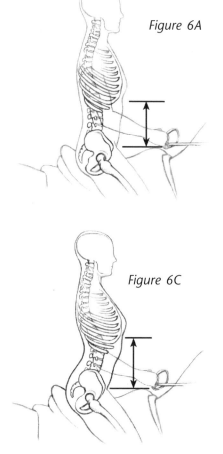
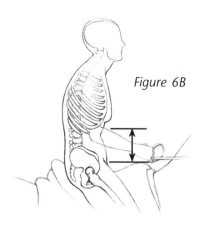

Figure 6A

Figure 6B

Figure 6C

Figures 6A, 6B, 6C: *The spatial relationship between the ribcage and the pelvis is altered when the alignment of the vertebral column is changed. When the back is flexed, the distance decreases* (Figure 6B). *When the back is arched the distance between the ribs and pelvis increases* (Figure 6C).

arches the back too much, Figure 6C), or one side moves closer to the pelvis (side bending). Becoming aware of changes in the relationship between the front of the rib cage and the pelvis can help the rider become aware of changes in the alignment of the spine.

While resting, it isn't terribly hard to balance the body in proper alignment, but alignment can get disrupted with movement. Preserving alignment with activity requires that the deep abdominal and back muscles of the trunk cooperate despite varying forces (gravity, carrying an unbalanced load of groceries, walking, etc).

While riding, to stay balanced in neutral alignment atop a moving horse, the rider needs to find a way to move forward in space with the horse. This can happen in a variety of ways. The rider can constantly play "catch-up" with the horse—that is, the horse pushes the rider's pelvis up and forward and this movement ripples up through the spine. This makes the rider looks a bit like a rag doll. Or, the rider might keep her balance by gripping with the legs and holding onto the reins. This stiff posture precludes the rider being effective, and is unpleasant for the horse. In contrast, a rider that engages the muscles of the trunk to maintain alignment (ribs over pelvis) is able to carry herself forward in space with the horse. This takes supple coordination of all the muscles of the trunk, relieves the legs and arms of balancing duty, and puts the rider in an interactive (a part of the movement), rather than a reactive (affected by the movement), riding position. This position of the rider looks fluid, and while it is tempting to call it "relaxed," it takes active muscle work to accomplish.

Nearly everyone has trunk muscles on one side of the body that are stronger than those on the other side. The side that is stronger is often related to handedness (that is, right-handed people tend to be stronger on the right side of the body). This stronger side of the body tends to be shorter, as the muscles are used more than those on the opposite side. It is as if the body comes to rely upon these muscles as the primary source of balance. This can show up dramatically on horseback. In the unstable situation of being atop a moving horse, this habitual balance mechanism will come into play. This leads to asymmetric posture on the horse (Figure 7). Usually, the side that is stronger, and therefore shorter, pulls the seat bone up on the same side and shifts weight onto the opposite side (Figure 7B). The knee of the stronger side tends to be pulled up (as this is often the stronger leg, as well), and the rider may frequently lose that stirrup. The saddle may become overly worn on the side on which the rider tends to sit more heavily. Strategies to eliminate this asymmetry include: 1) an awareness of how the stronger side engages to balance, 2) strengthening the weaker side and stretching the stronger side, and 3) encouraging the weaker side to participate in balance. Think of the weaker side becoming shorter, lifting up the more heavily weighted seat bone. This can help "take work away" from the stronger side, allowing it to "let go," the leg to hang more freely, and the seat bone to settle down onto the saddle. This might take some practice off the horse. One can start by learning to shift the weight from one seat bone to another sitting in a chair. Attention to symmetric use of the trunk muscles while exercising will also help.

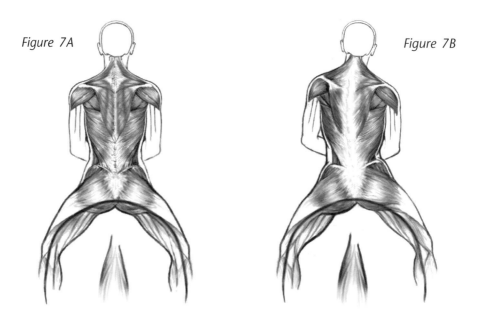

Figure 7A

Figure 7B

Figures 7A & 7B: *Figure 7A demonstrates symmetric muscle use. In Figure 7B, trunk muscle strength asymmetry can pull the rider out of alignment. In this example, the rider's stronger side (the right) pulls the ribcage closer to the pelvis on the right. This may be accompanied by tightness across the right hip joint with the knee pulled up. Weight is shifted over onto the left seat bone, and the left shoulder is higher than the right. Remembering that muscles only pull, the most productive strategy for correcting this misalignment is engaging the muscles of the left side and stretching the muscles of the right side.*

Effective use of the trunk muscles has benefits in addition to maintaining balance and posture on the horse. Use of these trunk muscles supports the back and prevents excessive movement of the intervertebral joints, which should reduce wear and tear on the back. This is not to say that movement of the back and pelvis is avoided while riding. Certainly shifting the weight over the seat bones (part of the pelvis) and changing the direction of the seat bones are means of aiding the horse. But these changes from neutral alignment are conscious, deliberate, and brief.

Supervised exercising can be very valuable in understanding how to use the trunk muscles correctly. One system of supervised exercise, Pilates, teaches use of the deep abdominal and back muscles for postural support. You learn to develop your own muscles to provide a built-in back and trunk support system. For example, "sit-ups" are taught in a way that exercises the deep abdominal muscles. They are done by first scooping in the deep abdominal muscles and then curling up a bit. The feeling should be of peeling off the floor. This method of exercising the abdominal muscles is different than the classic "crunches" that strengthen primarily the more superficial rectus abdominis muscle, which is not as important as the deeper muscles in preserving posture during movement. However, without guidance from an instructor it is difficult to know if you are getting exercises like this "right." It is challenging to change the way you use abdominal muscles, but it can be done. Most importantly, it can improve your ride.

ATTACHMENT OF THE LEG AT THE PELVIS

The upper leg—the thighbone or femur—attaches to the pelvis at the hip joint (Figure 1). It is a complicated joint with many muscles connecting the thighbone to the pelvis. The shape of the hip joint and its muscular attachments allow this joint to move in many directions: forward, back, towards and away from the body, rotating in and out, and in a circle.

Movement in many directions is a beneficial feature of the hip joint for riding. A supple hip joint (just the right amount of muscle tone at any given time) allows you to swing at the hip joint with the movements of the horse's back, while keeping the pelvis in a stable position. If any muscle of the thigh becomes excessively and constantly tight, the hip joint becomes locked up, supple movement of the hip joint is impossible, and you are bounced out of the saddle. Supple movement about the hip joint is only possible if you are not dependent upon the legs (gripping) for balance. By using the muscles of the trunk for balance, the muscles of the hip can remain supple and the hip mobile. Achieving this smooth action of muscles around the hip is the skill that makes good riders look like they are glued onto the back of the horse.

Important muscles of the hip joint

The psoas (pronounced "so'-az") is a unique muscle in that it is the only muscle that attaches the thighbone directly to the center of the body (Figure 8). When the spine is stable, the action of this muscle is to flex or "close" the hip angle. As a general rule, muscles

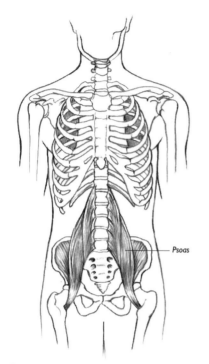

Figure 8: *The psoas muscle lies deep in the body beneath the abdominal organs. It is the only muscle that connects the thighbone, or femur, directly to the center of the body.*

that connect to the center of the body have the potential to help stabilize the body through movement. The psoas is no exception. It is a bit of a mysterious muscle in that it lives deep in the body, and is difficult to feel move. Movement of the thighbone that feels like it starts from the center of the body will probably access the psoas muscle and its stabilizing capabilities.

The hamstring muscle is the large muscle on the back of the thigh. It hooks onto the seat bones (ischial tuberosities) at one end, and just below the knee at the other, forming the two tough bands of tissue on either side of the knee (Figure 9). The action of the hamstrings is very important to riding. It pulls the thighbone back, or "opens" the hip, and it bends the lower leg at the knee, pulling the calf toward the horse. So when you use the lower leg, it is primarily the hamstring muscles of the thigh that are working (Figure 11).

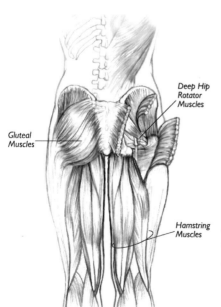

Figure 9: *The muscles of the posterior thigh. On the right side of the figure, note the hamstring muscles that insert on the seatbone (ischial tuberosity) and end on either side of the back of the knee. The large gluteal muscle overlies this muscle.*

The gluteal, or "butt" muscles (Figure 9) attach to the back of the pelvis and then to the thighbone. The action of this muscle group is to open up the hip joint, and, along with a complex group of deeper muscles, rotate the thighbone outwards. These muscles can get tight and fatigued in riders. The gluteal muscles are very strong. Watch that they are not engaged and "helping" when you are using the hamstrings to apply a lower leg aid (Figure 11B). Gluteal muscles that are tight tend to push you out of the saddle. Sitting "deep" necessitates releasing these muscles.

The quadriceps muscle group (Figure 10), for the most part, arises from the thighbone and combines together to form the tough tendon within which lies the kneecap. The main action of the quadriceps muscle is to straighten the knee joint. However, one part of this muscle does cross the hip joint and attaches to the pelvis. The action of this muscle, like that of the psoas, is to bend the hip joint toward the body. If you tend to pull the knee up in the saddle, this muscle is probably overworked. Again, this tightening will limit hip freedom and can be detected if the tendon in front of the hip joint pops out all the time. Because the quadriceps muscle also straightens the knee joint, use of this muscle can pull the lower leg forward (Figure 11C).

The adductors are a group of muscles that attach from the thighbone to the pelvis around the pubic bone (Figure 10). The action of these muscles is to pull the thighbone toward the center of the body. These muscles are the "grippers." Riders who squeeze their knees together to stay on the horse are using the adductor muscles. Overuse of these muscles will prevent free movement around the hip joint.

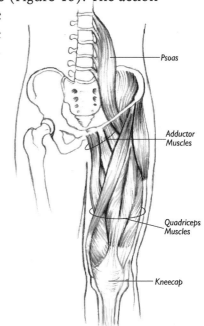

Psoas

Adductor Muscles

Quadriceps Muscles

Kneecap

Figure 10: *The muscles of the anterior thigh. Note the large quadriceps muscle that mostly arises from the thighbone and comes together at the knee to form the tendon that contains the kneecap. This muscle mostly straightens the knee, but part of it also crossed the hip joint and can flex the hip. Also note the strong adductor muscles.*

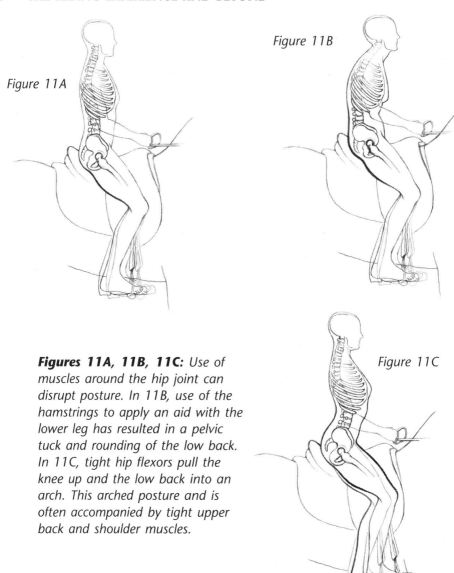

Figure 11A

Figure 11B

Figure 11C

Figures 11A, 11B, 11C: *Use of muscles around the hip joint can disrupt posture. In 11B, use of the hamstrings to apply an aid with the lower leg has resulted in a pelvic tuck and rounding of the low back. In 11C, tight hip flexors pull the knee up and the low back into an arch. This arched posture and is often accompanied by tight upper back and shoulder muscles.*

Successful operation of the muscles of the hip to move the leg is possible only if these muscles are not the rider's primary source of balance. Maintaining balance is the function of the trunk muscles. Further, in order for you to stay balanced while giving, for example, a leg aid, the trunk muscles must be able to counterbalance the movement of the leg. Then, your posture is not disrupted by use of the leg.

Proper functioning of the muscles about the hip is complicated by movement habits that might exist. One example is rounding of the back when using the hamstrings to apply a leg aid—often with added gluteal muscles (Figure 11B). It is as if the body "believes" it can achieve more power in this position. To a certain extent this is true, but it is clearly not the desired way to use the body. Posture is disrupted, and the back is strained in this position. In another example, a rider with tight quadriceps or psoas muscles may have difficulty opening the hip angle to use the leg; the body compensates by arching the back (Figure 11C). This arched posture often also includes tight upper back and shoulder muscles with the body dependent upon the shoulders and arms (and reins) for balance. By becoming more aware of neutral posture, you can learn to feel when use of the leg disrupts alignment.

Exercises that teach movement of the leg through the hip joint in all directions while maintaining neutral spine and pelvic position teach supple use of the hip muscles and help identify tightness in a muscle group. Doing exercises that increase and then clearly release the muscle engagement can enhance the awareness of the state of contraction in the muscle group. Consider the example of a rider that tends to pull the knees into the saddle to grip. Take a few moments (either off the horse or at a halt) and increase the gripping as much as possible, and then completely let go. Do this several times. Learn the feeling of freedom through the hip when the muscles are released. Note also that the trunk muscles now have to engage to keep balance when the grippers are gone. Awareness exercises like this can help the rider access effective tools for balance on horseback and give up those that are problematic.

THE SHOULDERS

The bones of the shoulder area include the upper arm bone, or humerus, the shoulder blade, or scapula, and the collarbone, or clavicle (Figure 1 and 5). Like the hip joint, the shoulder joint is a complex apparatus that can move in many directions.

Several muscles of the shoulder are easily recognized (Figures 12 & 13). The trapezius muscle has many actions; the most notable is the shoulder shrug. This is the muscle that fills the space between the neck and the shoulder. The lower part of the trapezius muscle pulls the shoulder and scapula back and down. The rhomboid

Figure 12

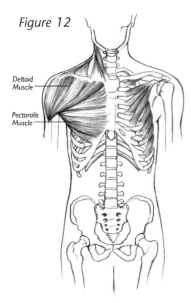

Deltoid
Muscle

Pectoralis
Muscle

Figures 12:
*Muscles of the
shoulder girdle,
anterior view.
Note the deltoid
muscle (forms
the contour of
the shoulder)
and the large
pectoralis muscle
that can become
tight from desk/
computer work
and pull the
shoulders
forward.*

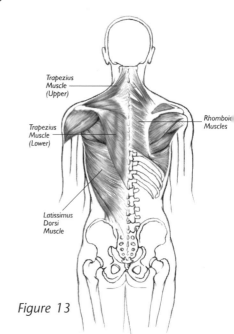

Trapezius
Muscle
(Upper)

Trapezius
Muscle
(Lower)

Latissimus
Dorsi
Muscle

Rhomboid
Muscles

Figure 13

Figure 13: *Muscles of the shoulder girdle, posterior view.
Note the fan shaped trapezius. The upper part of this muscle
is often overworked. Note the rhomboid muscle that pulls the
shoulder blades together. Finally, the latissimus dorsi muscle
attaches the humerus (arm bone) to the center of the body.
Accessing the lower trapezius, rhomboid, and lattisimus dorsi
muscles help keep the shoulder back and down.*

muscles bring the shoulder blades together in back. The pectoralis muscle forms the front part of the armpit, and can pull the shoulder forward. This muscle can become tight in individuals constantly working with the arms in front of the body (desk jobs, computer work, etc.) and contribute to a slouched posture. Periodic stretching of this muscle can help. The deltoid raises the arm, and forms the contour of the shoulder.

The arm has a strong connection to the back/trunk through the latissimus dorsi muscle. At one end, this muscle inserts at the top of the upper arm bone; at the other end, it fans out over much of the mid and lower back. This muscle, in combination with the lower part of the trapezius and the rhomboid muscles, supports the shoulders back and down. This group of muscles forms the stabilizing connection of the shoulder and arm to the center of the

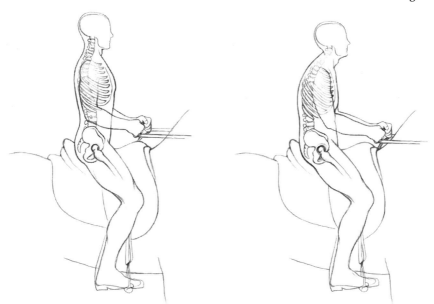

Figure 14: *Movement of the shoulder can disrupt posture. Here moving the arm forward* (rider on right) *is accompanied by forward bending (flexion) of the trunk.*

body. An arm hanging from a shoulder that is stabilized to the center of the body with these muscles can rest by your side and be used efficiently with ease of control. An arm lacking this shoulder stability is held in tightness and is unlikely to function in the supple manner needed for steady contact with the bridle.

Several problems with use of the muscles of the shoulder and arm can contribute to riding difficulties. First, as mentioned previously, our lifestyles tend to bring our attention to our hands and face, raising the perceived center of gravity, and causing movement of the body to originate from the shoulders rather than from the true center of gravity. Gaining a sense of the location of the true center of gravity is key to changing this movement pattern. Overuse of the muscles of the shoulder leads to tightness, lack of freedom of movement, and poor posture. Some riders who lack an understanding of balancing from their center tend to use their arms and shoulders against the reins for balance, putting them in a perched, precarious position. This is clearly undesirable, not only from a rider mechanics point of view, but also for the horse's well-being.

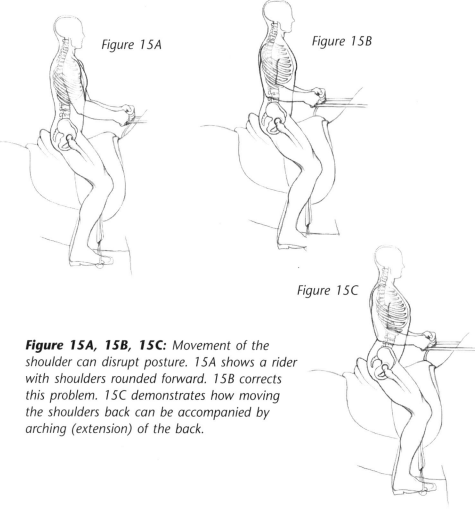

Figure 15A

Figure 15B

Figure 15C

Figure 15A, 15B, 15C: *Movement of the shoulder can disrupt posture. 15A shows a rider with shoulders rounded forward. 15B corrects this problem. 15C demonstrates how moving the shoulders back can be accompanied by arching (extension) of the back.*

Finally, tight shoulder muscles can pull the posture into a slouch—if this is one's posture for many hours a day at work, it is very difficult to change this posture while riding.

Proper movement of the shoulder/arm should not disrupt posture or alignment of the vertebral column. From the anatomy of the shoulder, it is apparent that the shoulder can move freely forward and back, and up and down, independent of any movement of the spine. But habits often link these movements, such that when the arm/shoulder reaches forward, the trunk bends forward, too (Figure 14B). Similarly, bringing the shoulders back and down, can result in arching the back (Figure 15C). These linked movements are not necessary, but changing these movement patterns takes practice. Try moving the shoulder up and down, forward and back, in front of a mirror. Make these motions with and without changing posture, or alignment of the spine. Note that moving the shoulder without changing posture requires an awareness of neutral alignment. It is the same when riding.

IMPROVE YOUR RIDING BY KNOWING YOUR BODY

A basic understanding of your own anatomy can help sort out problems with balance and position while riding. Of most importance is an understanding of neutral alignment and how to support it with the trunk (deep abdominal and back) muscles. Also important is taking full advantage of movement in joints meant to move (the hip) while limiting movement elsewhere (the back). Understanding the basic apparatus of the hip and shoulder will help recognize movement and/or holding patterns that are detrimental to good posture and riding. Untangling unproductive movement habits and replacing them with those that help with riding takes time and practice. Time spent off the horse learning how to use the body effectively is a great gift to yourself and your horse.

DEFINITIONS

Balance. A state of equilibrium in which all forces are opposed. For graceful movement, the minimum amount of muscle effort required is desired.

Bones. The dense, semirigid, calcified tissue that forms the skeleton of the body. Bones are attached together at joints via ligaments.

Center of gravity. That point of a body about which all its parts can be balanced despite the effects of gravity.

Feel. To examine, explore, or perceive the sense of touch and movement.

Relaxation. A loosening or slackening of muscles, or a state of refreshing tranquility. Since this term can refer to either a physical or mental state, in riding, a term such as "release" might be a more appropriate cue to relieve unnecessary muscle tightness. A state of relaxation of the muscles is an unusual goal on the horse; this would result in a floppy rider tossed about by the movement of the horse. "Supple" is a better term to describe the efficient use of muscles that allows a rider to follow the movement of the horse.

Skeletal muscles. Tissue composed of fibers capable of contracting to effect movement; these fibers are grouped into bundles to move a particular bone. Skeletal muscles (referred to as simply "muscles" in this chapter) attach to the bones they move via tendons. Muscles exert their effect only by contracting and releasing; they do not push.

Stability. The state of being steady without being moved or unbalanced.

Supple. Appropriate, efficient muscle use; only the necessary muscles are engaged or activated; there is no unnecessary muscle tightness.

Tension. The process or condition of being stretched tight, it can also refer to a state of mental anxiety. Since this term has both physical and mental definitions, it is good to use a more specific term, such as "muscle tightness" to refer to unnecessary muscle exertion.

Horse Insights

A horse is your most valued teacher,
let's understand a little about him.

Understanding the basic nature of the horse is essential to the development of your partnership and learning process.

The Mind of a Horse—by Jill K. Hassler-Scoop

Biomechanics of the Horse Made Simple—by Jill K. Hassler-Scoop and Kathy Kelly, Ph.D.

The "Right" Horse Through the Stages—by Jill K. Hassler-Scoop

THE MIND OF A HORSE
by Jill K. Hassler-Scoop

One of the most remarkable equine characteristics, common to nearly all horses, is a capability, even a willingness, to transfer the allegiance and loyalty normally extended to another remember of its own species to a human being and to obey orders transmitted to it through various channels.
—R. H. Smythe, The Mind of the Horse

Understanding a horse and knowing his needs are vital to becoming a good equestrian. The more you understand his mind and body, the better you can communicate successfully with him. Understanding your horse also creates opportunities for your own self-understanding.

Let's examine the characteristics that can help you understand a horse and give you insights into yourself as an equestrian: simplicity, leadership, routine, social interaction, senses, and intelligence are a few key traits. Understanding these points will help you to "get on the same page" as your horse, rather than expect him to get on "your page." Getting on the same page as your horse is very important for improving your riding performance. So often riders tend to attribute human characteristics to their horses rather than look at the horse and determine how to "get on the same page" from the horse's point of view. He, after all, is the partner with the greatest physical mass and presence in the team. Let us examine the key factors in a horse's character and compare them with our human characteristics. This will help you better understand the horse and communicate more effectively with him as well as understand more about yourself.

SIMPLICITY

A horse by nature, likes his life simple; his primary attention is on food and freedom (which many horses don't get today!). The simplicity of a horse is refreshing. As we discussed in the *Insights from Our Horse in Personal Insights*, horses live in the moment; they react and respond, they do not analyze and calculate.

If you go to the core of your own nature, do you understand the value of simplicity?

94

LEADERSHIP

A horse is a herd animal by nature. Once the leader is established, each horse assumes his place in the "pecking order." A horse can assume two roles in the herd: showing respect for the leader, and being the leader to those lower than him in the pecking order. If your horse is pastured, and he is the lowest in the pecking order, or if he is stabled and cannot honor his herd instinct, you may discover that he will try very hard to dominate you. You need to know how to deal with the "leader" in your horse. If you have a leader, consistent groundwork needs to take place so that your horse respects you. By nature you may be a leader or follower. If you are a natural leader you need to be careful to lead the partnership with love and consistency, not force. Creating a successful partnership will teach you much about the qualities of being a good leader. If you are a natural follower, you need to learn leadership qualities so you can take on the leader role in the partnership. Recognizing the roles in our partnerships is very important, each of the partners needs to respect the other. *(See Chapter—Personality Styles—Personal Insights)*

If your horse needs to learn respect, teach it to him with kindness. If you are a leader, you must be careful to insist upon respect with consistency and kindness. If you are a follower, you need to develop more strength of character to direct your horse. If you don't, even the kindest horse will develop bad habits due to your passiveness.

If you go to the core of your own nature, are you a leader or follower?

ROUTINE

A horse needs to be fed on a regular schedule or he may get sick. This is proof of his system sensitivity and his need for routine. Routine can be used in training sessions to teach a new skill. John Lyons claims a horse needs ten thousand repetitions to learn a new skill.

Characteristics to Understand
Simplicity
Leadership
Routine
Social Interaction
Senses
Intelligence

While that might be an exaggeration, a horse does need a lot of repetition. You need repetition to learn a new muscle memory. Who needs the most repetitions, you or your horse? It depends

"A horse will never do anything on purpose. This requires deductive reasoning, which horses simply do not have. Only highly intelligent beings do things on purpose and with planning. But the horse has a quick instinct for self preservation, an unbelievably good memory for good things and even more capacity for remembering bad things[1]."
—Walter Zettl,
Dressage in Harmony

upon the individual. You have an advantage over your horse because you are able to benefit from repetitions in your mind through mental practice, he can not. *(See Chapter—Mental Practice—Learning Insights)* The need for routine varies depending upon the nature of the horse and the rider.

If you go to the core of your nature, which do you like more, routine or change? How does that fit into your riding?

SOCIAL INTERACTION

Horses like to socialize, not with humans but with each other. If no other horses are around they will bond with a cat, a dog, or a goat. I even know one horse who had his own chicken who traveled everywhere with him. Horses do not like to be alone. Horses are happiest grazing in a field with their buddies, free to roam and interact. We are social creatures too, but are fundamentally different in that we can enjoy being alone.

If you go to the core of your nature, do you prefer being alone or with other people?

Tales From the Trip

Duchess and Choky

Duchess was about to have her first foal, and was uneasy, constantly whinnying. It took Mary, her owner, about three hours to figure out that she was calling to Choky, the experienced pony mare. Mary, went out to the far pasture and brought Choky into the stall next to her, and within twenty minutes Duchess had her foal.

THE SENSES

Horses have highly tuned senses of smell, hearing and touch. A small fly landing on a horse's tail will be immediately flicked off. If he can feel this, he is capable of feeling the slightest moves you make while riding. If you put medicine in the feed, you may discover that it is sorted out from the grain granules; he can't see it, but he can smell it. I often shudder when I hear people being loud around a horse, because their hearing is so sensitive. Our primary sense, on the other hand, is sight. We can develop all our senses if we wish to take the time, but it is often easier to rely on sight, thus our other senses remain underused. The one sense we must develop and refine to become a successful rider is that of touch, which allows us to "feel." Observe your horse, and consider how you can improve your sense of touch and feel.

Reflecting on your own nature, in what order do you rely on your senses?

INTELLIGENCE

A horse lives mainly in the present, in the here-and-now. Horses can remember the past, but only if the experiences in the past are particularly stimulating, good or bad. Because of a horse's moment-to-moment focus, he learns by repetition. He cannot process information in a complex way; the way you can. The experience remains as he felt it—either pleasurable, uncomfortable, or frightening. Normal day-to-day experiences do not affect him one way or another, only repeated experiences are remembered. However, painful or frightening experience may leave an everlasting scar because it is remembered particularly well, and the next time the horse is in a similar situation, he will recall the past, and become afraid. A traumatic experience (it needs to be really bad) may become implanted and, no matter what you try to do, will remain in his mind as he experienced it. Therefore, if you have had trouble during your training session, you must return to a pleasant activity before stopping, so that the positive experience is left in his mind, rather than the problem.

You, on the other hand, can live in the past, present, and future. You have the ability to process information, develop some understanding, and move beyond the bad experience. Some of us can do it better than others. One of the most important points to remember is that, because a horses cannot look towards the

It takes either a major trauma or a repeated negative experiences to leave a horse with a negative impact.

future as we do, they can not calculate and plan to do something to us—if he does something we don't expect or like, it is most likely a result of confusion, misunderstanding, or fear.

Do you spend most of your time with your horse living in the past, present, or future? Do you use your intelligence to understand what a horse thinks in his simple survival terms?

Tales From the Trip

Robby and Cindy

Cindy was on her way home from a show with her four horses in the trailer. She went around a turn on a back road and felt the trailer moving all over. She stopped to check on the horses and found Robby on the floor with his head held tight by the trailer ties. She quickly emptied the trailer and partitions so that Robby could get up. He did, and did not have one scratch. Cindy was thankful. She reloaded everyone, and as soon as she got Robby into the stall, he began to shake, scramble, and go down again. No matter what she tried, he remained panicked. The only way she was able to get him home was in a double stall. From that day on, Cindy had to ship Robby in a double stall, or leave him home. Robby never got over his trauma.

Cindy herself was so upset by the event that she shook the five hours it took her to drive home. She dreaded the next time she had to drive the horses to a show. Each time she drove, she held the steering wheel to the point that she found her arms exhausted, as well as feeling sick to her stomach. After six trips she decided this had to stop, and she sought counseling. Several sessions later, she was able to drive her horses free of stress. Cindy, with the help of a professional, was able to get over the trauma.

What a great combination—our highly refined brain and the horse's highly refined senses. We can learn from each other.

BIOMECHANICS OF THE HORSE MADE SIMPLE

by Jill K. Hassler-Scoop
and Kathy Kelly, Ph.D.

Conformation impacts performance!

Conformation plays a major role in your horse's ability to stay sound and to perform. Conformation refers to the way a horse's bones are put in place. For example conformation will tell us: 1) how easy or hard it will be for him to move balanced and, 2) how well he actually moves. We will now take you on a brief tour of the major conformation points so you can develop your "eye" for what makes a suitable horse when seeking a riding partner.

IDEAL CONFORMATION

The picture below is an example of a horse with good conformation. This next section explains in brief detail why we like the conformation of this "ideal horse". to help train your eye to see the underlying bone structure, we have also included an illustration of the skeletal system. Please note that deciding what is "good" versus "bad" conformation should take into consideration what kinds of work the horse is going to do. This ideal horse is built to perform in either dressage or jumping activities.

An example of good Conformation for a performance horse

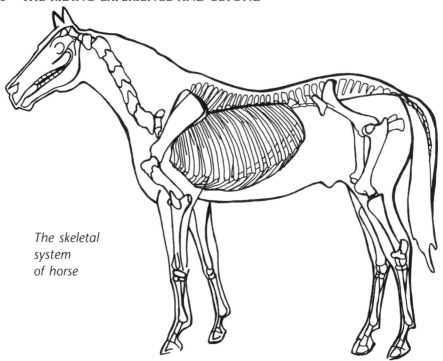

The skeletal system of horse

BASIC CONFORMATION

Eyes

Large eyes, combined with short, deeply arched ears, are a sign of sensitivity, kindness, and ability to learn. The eyes and ears show expression, and are clear indicators of the attitude and temperament of a horse.

Neck

The neck is well-carried and proportional with the body, with a wide gullet that thins as it approaches the head. It is set correctly on the shoulder, not low and not too long or short compared to the rest of the horse's body.

A low set neck is one of the most difficult conformation faults for horses that are asked to carry themselves in a light and balanced frame (dressage, eventing, hunters, jumpers).

Shoulders

The longer the length of shoulder blade, the longer the length of stride, while the slope of the shoulder dictates how much the horse will lift his knees. More upright slope of shoulder allows for the horse to lift his knees up towards his chin. Long length of shoulder blade combined with a more sloping shoulder is ideal for dressage horses. Long length of shoulder blade combined with a slightly upright slope of the shoulder is ideal for jumping horses.

Forearm

The forearm should be long compared to the cannon bone, connected at a right angle to the shoulder blade, and with well-contoured muscles. This combined with a good hindquarter allows for a long stride, which is great for galloping, extension, collection, and jumping.

Knee and Fetlock joints

Large joints are stronger than small joints. Clean joints, meaning no extra lumps, bumps, or swellings, stay sound longer. Knees should appear 'flat' when looking at them straight on, and be centered evenly over the cannon bone.

Front Pastern

Ideal length of pastern is not too long or short, but in the middle.

Too long leads to possible problems with tendons and ligaments stretching and pulling under work.

Too short leads to a more uncomfortable, jarring stride because of the shorter stride and increased concussion. Upright pasterns cause a horse to take short steps and may lead to future unsoundnesses. Too long pasterns can lead to hyper flexion of the tendons and ligaments.

Back

The back needs to be of appropriate length for the horse, not too long or too short when compared to rest of body (the wither is the beginning of the back, and the lumbosacral joint (L-S joint) is the end of the back).

Horses with backs that are too short or too long will find it difficult to use their backs correctly, and thus have a difficult time developing "throughness" (*See Chapter—Stage 4—Technical Insights*).

A little longer back tends to allow for greater body flexibility and more scope over fences. Backs that are not too long make it easier for a horse to engage and tend to be stronger. A 'good' back allows the unconstrained interaction of the circle of muscles from the croup through the back, the neck and the belly, this allows the back to swing freely. A horse should have well pronounced wither ('well-defined'). Horses with low or short withers have difficult time keeping the saddle in place and raising their backs while performing.

Chest

The chest should be deep and wide so as to allow room for the heart and lungs, as well freedom of movement for lateral work and speed. A narrow chest tends to cause the front legs to cross over in extended gaits and in lateral movements, because the hindlegs are wider.

Hindquarters

Hindquarters should be well muscled evenly on both sides with hips level. The distance between the hip and buttocks and hip and stifle joint should be long. This long distance provides the power, especially when the hock is close to the ground. The ability to engage is directly related to the right angle between the ilium and the thighbone at the hip. These points are the key to the horse's ability to engage, stretch, and bend without loss of power. Notice in the skeletal illustration—the angles of the joints in the hind end of the horse.

Hock

Ideally, the hock will be large and set close to the ground. They will be positioned slightly together so that the horse can stand with toes slightly out, with an angle not too bent (sickle hocks) and not too straight (post leg). The hock is responsible for distribution of the weight of the horse and the rider. It propels the weight forward.

Tail

The tail should hang down in a relaxed fashion, and swing gently with the side-to-side motion of the hips. It should also be long and full, so the horse can use it to keep flies away. The tail shows expression, attitude and temperament of the horse.

UNDERSTANDING MOVEMENT—THE CIRCLE OF MUSCLES

Energy moves through the horse's body via the circle of muscles. This movement begins when the hind legs step forward under the horse's body. When the legs move forward, with energy and straightness, the horse is said to be 'freely forward' and engaged. The abdominal muscles contract in rhythm with the horse's stride and the loin muscles (around the L-S joint) flex, and as these muscles are used correctly the back begins to get round. The more energy from the muscles, the rounder the back can become. The rounder the horse's back, the more swinging motion will be felt by the rider. An observer will see more motion in the horse's hips and swinging of the tail.

When the rider has the proper connection with the bit, referred to as contact, the energy will travel through the circle of muscles to the poll and the horse will make a telescoping gesture (reaching longer and lower with neck and head. The rider can maintain this feeling and ride the horse round, or ask the horse to stretch long and low. A horse begins by working in the "training-level frame," and as he develops and builds the correct muscles, the energy of the movement will be contained in an elastic receiving rein contact that will ask the horse to become even "rounder." Through the stages of the horse's education the horse's muscles will become stronger—as he advances in both his training and his strength he will be able to be correctly "on the bit."

 The Reference Feel: Once a horse is moving forward with a round back, and can flex and bend properly in both directions, you can feel the energy that is coming from the horse's hind legs, passing through the horse's back, and ending up in your hands. This is the "reference feel", which is felt in your hand when you have a consistent, elastic contact. When a horse moves forward into your hand, the horse is stretching and arching his head and neck (because his back is round), which allows him to give his mouth and jaw to your hand (providing the hand is receiving and educated). At this point the horse is relaxed, supple, obedient, and can be said to be "on the bit." *(See Chapter— Stage 3—Technical Insights)*

THE "RIGHT" HORSE
THROUGH THE STAGES

by Jill K. Hassler-Scoop

A horse is our most important teacher,
it is important to match his conformation,
temperament and education with our needs.

The three characteristics of a horse to consider in finding the "right" match for you are conformation, temperament, and education. It is good to know as much about yourself as possible, so that when you look for that right match you know what you are looking for. Throughout your riding journey the match of conformation and temperament remain the same; however, as you advance, your needs related to your horse's education change. The right match will depend upon your interests and goals. Seldom can one horse do the entire job of taking you all the way on your journey.

SIZE

The size of the right horse, as well as ideal conformation discussed earlier, must be physically compatible with your size. The horse should meet the needs of your body build in both height and width. A horse that is too large in either direction for your body conformation will reduce the flexibility of your joints and thus will make it difficult for you to relax and use your body effectively for communication. A horse that is too small will make it awkward for you to maintain contact with your legs and to feel in balance. Matching your conformation with your horse's is a very important ingredient that a professional can help you with, but you need to understand your body and be realistic about it.

Tales From the Trip

Lori

Lori had tried for years to lose the extra forty pounds that she carried. It was time to buy a new horse, and one professional told her to lose the weight first, while a second told her to buy a horse that matched her size. Either decision would have been fine; the key point was that a decision was made and followed. Lori, considering how many years she had tried to lose weight, realized that she needed to buy a horse who could carry her at her current weight.

104

Kelsey

Kelsey, who was only 5'2", bought a 16.3 hand horse as advised by her trainer. The idea was that she would look good and catch the judge's eye when they entered the arena. Kelsey continues to struggle with falling off more than she would like. She now realizes that her small body cannot absorb all the motion of her horse. Now she is faced with another decision; sell this horse and find a new one, or find a way to stay on him!

TEMPERAMENT

Each horse has a different temperament, and it is important to determine what will work best for you. While all *new* riders need a quiet, well-mannered horse, as you begin to advance you will discover that you may want to match your personality with your horse's. Passive people rarely like aggressive horses. Aggressive riders rarely like passive horses. Both combinations can lead to frustration. It is important not to mix sensitivity with an aggressive character. Most horses are very sensitive to the rider's balance, position, relaxation, and aids; it is how they react to your challenges while learning that are important. As you advance you will discover that your basic personality will have an impact on the horses you choose to ride. An aggressive rider can energize a lazy horse, and a passive rider can calm a nervous horse. Initially, however, during the learning periods of Stages 1 and 2, the ideal horse is one who is good-natured, well-educated, relaxed, and appropriately responsive.

Tales From the Trip
Indigo, Moonshine and Tom

Tom had reached Stage 3 in his learning journey and was looking for a horse to purchase. He tried Indigo several times because Tom loved Indigo's forward energy and response to the aids. Indigo, however, would become very wired after about twenty minutes of riding. The other horse that Tom was considering was Moonshine, who was less sensitive to the aids but responsive. While Tom liked the aggressive, forward Indigo, his instructor preferred Moonshine, who was obedient but less reactive. Tom was able to get Moonshine to do what he wanted without getting him wired. Both horses were sensitive, but Moonshine was by nature calmer and less aggressive. Tom took his instructor's suggestion and purchased Moonshine. They became long-term partners who enjoyed foxhunting and eventing.

EDUCATION

Throughout this book we refer to "schoolmasters." Schoolmasters are horses who are confirmed in their training. Their balance and response help you "feel" what you are learning and thus develop the correct muscle memory. The ideal schoolmaster is trained two levels above your level. Ideally, schoolmasters continue to be in some training in order to remain good at what they do.

 The qualities to look for in a schoolmaster: well-mannered, tolerant, calm, relaxed, and well-trained.

Schoolmasters Through the Stages

Stage 1 and 2 - solid individual who will not buck or run, is quiet and kind and listens
Stage 3 – supple, relaxed, and responsive to both the forward and lateral leg aids
Stage 4 and 5 – supple, relaxed, and responsive, with a higher degree of education

---

Stage 1 and 2 Riders

During these stages you need to learn on a horse who is properly trained, and who moves without stiffness and with rhythm, so that you develop the correct feeling from the very start of your riding. The horse you learn on must be of kind character, willing to please and trustworthy. It is during these stages of riding that the foundation for muscle memory is established, so a schoolmaster who has the appropriate education and movement is the most valued asset. If you have the chance to lease one, own one, or ride one in lessons, grab the opportunity. These valuable individuals are very difficult to find in the United States. As you will read in our Technical Insights section, one of the major differences in education in the United States as opposed to in Europe is the quality of the school horses. If you don't have the ideal schoolmaster, don't panic; look at our suggestions in the "Alternative Routes" section of each stage.

No matter what, don't try to learn to ride on a horse who frightens you. This is not only unsafe, but it will teach you all the wrong muscle memories.

Stage 3 Riders

It remains ideal to have a schoolmaster who is trained above your level so that you can learn on him, but at this point that is not absolutely necessary for your safety and proper muscle memory. It is also more difficult to find such an educated horse in the United States. If you don't have the "perfect" horse but you have good instruction and have had a solid foundation in Stage 1 and 2 skills, you will make it through this stage. However, you need to be prepared for it to take you quite a long time, and you will need to have realistic expectations, patience, and qualified help.

Stage 4 and 5 Riders

By now you have decided what you want to do with your riding pursuits. Often the horse that carried you through the earlier stages is no longer appropriate and you need to find a horse that matches your goals and future plans. It is at this point that some riders, because they love their horse more than their goals, will change their goals to match what their horse can do. Others make the mistake of trying to force a horse to do something that is not within his physical reach. This is not fair to the horse.

Thought process for problem solving your roadblocks

1. Check your position; alignment, spring in joints and relaxation
   - If you find a problem work on it and continue
   - If you feel fine…

2. Check your horse's response to your leg and rein aids and relaxation
   - If you find a problem work on it and continue
   - If you feel fine…

3. Return to the previous step you learned successfully, confirm that you feel good in it
   - If you have not solved your problem…

4. It is time to turn to your instructor to help you identify the cause (s) of the roadblock so that you can progress with your learning experience.

PROBLEMS: IS IT THE HORSE OR THE RIDER?

I would like to finish by explaining that often riders feel they are causing roadblocks during their riding. This may be the case, but more often it is a combination of the horse's lack of knowledge and your lack of experience. This is one of the truisms of riding. The better your balance and position, the better the horse will perform; and the better the horse performs, the better your balance and position. In the Technical Insights section we give you tips on how to deal with some of these roadblocks and confusions. The "Thought Process for Problem Solving Roadblocks" can be helpful from the first time you step onto a horse.

FACT INSIGHTS
Facts to help the discovery process!

The horse world, like all other aspects of the world we live in, will provide valuable experiences if we are educated consumers. We often get asked, "but how do I know if the information I am learning is correct?" The *Fact Insights* are the basic facts that will help you determine what is correct, and give you the factual information on which to base your decisions. Every rider needs to know what is in this chapter.

FITNESS FOR RIDERS
by Sophie H. Pirie Clifton
with Patrick Hanks

Never ask more of your horse than you are willing to give.
—Ray Hunt

When I was little, I thought that all I did to help my riding was ride—young and often naughty ponies and horses. In fact, I did a lot more, because I grew up on a farm and was constantly active. My best friend and I got our working student jollies by racing to see how many stalls we could muck before anyone else showed up at the barn. Even though I weighed under a hundred pounds through my teens, I could easily lift eighty-pound hay bales and tack trunks. It was not until I made the North American Young Riders Three-Day Event Team, however, that I undertook my first conscious supplemental training program – which consisted of running sprints uphill through long grass and then begging anyone I could find to put me through a session on the "bucking barrel." Had I known about strength training, I absolutely would have supplemented my efforts with that. As it turned out, at the Young Riders championship, my first ever full three-day event, I needed every bit of balance, physical strength, and endurance I possessed to pull off a clean cross-country round, as I rode Phase D (the actual cross-country) on a very keen and strong horse with sopping wet leather gloves (no one had told me about rubber gloves!) and wet reins that I had to wrap around my fists and then under my butt riding over most of the fences in order to have any control. Many of you have seen pictures of the famous New Zealand eventer, Mark Todd, jumping around Badminton minus one stirrup, but unlike me with my reins, he made his trip look like all his tack was in good working order, so phenomenal is his balance and strength.

Even under less demanding and less dramatic circumstances, riding safely and effectively will often require us to do and have done more than just ride. I have found this to be particularly true for people who have not spent their whole lives on a horse. I took twenty years off from riding. Coming back and seeking to achieve classical correctness and performance success for myself, my horses, and my students, I constantly draw upon the training, exercises, and body awareness that have come to me through having studied Tae Kwon Do, Gyrotonics, weight and interval training, and, to a lesser extent, Centered Riding, dance, T'ai Chi, several varieties of yoga, as well as nutrition, basic physiology, and anatomy *(See Chapters—Supplementary Learning Insights.)*

IMPORTANCE

Riding one horse does not cause you to be fit enough to ride that one horse well. We all know that the extra stress and demands of competition—traveling, performing in a strange place, and pressure to win—require extra fitness beyond what we might need at home to safely and correctly perform a given dressage test, cross-country round, or other exercise.

What many riders and trainers overlook, however, is that, on a day-to-day basis, **effective** riding requires considerably more physical fitness than many of us usually have. For example, how well you sit and use your aids is as much a function of your "rider's fitness" as it is of your technical proficiency as a rider. As an instructor, I can't tell you how many currently competing students I come across who are winded after a round of eight stadium jumps or find it difficult to use their back correctly for a half halt. *Your* fitness is an important ingredient in how well your horse goes and develops.

If you are not adequately fit, not only do you risk injury to or bad training for your horse, you also risk injuring yourself. The risks vary from straining tendons and ligaments because supporting muscles are not strong and flexible, to not being able to stop a runaway horse. Should you fall, your overall fitness, especially your flexibility, will often determine whether you suffer serious injury or jump back up with only a few bruises.

 Before beginning any fitness program, it is advisable to consult your physician to determine whether you have any special needs or concerns.

Just as you would never expect your horse to perform well and safely without appropriate conditioning, you also should not expect to perform well and safely yourself without appropriate conditioning. To paraphrase Ray Hunt, you should not ask more out of your horse than you demand out of yourself. Do not expect your horse to make up for your own lack of conditioning.

TIME

Just as *time* (i.e., the lack of time) is *never* an excuse for not getting and keeping your horse fit, neither is it an excuse for not being fit yourself. But because riding does build some physical fitness, we only need to think in terms of a *supplemental* fitness program. Unless you are quite unfit (in which case you may need to devote more time up front), most people can accomplish basic equestrian fitness needs (say, those adequate for pleasure riding and lower level competition) by devoting 15–20 minutes a day, 4–5 days a week to strength and flexibility and 20–30 minutes a day, 3 times a week to cardiovascular training (in addition to time spent riding at least one horse 4–5 days a week). If you ride more than one horse a day and regularly move hay and jumps, you may be able to reduce some of the strength training. If you exercise racehorses regularly, you may be able to reduce the cardiovascular requirement. If you are lunged regularly, you may be able to reduce some of the flexibility work. There may also be other things you do in life that can substitute; for example, yoga practitioners and ballet dancers typically do not need to worry about flexibility training; people who play basketball, soccer, or other running games 2–3 times a week tend to have sufficient cardiovascular fitness; and those who work for UPS lifting boxes tend to have sufficient muscular strength.

Even if you do not take dance classes, play soccer, or work for UPS, many of you will still be able to accomplish these fitness objectives without adding more than a few minutes onto your no doubt already busy schedule. If you watch TV or talk a lot on the phone, that is a great time to do your stretches and play with hand weights. If you have a treadmill or other cardiovascular machine (bike, Nordic Skier, etc.) at home, put it in front of the TV or move the TV to a place where you can jump rope. If you dispense with the snowblower and shovel your driveway, you can probably get in both a strength and a cardiovascular session at one time, especially if you race your neighbor to see who gets their driveway cleared fastest. There are even activities that you might not associate with exercise that can be used to help your overall fitness; for example, washing the dishes or talking on the phone can be a great time to stand on a balance platform (or just on one foot) to work on your balance and the strength and flexibility of your ankles and feet.

BASIC CATEGORIES, WHICH *TOGETHER* COMPRISE FITNESS

The key to fitness efficiency (time-saving) is combining the following five categories of fitness training and maintenance into an individualized equestrian-oriented fitness program:

- Structural Alignment and the Functional Body
- Breathing
- Cardiovascular (heart and lungs)
- Muscular Strength
- Flexibility
- Balance, Coordination, and Reflexes
- Nutrition and Hydration (including weight/body fat optimization)

While we all need to develop and maintain our fitness in all of these categories just to be healthy as human beings, *how* we each do that will vary with our goals and needs as riders, as well as with what else we do (and want to do!) in our lives besides ride.

Structural Alignment and the Functional Body

While traditional conditioning programs tend to focus on cardiovascular and muscular fitness, we can improve the efficiency of our fitness efforts, enhance our performance, and minimize the risks of injury by first focusing on our structural alignment. Our overall alignment determines how well we use our bodies to breath, balance, digest, and, most importantly, move. Like horses, some humans have well aligned and well functioning bodies. Most of us, however, at least after years of sitting still at school or office desks and in our cars, have significantly compromised postures and core body strength, much as can be true of horses that have been stall bound for lengthy periods. As a result, when we begin our conditioning programs, we find it harder to achieve fitness and are more likely to complain of sore backs and experience shinsplints or other injuries. Often, when someone starting a fitness program claims they don't like certain activities, whether it be swimming or running or biking, the problem is often that their bodies are not functioning well from a structural point of view and so the activity feels particularly onerous or uncomfortable. Even many very active people suffer from structural misalignments and dysfunctionality; this is because, while active, they are often only active in a few specific ways. Take, for example, the person who runs ten miles every day and walks two miles to work; you might think they would be very fit. However, by not engaging in the highly varied kinds of quite constant motion that was true of our ancestors who worked the land for a living, their fitness is limited and becomes increasingly unbalanced over time.

This does not mean, however, that we should all troop off to the chiropractor (though that can be extremely useful in some cases). Rather, we need first to evaluate our basic structure—our posture and gait—so that we tailor our conditioning efforts to improving our core or structural functionality. Then, the more strength and flexibility we develop, the more it will help us to maintain good structural alignment, which, as we all know, is critical to our own balance, straightness, and effectiveness as riders, and thus to our horses' straightness, balance and ability to respond to our aids. If, however, we build our strength on the basis of a crooked body, then we risk reinforcing that crookedness. Also, in contrast to runners or other athletes whose performance demands are highly specific, as riders and horse people we need to be multi-functional to perform well the wide variety of tasks we face in the barn, as well as on our horses. There is no point going to a competition and not being able to ride a good dressage test because we wrenched our backs lifting a hay bale out of the truck.

Evaluating Your Structural Alignment—
Giving Yourself a "Pre-Purchase Exam"

In order to move well—and enjoy moving—our load-bearing joints must line up vertically in the plane of gravity—i.e., perpendicular to the ground.

As you stand facing the mirror:

- Are your ears, the points of your shoulders, and the points of your hips all level (parallel to the horizon)?
- Can you draw a line down the center of your face, your torso, and between your legs that is straight, is perpendicular to the ground, and has equal amounts of your body on each side?
- Do your kneecaps and feet point straight forward?
- Does one or the other hip or shoulder seem to be closer to the mirror than the other?
- As you walk toward the mirror, do your legs swing forward under your body or do they "wing" or "dish" like a horse with faulty conformation?
- Do the feet land square from heel to toe and push off square?
- Now, from the side: Are your ear, shoulder tip, point of hip, knee, and ankle joint all in one line?

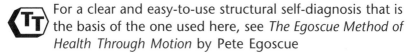 For a clear and easy-to-use structural self-diagnosis that is the basis of the one used here, see *The Egoscue Method of Health Through Motion* by Pete Egoscue

Very few people can answer, "yes" to all of these questions. If you can answer "yes" to all the above questions, have a friend take a picture of you in a bathing suit and then draw lines with a ruler through your body parts; most of us are so accustomed to how we look that we think we are much better aligned than we are. Most of us have our pelvis rolled under (thus curving our spines and making us sit on a horse in the all too classic "C seat" or slouch) or rolled back (thus arching our spines too much and causing us to sit in a "fork seat" or stiff arched position). Similarly, most of us tend to have one hip and/or one shoulder that is forward of the other, thus making us sit asymmetrically. No wonder our horses find straightness and thus balance such an ordeal!

Improving Your Structural Alignment and Functionality

On the basis of your own specific alignment issues, you have to work to engage the muscles that have become lazy through disuse, teach those that have incorrectly been doing work to chill out while the correct muscles work, stretch those muscles that have become constricted, and not overstretch those that have become too elongated. This rebalancing and reeducation of the body is the first step toward making sure that we work—and condition ourselves—in ways

THAT PERSISTENT SLUMP

Once we go to high school, most of us start a life of sitting at the desk or computer which wreaks havoc on our posture: Our shoulders slump, our abdominals collapse, our head looks like a turtle coming out of its shell, and many of us complain of lower back pain. Once on our horses, we *try* to align our head and neck over our shoulders, our shoulders over our hips, and our hips over our heels. We find, however, that the *best* we can do is to remain still quite slumped or to over-arch our lower back. Either way, we risk lower back pain; we are unable to fully absorb the horse's motion; our seat and back aids remain less than fully effective; and our legs are not really down around our horses.

How then to get that tall, straight back and elongated legs we see in every equitation manual? We need to regain flexibility of the vertebrae in the *mid-back* (especially at the base of the shoulder blades, i.e., the thoracic area of the spine) and flexibility of the muscles that have shortened and keep us curled over, especially the psoas, around the hip socket and across the front of the chest. Then, we need to strengthen the muscles that hold us erect, especially all the back muscles, but also the abdominals. While that ideal tall, effective position can remain challenging for those of us who don't ride all day, every day, we can all get closer and closer to the ideal as we work on all aspects of our fitness. And the closer we get, the easier we will find it to sit correctly and effectively, on the horse or at our desk. After all, both our own bodies and our horses *want* us to be aligned in balance with the center of gravity.

that enhance our functionality and ultimately our performance. For example, if you have a slouch, chances are that your stomach muscles are constricted, your back muscles are weak and over elongated, and your various leg and hip muscles are over- or under working relative to what is functionally correct. Without addressing these core issues you will tend to slouch on a horse and overuse your hands rather than your back, seat and legs.

There are many approaches to body biomechanics that can form the basis of an efficient and effective conditioning program that addresses your core strength and structural alignment issues:

yoga, Pilates, Gyrotonics and the Egoscue Method are a few such programs. You can certainly embark on any of these programs by reading a few books and analyzing your strengths and

"Ride your horse forward and set it straight." Similarly we need to set ourselves straight and then move forward.

weaknesses, but assistance from an exercise specialist with knowledge of biomechanics can be helpful, particularly at the beginning stages of a conditioning program. The critical step before you embark on a yoga or other program is the analysis of your own conformation and gait as indicated above, so that you can tailor your regime to what *your* body needs to perform better both in daily life and on a horse. You will find that if you work from the core—the hip, spine and abdominal areas—and emphasize structural alignment, then the rest of your conditioning will involve less pain and more gain. Additionally, this approach should reduce your chances of injury and allow you to notice very quickly the beneficial effects for your riding, a sport in which we are most effective when we act from our core. Just as the great classical dressage trainers like Steinbrecht and Podhajsky say, "Ride your horse forward and set it straight," similarly we need to set ourselves straight and then move forward.

Breathing

While many people think breathing concerns cardiovascular fitness, which it does, the concept goes beyond your lung capacity to also encompass the control you have over your breathing under different, especially stressful, situations. It is also integral to the healthy functioning of our bodies because of its influence on such things as our mental acuity and metabolism of foods and waste products.

In Asia, you would learn breathing exercises as part of learning most any sport; but in Western countries, breathing is rarely taught as part of sports training.

Further, those of us who sit long hours at a desk or lead otherwise quite immobile lives risk compromised movement functionality, not only because of the structural issues discussed above, but also because we are more likely to breathe only from our upper chest and with little control over our rhythm, particularly if we have ever had pneumonia, asthma, or other severe challenges to our lungs.

If, after a minute of running or galloping a horse, you are out of breath and start to breathe out of sync with your horse's stride, it is probably lack of control over your breathing, more than poor cardiovascular fitness that is the problem. Because being able to adjust your breathing rhythm relative to your horse's (whether to calm him, energize him, or enhance the definition of his gait) is critical to his performance, you need to develop the capacity to control your breathing for at least the 40–50 minutes of a typical training session. Yet, most of us find it hard to just sit in a chair and hold a specific breathing pattern for even 5 minutes.

The good news is that everyone can quite easily improve their breathing, no matter how weak their lungs may be. The other good news is that you can do breathing exercises any time. You do not need any special equipment or to allocate any special time to breathing, but you do need to allocate some focused attention. You can (and should) do breathing exercises when you are riding (at all of the gaits) as well as when you are focused on some other part of your fitness program, whether stretching, running, or lifting weights. Breathing is also something to work on when you are sitting.

First, evaluate your breathing:

- Is it deep or shallow?
- Do you take as long to exhale as to inhale?
- Does your rhythm change when you speak?
- Can you breathe in any desired rhythm at any time?
- Do you breathe deeply from the core of your body?
- Can you use your breath to energize different parts of your body and even your horse's body?
- Does your breathing become shorter and shallower when you are tense or nervous?

Then, start experimenting and challenging your breathing and notice how you feel afterward:

- Can you double the frequency or the duration of your inhales and exhales from your normal rate for even just five minutes?
- Can you breathe out of only your nose and then only your mouth for five minutes each?

Afterwards do you feel calmer? More Alert? Energized?

It is important to become aware of how different patterns of breathing produce different effects in your own body as well as in your horse. A good yoga manual can introduce you to some of the basic patterns and their effects on the human body. Following is a Tae Kwon Do-based breathing exercise that I have found useful for riders seeking increased breathing control and awareness:

Stand or sit comfortably, but sit up; don't slouch. Breathe in through your nose and push the air way down so your belly fills. Hold for a count of your choice (2-15 seconds). Then, push the air inside you up into the top of your chest. Finally, expel it forcefully and completely out through your mouth. (If you find it hard to repeat this exercise for ten minutes, you may want to evaluate your structural alignment, as dysfunctional alignment—e.g., a slouched posture with your head jutting forward—can hinder the effective use of your diaphragm which this exercise emphasizes. On the other hand, doing this exercise can help to maintain good posture and functionality because of the muscles it calls into play.)

If you do this exercise ten minutes a day (a long time for most of us to concentrate on something like breathing), you will develop considerable ability to control your breath. You will increase your lung capacity and health and strengthen your abdominal muscles, two components of core body strength. You will also increase your ability to be *aware* of your breathing at any time, which is critical for controlling nerves and is a first step toward learning how to incorporate correct breathing into your riding so as to sit deeper and use your aids more effectively. Ultimately, how well we breathe determines how well we develop those basic characteristics of good riding emphasized throughout this book: riding in rhythm, with feel and with ease.

Efficiency Tip for Breathing Fitness

You can practice breathing techniques as you groom, clean tack, and sweep the barn aisle; you will find them surprisingly meditative, relaxing or energizing, and grounding.

Cardiovascular Fitness

Cardiovascular fitness concerns the efficiency and capacity of our heart and lungs to deliver the oxygen and other blood-based components of energy to our entire musclo-skeletal system and to assist in ridding our bodies of the waste products of energy production like carbon dioxide. The basic message here is that cardiovascular improvement requires that you exert yourself (i.e., that you work within the target heart zone—see below) for at least *20 minutes* at a time, *not including* time to warm up and get your heart rate going or to cool down.

It is helpful to think of cardiovascular training as having two different components: *endurance training* and *capacity training.* You need both! For example, to survive cross-country day or a horse show, you need endurance fitness to be on your feet all day moving around—walking courses, tacking up, warming up, and cooling down your horses, as well as lugging water, hay, and bedding. Then, you also need to be able to call on significant cardiovascular capacity during the relatively short periods that you are actually on course. Because of the need for both kinds of cardiovascular fitness, I encourage riders to alternate their cardiovascular workouts between longer, slower workouts and intervals, hills, or other intensity training. Designing a cardiovascular training program to meet your riding needs is something that a personal trainer at a local gym can help you with.

To obtain cardiovascular benefits, almost any continuous movement activity will work—walking, running, biking, skiing, rowing, hiking, dancing, playing soccer, swimming, jumping rope, climbing stairs—as *long as you exert yourself.* If your knees hurt when you run, then you can walk, speed-walking uphill if necessary to get your heart rate going. If being on your feet hurts, then swim. (But, if you find these basic movement activities painful, you should also consider whether any aspects of your structural alignment and core strength are hindering your functionality—your ability to move well and easily.) If you get bored with one activity, switch to another. The point is to move—no excuses!

In fact, switching among aerobic activities—called *cross-training*—is a great way to improve the efficiency of your workouts. Because you will be using different muscles, you will find that you can get into your 20-minute cardiovascular productivity zone more quickly, and that it takes less speed or distance to accomplish 20 minutes of exertion. The other advantage to cross-training from an equestrian perspective is that you will be less likely to build substantial activity-specific muscles (e.g., big quadriceps (thighs) if you only bike or tight glutes (butt) if you only climb stairs) that may hinder optimal equitation.

Your *target heart range* is the zone you want to train in. To simplify this, and to avoid the need for pulse taking or a heart rate monitor, keep the following in mind:

- When you are working on cardiovascular *endurance*, you should just barely be able to talk to someone as you go along. (If you are a runner, you will find that you often need to slow down a bit; if you are a walker, you will probably need to speed up so you are working, not strolling.)
- When you are working on cardiovascular *capacity,* you should be beyond the point where you can hold a conversation, but *not* at the point where you feel like you are going to die!

It is critical to keep these sensations in mind; they are more important than the speed at, or distance over, which you train. Just as with conditioning your horses, it is as important to not over-stress as it is to not under stress during your workouts. If you can borrow a heart rate monitor from time to time, it will help you to correlate the feeling of different levels of stress with your actual heart rate.

Efficiency Tips for Cardiovascular Training

Use your time doing barn chores and turning the horses out as your warm-up time; then run a few sprints across the pasture or up and down any hill; then use bringing in some horses as cool down time. Have fun teaching your horse to trot well in hand by doing sprints with him. If you have access to a building with ten

---

TARGET HEART RATES

If you want to know what the two target heart range feelings translate into in terms of actual heart *rates,*

- subtract your age from 180
- multiply that number by 60% for *endurance* mode

OR

by 80% for *intensity* or *capacity building* mode.

Example

heart rates for a 15-year-old:

180-15 = 165 x 60% = 99 beats per minute (endurance)

180-15 = 165 x 80% = 132 beats per minute (intensity)

flights of stairs or more, run up the stairs (working toward doing 100 or more flights with all the flights two steps at a time). Jump rope while filling water buckets.

Muscular Strength

As with cardiovascular conditioning, it is useful to think in terms of two kinds of muscular strength: *endurance strength* (e.g., the ability to lift a given weight 50 – 100 times without stopping) and *maximum or brute strength* (e.g., the ability to lift a given weight 2 – 5 times). For riding, you will need both, but you will need much more of the endurance type.

When you start riding at the upper levels (e.g., riding in full three-day events), many women find that they need to increase their capacity in both brute and endurance strength substantially. At the lower levels of competition and for recreational riding, it should suffice to target your strength training to those muscle groups that need to be challenged to improve your structural functionality and to those not exercised in the course of your cardiovascular work.

To determine exactly which muscle groups you need to target and how to condition them, it is worthwhile finding a good personal trainer or other physical fitness expert to give you a physical evaluation and then design a training program for you and teach you how to do the appropriate exercises with correct form to prevent injury and enhance effectiveness. Ideal is a fitness expert who is at least somewhat knowledgeable about riding, but you could also take a trainer a video of good riders in your discipline to show how comprehensive are riding's demands.

I have found that effective riding, in the sense of being able at all times to call upon strong and correct equitation, requires almost all riders to develop the following muscle groups (though many of us do develop the lower body parts in the course of our cardiovascular training if we, for example, run, ski, or bike):

- Back muscles (especially the rhomboids, trapezius, lattisimus dorsae, and erector spinae) for, among other things, sitting tall and effectively using your back;

- Abdominals (including the obliques)—for sitting tall, centering yourself and your seat, and collecting your horse's gaits;
- Triceps and biceps—for controlled use of arms and hands;
- Chest (e.g., pectorals)—for sitting tall and balancing your horse;
- Thighs, hamstrings, adductors—for galloping and jumping in balance and using thigh aids on the flat;
- Gluteals ("glutes," butt)—for half halts and use of seat aids;
- Calves, ankles, and feet—for many different aids and grounding your position.

Efficiency Tips for Muscular Strength Training
- Because muscles have an amazing ability to learn routines, it is usually preferable to do your strength exercises in a different order each day and rotate among different exercises that target a given muscle. This will allow you to do fewer repetitions while still challenging the muscles.
- Always concentrate on correct form to get more out of each exercise and prevent injury. Slower is almost always better than faster!
- Remember to breathe. Usually optimal is breathing out when you exert (e.g., when you push up) and breathing in when you return (e.g., lower from a push up). For riding, it is especially important to train your body to breathe as you exert yourself so that you do not tense when you call upon specific muscles and thereby lose independence of the aids or cause tension in your horse.
- Don't do weight training for any specific muscle groups more than every other day.
- Buy yourself a set of five, eight or ten pound hand weights (small dumb bells) and a set of ankle weights and put them, along with a few bath mats, near the TV, in your tack room, in your bedroom, or anywhere you can take ten minutes a day or every other day to do several sets of strength exercises to supplement what you are doing around the barn and elsewhere in your life.

Flexibility

Flexibility is critical. There is no way to sit deep in the saddle and use your legs independently unless you have lots of flexibility all around the hip sockets most critically, but also in the back, hips, butt, legs, and ankles, along with the shoulder girdle, neck, and arms.

Flexibility must also be worked on regularly. Even correct riding tends to tighten a few muscles (e.g., adductors and muscles around the arm and hip sockets). But incorrect, especially tense, riding will cause many muscles to tighten, particularly in the neck, arms, back, hips, and upper legs. Additionally, many strength and cardiovascular training exercises can tighten at least some muscles: For example, running may tighten hamstrings, and push-ups may tighten pectorals.

You need to think in terms of stretching both the muscles tightened by riding and those tightened by your other exercises and daily activities (especially if that involves sitting hunched over at the computer all day!). Additionally, there are specific stretching related movements that are extremely beneficial if you want to increase the elegance and effectiveness of your position, especially your seat and back.

Stretching prior to exercise is not necessary in most cases, unless you have a particular injury or position problem for which pre-stretching is appropriate. Stretching is safest and most effective when your muscles are warm from doing your cardiovascular exercise or some other movement for at least five to ten minutes. (So, if you run in the morning and want to stretch in the evening, I would recommend that you stretch your hamstrings and calves right after running and then, in the evening, put on some disco music for five minutes and dance to it; then do your other stretches.)

How to stretch:

There are many theories that come in and out of vogue about the Golgi reflex, about bouncing or not bouncing, about 3-minute stretches versus repeated 30-second stretches versus 5-minute stretches . . . An easier way to deal with these issues is to keep the following in mind:

- Always be *very* careful when stretching your neck and lower back.
- Stretch until there is some pain (good pain, not tearing pain). Then, vary holding that stretch and pushing further as the pain alleviates with backing off and then coming back into the stretch repeatedly.
- Breathe into your stretch; focus your breath into the particular muscle you are working on in order to increase the stretch and to remind yourself to breathe.
- Combine *dynamic* stretching (extending range of motion while moving) with *static stretching*.

You will need to create your own stretch routines (but, again, they need to be varied) depending upon your body and your other activities. You may want to work with a yoga instructor, sports medicine practitioner, or personal trainer to evaluate your current (in)flexibility and design a stretching program. As a rider, you will want to make particularly sure that you have full range of motion and flexibility of the muscles, tendons, and ligaments in the following areas: hip and arm sockets, neck and spinal column, knees and ankles, adductors, abductors and hamstrings, pectorals and trapezius, and finally, but so often overlooked, the psoas, which is critical to your ability to sit tall over your seat bones and use your legs independently of your hands.

Efficiency Tips for Flexibility Training

Do some concentrated stretching (10 – 15 minutes) at least every other day. During that time, choose one or two stretches that you will hold for 3 – 5 minutes (which is a very long time, so be somewhere comfortable and warm) and then hold the others for 30 – 60 seconds each. On the in-between days, look for places in the barn to do some stretches as part of your barn work; for example, put your leg up on a fence and stretch your hamstrings while you are watching someone jump, or do psoas stretching lunges while hand grazing your horse. (Just be sure your muscles are warmed up from walking around or some other activity.) And remember to incorporate breathing exercises into your stretching: Yoga practitioners talk about "breathing into an area" that you are stretching to enhance the stretch.

Balance, Coordination and Reflexes

Riding is a balance sport that requires considerable coordination and fast reflexes to have aids that are quick and clear and to enable you to respond to the unforseen. Additionally, many of the things you do around the barn, from bandaging and leading multiple horses to handling fractious youngsters, require well-developed coordination, balance, and quick reflexes.

Balance

Riding requires dynamic balance, which involves being able to adjust to changes in balance in your environment or caused by your own movement—for example, adjusting to changes in your horse's balance as he goes over a jump. T'ai Chi and other martial arts, gymnastics, rock climbing, and dance, but also walking on fence rails, playing soccer, working on a sailing boat, and windsurfing all develop dynamic balance. Again, a personal trainer can help you learn balance exercises useful for your riding needs. Many great exercises, like boulder jumping and playing hopscotch, don't need a gym or special equipment.

To test and work on your dynamic balance while on a horse try the following:

- While you are trotting or cantering, let your legs hang down loose and grab a piece of mane, first in one hand and then in another: If you feel any pull against the mane as you continue trotting or cantering, then you are not in balance, but most likely are usually using the reins or a tight, gripping leg for balance.

- Riding, including jumping, with your eyes shut: If you can ride a straight line with your eyes shut, you have good balance and feel for your horse's straightness. Try trotting over poles on the ground and doing lateral work with closed eyes. If you think this is impossible, just remember that blind people can ride— often extremely well. (It is best to have someone there to help spot for you or call out movements for you to try.)

- Walk, trot, and canter with your legs raised out to the sides from the hip so they are completely away from the saddle, but keep your butt, hips, and lower back loose and able to absorb the motion. It is OK to *lightly* hold the pommel with one hand, but do *not* pull back against the pommel or slump your back. As long as you don't let your legs come forward as you raise them, this is a great exercise to teach you where your center of gravity is relative to the horse's; it will make you sit correctly, that is, down on and up over your seat bones.

- At the walk, trot, and canter, do a variety of arm rotations and other exercises without changing your leg position or increasing the grip of your legs.

- If you tend toward a slouch or "C seat," try clasping your hands together with your hands out in front of you and then slowly raising your hands up over your head without letting any air come between your palms to give you a sense of how your current sense of balance is intertwined with your structural alignment.

- Get someone to lunge you, and then lunge you some more, and then some more! I have been told that the Spanish Riding

School in Vienna, Austria does not let its riders have reins or stirrups until they have been trained exclusively on the lunge for two *years.*

The goal to strive for with this balance work is to be able to ride without using any holding muscles (whether your legs or, heaven forbid, your hands) to keep you on the horse. Rather, if you stay with your horse's center of gravity, you will stay on the horse. The easiest way to fall out of alignment with your horse's center of gravity is to start holding with any of your muscles: The more you hold, the more you need to hold and the tenser and more out of balance you and your horse will get. Instead, let go and trust that the force of gravity and your developing sense of balance will keep you on top of your horse. As I tell my students, "It is your job to relax and then, but only then, it is God's job to keep you on the horse."

Coordination

Coordination combines both mental and physical aspects. On a horse, as in many other areas of life from skiing, to surgery, to changing the diapers on a wriggling baby, you need to be able to assign different and often fast-paced tasks to different parts of your body. With riding, you also often need to be able to tell some parts of your body to work with strength (e.g., a strong driving leg and seat) while others work with extreme delicacy (e.g., super light hands, especially if you are jumping with a gag bit or refining collection with a double bridle).

Want to learn balance the way four time Olympic show jumper Anne Kursinski did?

"*Back at Flintridge, in the days of Jimmy Williams, we had a round jumping chute . . . We'd get in there with no reins, Jimmy would crack the whip, and off we'd go jumping round and round—hands on our hips, hands out to the side, hands on our heads. Another way he'd get his point across about balance was to give us reins and stirrups but blindfold us. You had to be out of the saddle, in two-point, to be ready for the jump, so it taught you feeling; to be with the horse, you had to gallop and jump through feeling. We started over little jumps, but we progressed to jumping five feet . . . We thought it was great fun, and the horses jumped so much better. It truly made me the rider I am today. Unfortunately, we've lost a lot of that natural kind of teaching (and riding).*"

To test and develop your coordination:

- Practice *multi-tasking* without compromising the quality of how you do either task. For example, stroke your dog very smoothly while you hammer nails into a board. On a horse, stroke the top of your head to one rhythm while you pat your stomach to a different rhythm, so that you can some day tap your horse with your dressage whip on his hocks to encourage the elevation of his piaffe while quietly stroking his neck to calm him; or, more immediately, so you can use your crop to send him over a cross-country jump he is balking at without grabbing him in the mouth, which would encourage him to stop or jump poorly.

- Make sure you vary these multi-tasking exercises so you are always challenging yourself.

- Develop *equal left-right dexterity* by doing as many things as possible with your left (or non-dominant) hand and side that you ordinarily do with your right (or dominant) side. Curry and brush your horse with your non-dominant side. Sometimes, get on and off your horse on the off (right hand) side. (This is also good for your horse's spinal alignment). Write down telephone messages and the grocery list with your non-dominant hand. Alternate which hand you carry your whip in or have on the back of the pitch fork when mucking. (Watch the movie *Karate Kid* for a wonderful lesson about training your non-dominant side.)

Reflexes

Quick reflexes are critical to staying on and regaining control when a horse spooks suddenly, reacting appropriately when a horse pulls back or a small child or dog goes under your horse's feet, or deciding to kick on or pull up when you see two strides out that a rail is in the way of your take off spot or landing. But even when everything is proceeding quite normally, the quickness of your reflexes—then called having "good feeling"—significantly affects your training. The quicker you can sense and respond to a resistance or the quicker you can release and reward your horse when he yields or answers a request, the quicker your training will progress and the lighter your aids can be. While all good riders, almost by definition, have quick reflexes, anyone can significantly improve their reflexes with practice.

The key to quick reflexes is having taught both your mind and body how to respond to a wide variety of situations without you having to do any conscious mental processing. Think about the first time you drove a car. You probably had to be told that you were getting too close to a car in front of you and to brake; then you progressed to consciously

The key to quick reflexes is having taught both your mind and body how to respond to a wide variety of situations without you having to do any conscious mental processing.

saying to yourself, "That car looks too close; I had better make my foot press on the brake pedal." But after years of driving you don't even need to consciously notice that you are getting too close; you just regulate your speed to keep your desired distance with no lurching forward and backward. This quickness, this automatic, natural ability to respond, requires both the accumulated experience of doing something like driving that your mind relies on to perceive and evaluate a situation and then determine an appropriate response and your allowing an automatic mind/body reaction to take place. You have no doubt heard the expression, "Just trust your reflexes." That is absolutely necessary, but you do need first to develop relevant reflexes!

Two things will help you to develop your reflexes for riding: First is riding as much as you can, as many horses as you can, and under as many different situations as you can, especially situations that involve the unpredictable, in order to develop your mind and body's repertoire of horse experiences and successful reactions. This thinking underlies the U.S. Pony Clubs' requirement that all their members develop proficiency at riding in the open over uneven terrain like one encounters on cross-country or out fox hunting. Second is developing the quickness of your reflexes off your horse by, for example, playing team ball games or sparring in martial arts. You will find that the quicker your reflexes are off the horse, the quicker you can develop your more equestrian-specific reflexes, because you will already know how to trust your mind/body response system and will have taught it about the importance of always perceiving any changes in the environment or anyone's behavior instantly, whether a reaction is called for or not.

Nutrition and Hydration

Proper nutrition and adequate hydration are critical not only as sources of fuel for our bodies but also to the health (and thus the strength and flexibility) of our muscles, to injury prevention,

and to our overall physical and mental fitness.
They also play a significant role in our ability
to concentrate and use our bodies well during
a riding session. Similarly, our core fitness
and alignment can affect our nutrition: For
example, the enervating effects of poor
posture and lack of movement can cause
cravings for coffee, soda, and other "pick me ups."

Eating

- Day to day: You worry that your horse gets good quality, balanced, and adequate meals everyday; do yourself the same favor. You know about the food pyramid, the importance of eating fruits and vegetables, the arguments for organic produce, and avoiding junk food. Following healthy nutritional guidelines really will help your riding!

- After strenuous exercise, like doing a cardiovascular workout, it is a good idea to immediately eat something high in glucose (e.g., a small box of raisins or an orange), as this is the best time to replace your glycogen stores so that your body will respond well to exercise on the following day.

- For day-long activities like competition and during other periods of extra stress, avoid junk food. If you can make yourself eat fruit instead of candy, drink juice instead of soda, and eat pasta or chicken with a vegetable instead of pizza, you will feel and ride better, as you will be less likely to be carrying around excess sodium (salt), excess fats in your stomach (which are slow to digest and hard to access for energy), or to suffer from sugar highs and lows. Just as you take your own grain and hay for your horse when you go to a competition, take healthy food for yourself, rather than relying on concession stands that often provide only donuts, greasy burgers, and soda pop.

- Supplementary vitamins and minerals: Consult a good nutritionist or your doctor as you may need to supplement your regular diet. For example, I have found that many thin girls in their teens who work at the barn and ride several hours strenuously need electrolytes (salt and potassium, in particular) to combat dizziness when it gets very hot in the summer.

Hydration

- Day to day: You worry about your horse's water needs, so worry about your own too. The rule of thumb is 6–8 eight-ounce glasses of water per day, just to meet your body's maintenance needs.

(For each cup or glass of caffeine, including caffeinated sodas, or alcohol, which are dehydrating, you need to add at least one additional glass of water to your daily needs.) You may need to drink more if you live in a particularly dry climate. If you find it hard to drink this much water, try flavoring it with a squeeze of lemon or a bit of cranberry juice. Keep water with you at all times. (I find those bottles with pop-up tops helpful.) If it is with you, you will likely drink more. Also, the fitter you become, presuming it is on the basis of proper musculo-skeletal alignment, the more you will likely crave sufficient hydration, just as you will crave healthier nutrition.

2. During strenuous exercise: Many doctors recommend drinking during exercise, particularly long, continuous exercise like running a marathon. Most riding sessions, except endurance riding and some ranch work, do not involve being on a horse for extended, strenuous periods of time. Thus, in most circumstances, a fit rider who has eaten and drunk properly and sufficiently *prior* to coming into the arena should not need to drink during a riding lesson or training session (despite the current vogue of having riders ask their instructors to go get them water during their lesson). If your horse needs water during your training session, then you probably also need water; but if he doesn't need it until you dismount, then you probably don't either.

3. After strenuous exercise: You will need to drink more and, just like your horse after you gallop him, you should drink right after exercising, particularly to aid in removal of lactic acids that can cause sore muscles.

4. At times of extra stress: As you do for your horse, you may wish to consider some form of electrolytes as in Gatorade, though fruit juice and extra water should suffice.

Before beginning any diet program, consult your physician. The information in this section is intended only to indicate the basic relationship between percentage of body fat and overall fitness for equestrian purposes.

A Few Words on Weight and Physical Fitness:

We all know that George Morris, co-chef d'equipe of the USET show jumping team and renowned hunter/jumper trainer, has been heavily criticized for his remarks over the years about overweight riders, particularly women. While I would not recommend that someone lose weight just to look better on a horse, I do agree with Mr. Morris that carrying excess weight (i.e., weight in the form of fat, not muscle) can compromise both effectiveness and safety. I also believe that being too thin—not having enough body fat and muscle mass—can also compromise effectiveness and safety.

What I have found watching many riders at all levels over many years is that *if* you are fit (i.e., strong in cardiovascular and muscular strength, flexible, and with good nutrition), then being *somewhat* overweight (in terms of total body fat percentage or weight relative to your height and bone mass) is not likely to adversely affect your riding substantially. However, if you are fit, then you are also unlikely to be carrying much extra body fat beyond what is appropriate for your body's health. This is because a fit body tends to be a functional, moving body, and a functional, moving body will tend over time toward overall efficiency and health, including an appropriate percentage of body fat.

 For disciplines requiring extensive conditioning, mileage, and/or speed, like endurance riding and full-fledged three-day events, the risk of lameness can be reduced by shedding any excess (i.e., fat) pounds your horse has to carry over the many miles involved in both the long conditioning phase and the actual competition itself. But as 100 mile endurance riders have learned, horses can also be too thin to compete a competition in good health. Similarly, if you are too thin to yourself endure the rigors of your conditioning and competition, you will tire quickly and risk laming your horse through poor riding. You want your horse neither pudgy nor scrawny to meet rigorous endurance demands; applying the same to yourself will help you and your horse remain sound and perform well.

But don't confuse body shape with optimum weight. We all know of some Olympic-level riders who would not get jobs as fashion models; however, these riders are not carrying excess fat. They are extremely fit and functional, but have body types that tend toward bulky muscles. You cannot change your body type, but you can become fitter (i.e., leaner). You will find that the fitter you become as a rider, the less body fat you will carry (though you may end up weighing more because muscle weighs more than fat). For women, whose body fat tends to gather around the hips and thighs, being lean also significantly helps us to sit deeper in the saddle and get our legs, especially our thighs, down around the horse.

But it is only up to a certain point that having less body fat is desirable from a riding perspective. Being too thin can cause you to lose muscular strength and cardiovascular conditioning, risk injury from muscle tears and bone fractures, and experience metabolic problems. Particularly if you participate in the more strenuous equestrian disciplines, like steeplechasing, working cows, and three-day eventing, or ride at the elite levels of any discipline, then being too thin will likely compromise your performance. Riding is, after all, partly a strength sport. However, if you are fit in the ways discussed in this chapter, including proper nutrition, you are unlikely to be too thin.

If you eat healthfully, then building your structural, cardiovascular and muscular fitness will tend to bring your body toward an optimum level of body fat without the dreaded D (for diet) word ever being mentioned. Working at the lower end of the target heart zone (i.e., at 60% of your maximum heart rate) is credited by many health specialists with efficiently burning calories and converting fat to energy. Because muscles burn more calories per day (even when you are sitting at your desk) than do fat cells or bones and other body components, building your muscle mass through strength training can also be an efficient and healthy way to "lose" weight. For people who are too thin, strength training can help to add healthy body mass. In other words, conditioning work tends to act as a virtuous circle: The fitter you become, the easier it is to get fit; and the fitter you become, the more likely you will be to progress in and enjoy your riding, and then the more fit you will want to become, and so on.

Author's note: I would like to thank Pat Hanks of Bozeman, Montana, a certified strength and conditioning specialist and an exercise biomechanics expert, for his insights into the central role of structural functionality in any conditioning program or performance effort. The section of this chapter on structure and function is based on his research, experience, and ideas.

WHAT YOU SHOULD EXPECT
by Elizabeth N. Clarke

*Your Rights and Responsibilities as a
Consumer of Horse Related Services*

When you purchase services from a professional equestrian, and whether you are yourself a total beginner or a very accomplished rider, there are certain things you should be able to expect from any stable.

The very basics:

• *Humane and caring treatment of horses*: If a professional you are considering dealing with, or anyone who works directly with that professional, demonstrates or expresses disdain, contempt or worse for the horses, look elsewhere. Horses don't choose to live confined and work at the whim of human beings. They are generous enough to do so, and they deserve the best of care and understanding in return. Anyone demonstrating anything less than caring consideration for the horses' well-being is not a good horseman. Watch a training session or two. Is the trainer setting the horse up to succeed and improve in a way that emphasizes reward or constantly punishing the horse and going for bigger and stronger spurs, bits, and restraining devices? Even the kindest trainer will have to discipline a horse occasionally, but it should be the exception rather than the rule, and it must be immediate, brief, clear to the horse, and *over.* A horse doesn't relate ongoing pain to something the horse did even several seconds earlier. It is just pain. People who don't understand that fact don't understand horses. There are many professionals who truly do care for the horses, and who truly will help you find the joy of building a partnership with these magnificent beings. Don't settle for anything less.

• *A safe environment for humans and horses:* There are and always will be accidents around horses. It's the nature of working around large, fast, flighty animals. That said, there is much to be done both to the physical environment and with the operation of it that minimizes risk to horse and human. If safety is not emphasized and practiced, look elsewhere.

• *Basic courtesy and respect:* The American systems of riding, especially the English disciplines, evolved largely out of military schools. Orders were barked and followed without question. Students were considered and treated as inferiors. To some extent that tradition lives on, but more enlightened teaching methods are beginning to emerge in American riding schools. It is imperative that during instruction every student follow the direction of the instructor without delay. Failing to do so can create problematic and even dangerous situations for the student, the horses, and other riders. That said, it is not necessary for instructors to belittle, insult, or speak ill of students who are paying them for instruction. Every client is entitled to be treated with respect and dignity. So is every instructor, trainer, or clinician. If you don't see a trusting and respectful relationship between the trainer and other clients, look elsewhere. Since it is often the trainer or head instructor who sets the tone, it is not likely that the situation will be different for you or your horse than it is for other clients. If you are riding for your recreation (and indeed, even if you are riding for your profession) you don't need your time with horses tainted with largely negative, destructively critical discourse. Listen to a lesson or two. Is the instructor telling the student what *to* do in a way that enables the student to improve and gain confidence, or continually telling the student what *not* to do in a way that undermines confidence and creates tension?

• *Honest dealing*: Much of the horse industry is more accepting than it should be of behavior that is not tolerated in other facets of life. Many of the worst stories have to do with the buying and selling of horses, but the truth is that the horse industry has a habit of turning a blind eye to practices that are at best questionable, sometimes not in the interest of either the horse or the owner, and not infrequently against the law. I have actually seen training agreements that gave the trainer discretion to medicate the horse without the owner being informed or consulted, regardless of the legality of the substance or its permissibility under applicable horse show rules. This is the extreme end of the spectrum, but it is not necessarily an isolated case. The fact that ethical problems exist within the industry does not mean that one has to accept them in order to participate in the sport. There are very honest horsemen and horsewomen who truly care about both the good of the horses and the good of the sport. If you ask smart questions, you can find them. If you discover that someone has been less than honest with you, you may or may not have legal recourse, but at the very least you have the choice not to reward dishonest or unethical behavior with any more of your money. When dealing with a new trainer, it is easy to be excited and optimistic. Make sure to look a little underneath the polished presentation. Some healthy skepticism may save you a lot of grief. Better to find out, up front if possible, that things may not look so rosy later. If you ask reasonable questions and the person you are dealing with becomes dismissive or even defensive, ask yourself how they will be to deal with when the chips are down.

People very often get involved in the horse world for emotional reasons and put their rational sides away the moment they walk into a barn. I've seen it happen. Individuals who run major corporations or universities, who carefully negotiate large commercial deals, who are businesslike and clear thinking in every other aspect of their lives, get dreamy when they walk into a stable. They have hopes and dreams and assumptions about how wonderful it will all be. It is in some way a part of that magical thing horses can do to all of us. We allow ourselves to be vulnerable around horses. That can be a very cathartic and refreshing thing and the horses

---

Questions to ask of yourself when evaluating a new situation:

- Do the horses look content and relaxed in the stable and turn out areas?
- Do they look healthy and well cared for? Coats glossy? Well groomed and neatly turned out? In good weight? Feet in good condition?
- Do the horses appear to be relatively happy in their work? Is there more praise than correction? Tack well fitted and relatively mild in terms of bits, spurs, and restraint devices?
- Is the atmosphere at the facility friendly and cheerful? Are the clients treated with the respect that paying customers deserve?
- Does what instructors are saying to students make sense to you? And are the students generally able to carry out what they are asked to do?
- Does communication appear to go both ways? Are students encouraged to ask questions? Boarders encouraged to give feedback?
- Does the facility reflect attention to detail? Stalls clean and well bedded? Things neatly organized and put away? Fencing safe and in good repair?
- Is the person who is running the operation someone you would readily trust with the care of your horse?

can respond beautifully to it. Remember, though, that for the person on the other side of the transaction it is also a business. If well run it is a business with routines and rules and a certain order into which clients are expected to fit. Beautiful as the stable and the horses may be, the business operation may or may not fit your expectations for your relationship with horses.

Some rules of thumb to prevent dashed expectations:

• *Assume nothing.* This is a good rule for life in general, and it is a very good rule for evaluating horses and services related to horses. We all have ideas of how things will or should be. Beware that standards in the horse industry vary widely by region, by discipline, and by personal style. When I was in Massachusetts, "board" included a stall that was cleaned once a day, picked again if weather kept the horses in and that was bedded as needed. It also included daily turn-out, blanketing and unblanketing as needed. Grain provided by the stable with owner-provided supplements added by the stable staff was fed two to three times a day, as was hay in whatever quantities the horses required. Each boarder was accorded space in the tackroom and time in the riding areas, which the boarders pitched in to maintain. When I moved to California, "board" at almost twice the Massachusetts rate included a stall that was mucked once a day, bedded once a week, and hay fed once a day with an extra fee for more than four flakes. Turn-out was extra, or for a lesser additional fee for paddock use I could turn my own horses out and bring them in. Tackroom space was also extra. Blanketing was not even considered. Owners or trainers were expected to provide grain, salt, and whatever else the horses required. On the other hand the arenas and grounds were beautifully maintained by the facility management. In fact the latter arrangement was much more like renting space than purchasing services, but it was called the same thing. If I hadn't asked, it would have been a very rude surprise. Ask what's included and what isn't. Don't assume services are the same as you are used to at another facility, or the way you read they should be in a book. Be sure to find out how things actually are at the places you are evaluating.

• *Start your relationship with good communications.* Riding instructors can be a lot of things, and some have been thought to read minds, but don't expect them to be able to read yours. It is also dangerous to think you can read theirs. Think about and know your expectations, goals, and questions. Better still, write them down. Discuss them with the instructor or trainer. That person should in turn be honest with you about whether their program is a good place for you to try to reach your goals. What might be a very good, very well run barn may still not be exactly the right program for you. Once you have expressed serious interest, if the trainer or instructor won't make time to discuss your goals and expectations with you when you are a potential client, it probably won't get easier to have such conversations later. Expect to be able to be candid with your instructor or trainer, and expect them to be the same with you.

• *Don't expect special treatment.* Read the stable rules and any relevant agreements. Ask what is and what is not allowed or provided in terms of what you think you will need. Expect the rules and terms to apply to you. If you can't live within them you're in the wrong place. If they seem unreasonably strict you may need a less formal setting. If they seem lax you may want to look further to see if that means that the person in charge hates paperwork but in practice runs a very organized operation, or if it is a sign that the organization is more casual in other ways than meets your comfort level. If you or your horse needs more help or attention than the average client because of special needs, ask up front whether your special needs (odd work schedule that requires you to ride very early in the morning, horse that has a vice or needs special food or turnout) can be accommodated and expect to pay others for their extra effort on your behalf if they need to break the normal routine to meet your needs. Which brings me to my next point. . . .

• *Expect to get what you pay for and pay for what you get.* Except for the sale of the horses themselves, what people in the horse industry are primarily selling is their time and the knowledge they have spent time, effort, and money accumulating. Because time is what they sell, it is a valuable commodity to them, and their time should be valuable to you as well. If you arrange for a lesson or training session, and pay the quoted rate, you should get the instructor's full attention and engaged assistance for the allotted time. You should only be asked to share it with others who are scheduled to be in the same lesson. You should be learning something in each session, and should over a period of several lessons

> ### Services versus Goods
>
> This chapter only addresses the purchase of ***services*** from equine professionals. When you purchase "goods" (horses, tack, etc.) or engage the services of an equine professional to help you purchase or sell goods, in addition to ethics and basic honesty, two very specific bodies of law govern your rights. The Uniform Commercial Code governs the sale of goods and implied and express warranties. The law of agency governs the rights and responsibilities when one party is engaged to act on behalf of another in a transaction. These bodies of law are rather specialized and the subject of other books, but are not addressed here. If you are buying and selling horses, and using (or being) an agent in such transaction, it is well worth educating yourself about the law surrounding these transactions.

be able to look back and see your progress. In the same vein, if you need help that doesn't fall within the structure of a lesson—help with saddle fitting, a look at a potential horse, or discussion about show strategy—you are still using the instructor's time and knowledge. Some professionals will include these other services as part of a "package" of what they provide, but don't assume that is the case. If you are not paying a monthly flat fee for full training, ask about paying for the extra time, or at the least about returning the favor in some way. Even if the trainer doesn't expect it, they will appreciate the fact that you value the time and knowledge they are sharing with you.

In specific situations, expectations can be more exact. Again, depending on location, discipline, and the activity at hand, some situations need to be more specifically defined than others.

LESSONS

Lesson situations are generally pretty straightforward. The student pays for a fixed amount of time with an instructor, either with two or more other people (group lesson), with one other person (semi-private lesson) or alone (private lesson) at some regularly occurring time interval (weekly, daily, or something in between). The student either rides her own horse or one provided by the instructor. The instructor may occasionally get on the student's mount to demonstrate a particular movement or technique, or to move along a situation where the horse needs more help than the instructor can give by teaching the student from the ground, but this is the exception. The focus is on the student learning to ride the particular horse better. Fees are generally set depending on how much of the instructor's attention is focused on the student (private, semi-private or group) and how long the lesson will last. The instructor's experience and reputation may also have some impact on the price of the lesson.

While the specifics will vary from place to place and with different instructors, the student is entitled to the following:

- *The instructor's undivided attention to the riders in the lesson.*

- *To learn something in every lesson.* Sometimes it may be something unexpected, like how to feel if a horse is lame, but every session should improve the student's horsemanship as well as her riding. An instructor who tells you only what they think you want to hear is not honestly helping you to improve your riding, and is selling you a defective product.

- *To feel safe and appropriately mounted.* If the student's own horse is difficult or inappropriate, the instructor owes it to the student to give an honest evaluation of the possibility for likely success in attaining the student's stated goals with that horse. On the other hand, as long as the student is dedicated to improving her horse, and the horse is sound and does not actually present a danger to the student or to others, the instructor should be able to help the student improve her riding on that horse and even improve that horse over time.

- *To have fun.* Some people call riding an art, others call it a sport. Either way, while it does require dedication and discipline, it should not be or feel like torture. Everyone has an occasional bad day, but if it is hard to recall the last time you got off the horse with a feeling of real satisfaction, it's time to reassess.

Be willing to try what is asked of you, and able to say when it feels beyond your comfort level. You are paying for someone's expertise. If you don't respect their opinion enough to try what they say, you are working with the wrong person. You have to try new things in order to learn new things. That said, riding is a sport where physical danger and the need to control a very large, fast-moving animal are daily realities. Your instructor needs to understand the rate at which you are comfortable progressing and help you find a balance in trying new things as you are ready for them without pressing you too far past your comfort zone. A good instructor has a sense of how much you are capable of trying at a given time without being over-faced, but cannot be expected to guess that you have a cramp in your thigh, butterflies in your stomach, or a headache from a bad day at the office. Asking for an easier jump or two to make sure your timing is good before you try the bigger course, or a session to review the things you do well rather than trying something new when you're not feeling entirely secure, is reasonable on occasion. Everyone has an occasional bad day, a day where you and the horse don't "click" as well as usual, a day where it would just be nice to enjoy the ride rather than push on to something new. If you find yourself pushed beyond your comfort zone on a regular basis, however, you need to ask two hard questions: 1) How much are you really enjoying riding? And 2) If you really do want to ride, is this the right situation in which to be doing it? Constantly feeling insecure or pushed beyond your capabilities isn't safe for you and isn't fair to your horse. This is one topic you *need* to be able to discuss with your instructor. If you aren't comfortable doing so, ask yourself whether it is that you are uncomfortable raising the subject because of your own issues, or whether you are in an environment that is wrong for you in terms of pace and expectations.

Questions to ask of a potential trainer or teacher:

- What is the length, frequency, and cost of sessions? Payment terms?
- Who is responsible for having horses ready for lessons/training sessions?
- Are riders not participating in lessons present in the working area during lessons?
- Does the head trainer conduct all sessions, or do assistants sometimes teach lessons or ride horses in training?
- What are the cancellation policies if you need to miss a scheduled lesson? Is there a notice period? Under what conditions might you be expected to pay for a missed lesson?
- Are clients/students expected to purchase extra services or go to a certain number of competitions? If so, what's the estimated additional cost?

TRAINING

Training situations vary a good deal more than lesson programs, and while lessons for the owner on the horse may be part of the program, training generally envisions more comprehensive supervision of the horse's schooling by the trainer with the primary goal of improving the horse. The trainer may ride the horse a good deal of the time, a part of the time, or even just supervise the student whenever she rides the horse rather than just on occasion. Training packages may include other services such as regular grooming or the trainer showing the horse, or these services may be extra, sometimes quite a bit extra. Often there is a minimum expectation for additional services over and above the basic training rate. For example, clients may be expected to utilize the trainer's services at shows, and may be required to show at least once or twice a month. Be sure to know in advance what is included, what isn't, and how much the additional services will cost. It is fair and prudent to expect a training agreement to be in writing, setting out the costs, the expectations and responsibilities of both trainer and client, what happens if the horse is injured and can't be in training, and the like. It is very important in training situations for the trainer and the client to both retain a healthy perspective regarding what's right for the horse. Horses progress at very different rates. As long as the horse is improving, and does not show signs of being unhappy or uncomfortable, patience is a critical element of any training situation.

CLINICS

Clinics are occasional lessons, not part of a regular ongoing program. Rather they are an opportunity to take advantage of a different point of view, perhaps with someone you admire or who has had more or different experiences than your regular trainer. Because your relationship with the clinician is of necessarily short duration, make the most of it by informing the clinician honestly about your horse, your own experience, any special issues the two of you face, or particular things you would like to work on. Then let the clinician guide the lesson as she sees fit. It may be that what you would like to work on is hampered by a "building block" the clinician would like to see you demonstrate first. It may be that the clinician has a different agenda for that day. Try to stay open to what each particular clinician has to offer. You should expect to be pushed a little, but not to be confused or to start something new that you and your horse cannot substantially accomplish within the clinic session. Because you don't ride with her regularly, the clinician should be careful not to leave you or your horse confused or try to totally change your system in one session.

WORKING STUDENT POSITIONS

Working student experiences can be among the best learning experiences or among the worst incidences of exploitation in the horse industry. Managed well, both parties benefit. The trainer gets low cost, highly motivated help and the working student gets a good general education in stable and horse management as well as good riding instruction. Managed badly, the arrangement is not far short of slave labor.

If you are considering a working student position consider the following:

- Do your homework ahead of time. Find out what is expected of working students and what you will get in return. What hours are you expected to work? How many days a week? Can you bring your own horse? If so, is board part of your compensation or do you have to pay for it? If not, will you be able to ride horses at the stable? Will you get scheduled formal lessons, or just a helpful comment here and there? Will your riding time be part of the workday, or do you have to find the energy to ride after a 10 or 12-hour day?

- Ask specific questions about the non-riding part of your education. Will your work consist entirely of mucking stalls, or will you get to participate in other aspects of stable and horse management? Will you be able to observe vets and other practitioners at work? Will there be opportunities for you to learn about managing the business aspect of things if you are interested? Will you be able to go to competitions or will you be the stay-at-home groom while everyone else goes away? The biggest advantage of a working student position is the opportunity for total immersion in the horse business. Make sure before you make a 6-month or even a year commitment that the immersion you will experience won't drown you.

- Do the numbers. If you will work 10 hours a day 6 days a week and get one lesson a week in return, then if you consider the equivalent wage you could make at Burger King or MacDonald's you will be paying approximately $360 for each lesson. At that rate, you'd better hope the stable management aspect of things is pretty interesting. On the other hand, if you work those same hours but as part of your "work time" get a group lesson with other working students four mornings a week on your own horse, for which board is provided at no additional cost, plus you get to watch the trainer work with another more experienced trainer one day a week, and get to go to at least one show every month where you really learn how things should be done to prepare for the show ring, you are getting quite an education bargain, even if you are tired!

- Expect to work hard and put in long days. The horse business is a 24/7 proposition. Horses need to be fed, be turned out, have their injuries treated, and have their other assorted needs tended every day of the week, holidays included. They colic at night, and the day starts very early in most stables. If the head rider plans to put a foot in the first stirrup at 8:00, expect to be feeding, mucking, and grooming by 6:00. If that same rider gets off the last horse or finishes the last lesson at 5:00, expect to be cooling out, cleaning tack, and feeding until 7:00 or so. Working student positions are a very good way to learn what the horse business is really like. That said, make sure that what you are taking on is not beyond your capacity or your energy level.

- Find out where you will be in the stable hierarchy. If you get a position with a famous trainer, lucky you! Maybe. In larger operations you may rarely even speak to the head trainer, much less be directly supervised by or taught by him. That doesn't mean your instruction or your experience won't be wonderful. It very well may be. It may also be that in a smaller operation you not only clean stalls and tack but warm up and hack out horses and, depending on your ability level, maybe even teach a few beginner lessons. Figure out what you want to get out of your working student experience, then find the situation that will provide it. Diving right in with someone because you've seen their name in a magazine may or may not be good way to get good experience. Aim for the highest quality of experience you can get with the highest quality trainer you can hook up with.

- The above caution notwithstanding, if you don't ask, you'll never know what opportunities you may miss. Many of the best riders in the country have working student positions in their programs. Someone will get those positions. If you do your homework, present yourself well, and ask the right questions, it may very well be you.

- A big caution about insurance is in order with regard to working students. Trainers don't like to consider working students "employees" because of the associated employment tax and workers compensation insurance expense. Beware that if you are injured, and your health insurance company considers the injury to have occurred "at work," your health insurance will not cover the related medical expenses. Make sure that the person you are working for has workers compensation insurance and that you are covered while working for them. Otherwise you could face potentially devastating medical costs, and they could face severe penalties for failing to secure insurance that is required by law.

BOARD ARRANGEMENTS

If you board your horse at someone else's stable, whether part of a training program or not, you have a responsibility to your horse to make sure the arrangement works well both for the horse and for you. As mentioned above, what is included in "board" at different stables can be starkly different. Costs, feed arrangements, services such as turn-out and blanketing, routine veterinary arrangements, and owner responsibilities all differ from stable to stable. Know in advance how much the stable will provide, how much you must provide, and what it will cost you to obtain the "extras" that aren't necessarily included. Know also any restrictions that are imposed. Some stables will limit what owners can do (Will you have access to the arena at a time your other commitments allow you to ride? Can you get into the barn early if you need to leave for a show?...) and who can provide services to the horse (Do they require that you use particular vets, farriers, etc.?). If you are paying for full service board, are the services up to your standards? Are stalls cleaned regularly and bedded deeply enough? Does the turn-out arrangement work for your horse? You have the right to expect that your horse will be well cared for, and that he will be treated with kindness and respect. Do not expect, however, that you will change the existing system. Investigate it thoroughly beforehand. It is a good idea to have a written board agreement listing what is provided, what is not included, and who is responsible for what. Putting things in writing often helps to clarify terms and reveal the different assumptions the parties may be making. If the stable doesn't have a written board agreement, ask if they will make you a list of what's included in board and what you need to provide yourself.

Over the course of a riding career most of us will spend a considerable amount of money on horse-related services. Approach them as an intelligent consumer. Know the product you want and shop for it. Investigate the quality and terms of the various options available. Ask smart questions. Look beyond the answers to what people are not saying. Be your own and your horse's best advocate going into situations and you will be much more likely to be happy with the result. Since your purchases are ongoing, stop and re-evaluate once in awhile. Are the services you are buying moving you toward your goals? Are you getting what you are paying for? Is the level of service what was promised? One or two years into an arrangement, is it working as well as you hoped it would?

Questions to ask at a facility you are evaluating for boarding:

- What is included in the standard board rate? What other services are provided at additional cost, and what is the cost?
- What is the horse owner expected to provide?
- Does the stable make regular arrangements for deworming, vaccinations, teeth floating and other regular care, or are boarders responsible for their own arrangements? If boarders are on their own, does the management require proof that boarded horses are in fact getting routine vaccinations and deworming?
- Is there anything required of boarders other than regular deworming and vaccinations that is not included in the board rate?
- Are there any restrictions on farriers, vets, or other therapists that you can use for your horse?
- What restrictions are there on stable access, riding hours, etc.?
- If there is a lesson program at the stable, are there times that boarders cannot use the arena(s)?
- If there is not a resident trainer, are you allowed to bring an instructor to the stable for lessons?
- Who will actually be handling your horse? What training is provided for new employees? If there are children or volunteers working at the stable, who supervises them?
- For what periods is the stable unattended? Does someone do a nighttime check on the horses?

AMATEUR VERSES PROFESSIONAL
By Elizabeth N. Clarke

Where Does the Line Fall?

When you pay someone for services, you want a "professional." In riding terms this word, and its converse, "amateur," have several different meanings.

According to *Webster's New Universal Unabridged Dictionary* a professional is someone "following an occupation as a means of livelihood or for gain," and with regard to sports is one who is "an expert player...serving as a teacher, consultant, performer or contestant."[1], In the equestrian world there are many who fit the first definition but who do not necessarily fit the second. Because riding instruction is not regulated in the United States, anyone can claim to be a riding instructor, regardless of talent or training.

The same dictionary defines an "amateur" as one who "engages in a study, sport, or other activity for pleasure rather than for financial benefit or professional reasons," or alternatively as, "an athlete who has never competed for payment or for a monetary prize," or "a person inexperienced or unskilled in a particular activity."[2]

For purposes of competition in regulated aspects of our sport, the lines are drawn in somewhat different places. According to the USA Equestrian 2002 Rule Book, any of the following will make an individual who has reached eighteen years of age a professional rather than an amateur, "Regardless of one's equestrian skills and/or accomplishments. . . . "

1. Accepting remuneration for riding, driving, showing (under saddle or in hand), training, schooling, conducting clinics or seminars, or giving riding instruction. The same activities will classify one as a professional if any member of the individual's family or a corporation owned or controlled by a member of the individual's family is paid for boarding, riding, driving, training, or showing the horse, even if the individual is not paid. Theoretically this means that if my mother runs a boarding stable and I come for a visit, and she borrows a boarder's horse for me to ride while I am home, I am a professional under the rules of our National Equestrian Federation.

2. Riding, driving, showing, training, or schooling horses that are owned, trained, or boarded by the individual's employer, a

member of the employer's family, or a corporation controlled by the employer or a member of the employer's family. So, if I work in a hair salon owned by someone who owns horses, and I agree to exercise my boss's horses as a favor while she is away on vacation, I have just become a professional under National Federation rules.

3. Accepting remuneration for the use of one's name, photograph, or other form of personal association as a horseman in connection with any advertisement or article to be sold. So if I am a model and want to show as an amateur, I'd better turn down any modeling assignments for tack catalogs.

4. Accepting prize money in horsemanship or equitation classes, except in dressage.

5. Accepting remuneration for helping to sell a horse or taking a horse on consignment.[3]

However judges, stewards, technical delegates, course designers, announcers, and TV commentators may compete as amateurs if they aren't otherwise considered a professional for the above reasons.[4] That someone qualified to judge the sport can be considered an amateur and a hairdresser doing her boss a favor is considered a professional may not be exactly what Webster's definition had in mind. These very convoluted and not necessarily logical categories came about in equestrian sport as a result of professional riders and trainers doing very creative things in order to be able to compete as amateurs.

If you are looking for good instruction, who is a professional? Think more along the lines of "professionalism." Not everyone who earns money training, showing, or otherwise dealing with horses, and who may or may not call himself a professional fits the description of "an expert player."[5] Professionalism, on the other hand, is reasonably easy to discern. A professional with whom you want to entrust your equestrian education should exhibit the following characteristics:

• Significant experience and knowledge in the discipline for which you are seeking help, preferably measured by demonstrable achievements in terms of horses and riders trained, a competitive record, or the like.

• A desire to continue her own education and maintain her skills, demonstrated by participation in clinics, workshops, or working with another trainer.

- A willingness to have her skills tested, either through competition, an instructor certification program, or other forum where she will be evaluated by respected experts.

- Honest and ethical business dealings, openness with regard to the terms of your arrangement with her, including the costs involved and full disclosure as to the treatment of your horse.

- Presentation of self, horses, and premises that demonstrates attention to detail, appreciation of the aesthetic aspects of the sport, and, most importantly, attention to the well being of the horses.

---

[1] Webster's New Universal Unabridged Dictionary, Random House Value Publishing, Inc., 1996, p. 1544

[2] Ibid., p.63

[3] Rule VIII, Chapter III, Article 808.

[4] Id.

[5] *Webster's* p. 1544.

Only that day dawns to which we are awake. —Henry David Thoreau

LEARNING INSIGHTS

The skills needed to learn most effectively

This section is filled with a variety of learning tools that are instrumental to being a good learner and, more importantly that will help you learn to "feel." These fundamental learning skills are the core of your learning process and will help your journey be more satisfying and fun.

AWARENESS LEADS TO FEEL
by Cathy Frederickson

Feel the moment, only then can you influence it.
—Dr. Reiner Klimke

When we talk about feel in reference to riding horses, we are actually talking about many things. The *Webster's Dictionary* defines feel as a verb that means "to examine, explore, or perceive through the sense of touch." That definition has real meaning to riders, because we essentially strive to communicate our wishes on horseback by touch. In the beginning stages we all must go through the process of learning the correct aids to communicate a command, and to discipline our bodies to maintain correct posture. How often have we watched riders doing those very things and thought they looked wooden? What is that elusive element that transforms the ride from mechanical to artistic? We must go further that simple sensory perception of hot, cold, soft, or hard. Over a period of time, we add an aspect of emotion or intuition, especially as we climb the ladder of achievement in the training of horses. We love being able to report after a lesson or competition that we were really working together as a team, and that the horse seemed to do whatever we wanted simply by our "thinking it".

So how do you learn about this illusive thing called feel? There are actually many ways to accomplish high levels of feel. Let me explore a few of the pathways with you and see if it will help you and your horse.

First of all, try to establish what area of horsemanship you are addressing. Feel comes in many different forms. You do not need to be sitting on horseback to have understanding and harmony with your horse. An integral part of many successful trainers' programs includes work on the ground in many forms. For a beginner with no previous experience with large animals, the groundwork becomes enormously important. The instructor is planting the seeds of understanding the animal as he walks the beginner through the steps of leading, grooming, and tacking up. The student is learning to observe the horse's mood and attitudes, and to respond appropriately. If you want to learn how to load a troublesome animal into a trailer, your references and instruction will be quite different from learning to ride upper-level cross-country techniques, or to canter tempi changes for dressage. The majority of you are striving to master techniques of low-level and middle-level competition and pleasure riding. That generally means you will be taking a multi-pronged approach. You might be utilizing a well-respected local competition rider whom has a reputation for patience with those who are less experienced. Perhaps you live where the only instruction is in the form of traveling clinicians, but you and a friend share the same passion to learn, and help each other. Or, maybe you live in an area that is full of Olympic riders, but they don't teach novices. Each and every one of you will still be able to learn to feel. It simply may be by different pathways and over different periods of time.

Let's begin by discussing some of the things you must consider. First on my list will be instruction. Then, we must discuss the horse that you choose to accomplish your goals upon. How do you as a rider fit into the picture? And lastly, we will look at some of the ways to combine these into a successful and fulfilling experience with horses.Instruction

It is so easy to say, "Get the best instruction that you can." The dilemma begins when you start the search. How do I find good instructors? How do I know they are good? Will our personalities match? Will they be able to help me as much as I think I need it? *(See Chapter—Finding the Right Instruction Plan—Discovery Insights)*.

Once again, try to establish what you want from an instructor initially, and then formulate some future goals. A good instructor will be more than willing to discuss goals and plans with you, and most now insist on some kind of initial evaluation process. It is important to find an instructor who has adequate technical training and knowledge for your needs. There are several ratings and certifications in the United States including clinician lists that can give you an idea of a person's experience and qualifications. Many Americans have also taken advantage of training and certification programs offered over seas. Most of these put their emphasis on teaching and training, not on competitive riding. Do your homework. Get referrals from people who have similar riding and training needs. Observe a lesson or clinic. Ask the instructor questions that are important to you. Ask yourself if you think they will be compatible with your personality and that of your horse? Why is all of this important to the subject of feel? Because it is vital that, whenever possible, you understand and are comfortable following your instructor's directions so that the process of developing feel in your work can progress.

LEARNING FEEL
Guided Feel

It is so important to have instructors throughout your development who ask things like, "Why do you think your horse responded that way? What were your aids? Were they too weak? Too strong? Wrong position with your leg?" You are looking for someone who can guide you forward from the commands of position, and guide you with correct feedback. I will refer to that as "guided feel." An instructor can give you specific directions, allow you to follow the directions on the horse, and give you feedback on the outcome until you can get the consistent results you want on your own. When you begin to get positive feedback from your instructor, you know that you are beginning to *feel* correctly. Guided feel can be utilized throughout a rider's career. A pleasure rider may take a lesson periodically to tune up. A novice or amateur adult will seek instruction as their work, school, family, or other commitments will allow. Any rider may seek guidance when they acquire a new horse or want to move up to a higher level of competition. But the commonality here is that all types of riders can develop a feel for what is correct in their horses, and seek feedback when they are not achieving desired results or want to learn something new.

If you want to improve, learn something new, or communicate more successfully with your horse you should continue to seek instruction. You *need* guided feel! In the beginning stages, the instructor gives you a very structured program consisting of simple basic tasks to practice and perfect. For example, you would learn to mount, walk forward, turn, stop, and maybe to trot a little in the first lessons. Sounds simple! But, a good instructor is busy assessing and then building many more essential elements. Balance of the human on the horse is a hugh issue! The instructor wants you to stay in balance as much as possible. This is essential for your confidence! A rider who falls off or feels unsteady is not likely to keep riding. The instructor will have you stretch and do various exercises to improve your strength and co-ordination. Simultaneously you will learn the aids to send the horse forward, stop, and turn. As you get more balance, and become stronger and more coordinated, you also become more confident! This is nurtured by the instructor's feedback, both corrective and encouraging. It is also important for you to have short periods of time between instructions to ride and *feel*. You will also progress faster and with more understanding if the instructor asks you to verbalize what you feel, and then offers feedback on your verbalization.

> **Instructor:** "I would like you to trot rising around the circle and make a transition to walk as you complete the circle. Stay aware of your shoulders staying up and straight, and your seat and heels staying gently down."
>
> **Rider:** Goes out and performs exercise.
>
> **Instructor:** "How did that go for you?"
>
> **Rider:** "I'm still struggling with a round circle, but it is less egg shaped. I really concentrated on my shoulders and that helped a lot with my heels, but my seat bounces a bit in the transition."
>
> **Instructor:** "Good, accurate assessment! You need to do this exercise a few more times and concentrate on the circle and your bending aids. Then add the transition after two circles. Continue with the good shoulder position, this will help your seat. Go ahead and begin."

The rider is rapidly learning to feel basic issues (the roundness of the circle and awareness of the various parts of the body) while the knowledgeable guidance of the instructor is making it all go faster and with a lot less frustration than if the rider were trying to do it alone.

As you master the next item, you accumulate an understanding or *feel* for the previous items. (This rider has already had explanations and practice on how to make a round circle, as well as practice on position and aids for transitions.) The instructor now guides the rider in putting skills together. This is the beginning stage of what I call "independent feel."

Independent Feel

Independent feel comes about as the rider accumulates experience and knowledge. Remember when we talked about how important the instructor's information is to the beginner about how to lead and handle the horse? Well, after a few sessions of leading the horse on their own, new riders will often experience the pain of having their feet stepped on! This experience strongly reinforces the instructor's vital piece of information about staying closer to the horse's shoulder to avoid the feet! The rider now knows independently how to better lead a horse.

The learning process doesn't need to be negative. A rider might sign up for a clinic with an expert event rider because he or she is having problems with balance issues after moving up a level in competition. The comments on the dressage test and the occasional stop on cross-country, especially if steep terrain are involved, and rails down in show jumping tell the story that sends a rider looking for help. After a conversation with a clinician, followed by some work on the flat, the rider has a couple of specific suggestions from the clinician about how to increase the horse's engagement and encourage him to change his balance to a more "uphill" position. This theme is carried through to the jumping that afternoon. The rider is beginning to feel a consistent change and improvement in the performance. Finally, during the cross-country session on the second day, the rider is really understanding the new concept, and balancing the horse on his or her own, with few reminders from the clinician. The horse has a wonderful cross-country school, performing on some difficult terrain successfully as well.

Finally, to turn this knowledge into independent feel, the rider must be able to continue the corrections at home, and perform at this new level the next time in schooling or competition. The rider may need to seek guided feel and feedback several times before achieving independent feel at the new level, especially when a difficult concept is being mastered.

Some riders will have the opportunity to receive guided feel from their instructor every time they ride. This is enormously beneficial, particularly if the instructor is able to integrate periods of independent feel. In such a case riders are less likely to make big mistakes with their horse, more likely to spend adequate time building a proper foundation, and will learn how to compete more easily while utilizing their everyday work. A higher level of independent feel, achieved more quickly, will be the result of consistent guided feel.

This is the traditional path, but some riders are also very good at using information from books and magazine articles. These can often reinforce what you are trying to do, and sometimes offer completely new information. They can be very useful along with regular instruction. Videos offer another avenue. Sometimes a little piece of information at the beginning or the end of a movement really helps us to understand the whole. Well-made videos can really help us see the whole picture. Remember, so many of us learn visually that, short of seeing a live horse and rider, a video can be the next best choice, particularly if you are very isolated from instruction.

 The rider may need to seek guided feel and feedback several times before independent feel is gained at the new level.

The highest level of independent feel usually belongs to a trainer of many years and diversified experiences. They have mastered the technical skills of their sport, and have added years of experience riding, training, and often retraining hundreds of horses successfully. These people are few, and if you have the fortune of observing or working with one, you understand the term "Master"

FEEL—THE ROLE OF THE HORSE

The horse has an enormous impact on how the rider learns to feel. Americans are a "can do" people, and like the idea of doing things themselves. We also have a great tradition of "informal horsemanship" from the Native American and the western ranch traditions. You can be successful coming from a "seat of the pants" learning process, but it usually means that you have talent as well as good luck. The majority of European riders are much more regimented in their programs than we are. Land is scarcer, and most start in riding school situations.

The big difference is the school horses. The ideal situation is a very experienced and tolerant horse for the inexperienced rider. Inexperience can range from the beginner learning to walk, trot, canter, to a rider beginning to learn first FEI movements. As America is becoming more suburbanized, with less land to ride across the country, new enthusiasts are turning to riding stables. Instructors in American establishments are learning to put more value in schoolmasters. Some riding school owners have long understood the value of horses that can teach a rider to canter with confidence, or to jump calmly and quietly, often forgiving a rider's mistakes.

A suitable horse can help a rider quickly learn to balance under saddle, develop consistent aids, and feel the correct response from the horse. Such a rider will have the advantage of learning "feel" more quickly and correctly.

 The horse has an enormous impact on how the rider learns to feel.

If you have aspirations of competing or riding at upper levels of horse sports, an experienced horse can be one of the most valuable assets in your learning process. If you are fortunate enough to ride a horse that will teach you to "feel," you are truly advantaged over the rider struggling to understand the "feel" on a less experienced horse.

Now let's go to a much more common scenerio: The somewhat green, but kind horse for the inexperienced rider. This situation can work, but it usually means some extra effort on the part of the rider and instructor. A workable situation occurs when the inexperienced rider seeks the guidance of an instructor familiar and comfortable with green horses. The rider can receive regular instruction and, in addition, regular or even occasional schooling/riding of the green horse by the experienced rider. There might even be a schoolmaster for the riders to hone their skills on. This will keep the green horse understanding what it needs to do, while the riders develop their skill to ask correctly. This reinforces guided feel by the instructor and the horse.

One of the big parts of the equation we haven't discussed is *time.* Many things can be accomplished with horses if riders are willing to be patient and invest the time it can take to develop their full potential. Different paths will reflect your drive, your time availability (maybe you have a family and/or job), and your resources, financial and otherwise *(See Chapter—Crossroad 1—Technical Insights.)* If you are a "type A" overachiever who wants to learn to ride and make an Olympic team in two to five years' time, then you definitely do not want to start on a green horse. Experience is your key. Choose the best instructors and horses you can find. These will shorten but not eliminate the learning curve. This path can definitely strain your finances, and will *not* guarantee success.

Most people must make a compromise somewhere. Many do it by acknowledging that their process will take a bit longer. They choose the best instructor and the most experienced horse they can afford, and they put in the sweat equity. Their learning curve is longer, but often has a very satisfactory outcome. Time can be a singularly important element leading to the learning of feel.

There are many scenerios in between, but let's take a look at the worst case: The green or inexperienced horse, and the green rider. This situation can be difficult in the best of circumstances, but if either or both of the team have an unkind disposition, it can really add to the difficulties. Both parties will magnify mistakes, and a downward, negative spiral can easily begin. The simplest thing can present roadblocks; not going forward, bending in both directions, jumping, and leaving groups, are all common tendencies of green horses. But if they are unkind or feel forced by an unkind rider, it can lead to serious resistance. Communication breaks down completely, so that even if good instruction is sought, the feel of the rider is so blocked by tension, anger, and frustration that the directives to the horse simply cannot be made. This is a sad case, and major adjustments must be made in order to salvage the horse or the rider. This is an extreme example, but many of these types of problems affect horses and riders every day. Choosing a horse that is appropriate for *your* needs is enormously important.

Time can be the singularly most important element in learning to feel.

THE NATURAL, DEVELOPED AND INTELLECTUAL RIDER

Most riders are not "natural riders" but have a love of the sport, a terrific learning attitude and a willingness to work hard. I call these 'developed riders.' Natural riders are those who are born with feel, they intuitively learn, feel and communicate with the horse. Natural riders often have a hard time "working hard" or explaining what they do, as it comes so naturally to them. It takes considerable effort for natural riders to explain the steps of what comes naturally to them. Intellectual riders are those who want to process everything with their mind, and have the most difficult time developing "feel." *(See Chapters—Learning Styles—Personal Insights).*

Natural Rider

You won't be around the barn or show ring very long before you hear someone say, "That rider is a natural." What do they mean? Let's go back to the definition of feel; to examine, explore, or perceive through the sense of touch. For most riders emotion and intuition are developed. Over a period of time and aspect of emotion and intuition is *developed* over a period of time. We all have the capacity to develop emotion and intuition in our riding, but the natural rider seems to innately possess this natural feel along with a great sense of balance and a high level of coordination. They don't seem to think about the process, they just do it. These riders seem to be attracted to extreme aspects of horse sports such as rodeos, steeplechasing, horse racing, and the cross-country phase of three-day eventing.

Now, I am only addressing a small percentage of riders who seem to rise meteorically to the top. The really successful riders, year after year, who ride many horses to the top, are a combination of a natural feel, and years of hard work and development.

Developed Rider

Many riders who do not have natural feel achieve great success in their sports. The vast majority of these riders have worked tirelessly, often with very talented instructors who have helped them master the skills of their sport. They are often more analytical about their riding because they have had to be. Students often benefit enormously from instruction of this kind of rider, who may be able to communicate their skills more easily as instructors. They had to examine the process more carefully and become more intellectual and often creative in their teaching and training styles. Their horses also reap the rewards of the years of experience and thought process that these riders have developed. These riders often acknowledge that they "never stop learning."

The Intellectual Rider

The third type of rider is the person with very little feel, and little riding experience, but good intellect. They often read and study, but don't ride much. It is very difficult to teach feel if it has not been learned on horseback. Books can deepen your understanding and can even show you new paths, but riding feel must be developed on horseback. This type of person can instruct in many areas of horse care, handling, and management, but you must try to seek an instructor who understands how to develop feel from the beginning stages of riding if you wish to move most successfully through the learning steps.

Those who choose instructors based only on successful competitive careers are sometimes disappointed. Remember that feel, both guided and independent is developed and learned. The rider who goes through this process is often your best-equipped instructor.

You have probably concluded by now that feel is complex and multifaceted. As I have discussed only a few scenarios in this chapter, I leave you now to go to your next lesson or clinic (mounted or unmounted) and have a dialog with your instructor. Try to honestly assess what your level of feel might be. Take into account the horse you've choosen, what your learning process might be, and how your instructor fits into the picture. Then continue to develop your feel for future success!

TRAINING FRAMEWORK
By Jill K. Hassler-Scoop

Simple, consistent structure to training sessions makes learning faster and more fun. This valuable daily training plan is good for riders of all levels.

Following a plan for your ride leads to consistency that influences several aspects of your riding: It reduces the thinking time, which increases the feeling time, provides the basis for quick, solid decision making, provides information that affects long term goals by staying on route in your short term goals, and creates a deeper awareness that allows you to respond to the horse through feel.

My suggested training session has seven phases or steps. Each of these steps provides a valuable time to observe, compare, and record.

CLEAR YOUR MIND

Before you arrive in the stable, it is important to clear your mind. Take a few minutes to separate your "normal" life from your riding time. Find an ideal way for you to clear you mind, whether it is making a list, mediation, or listening to your favorite music . . . discover what it is and use it. Enter your "horse life" with a full focus and a heartfelt intent to enjoy the time.

GREET AND OBSERVE

Beginning when you arrive at your horse's stall, pen, or pasture, notice his behavior and reactions to you, the environment, and other horses. Notice his response to your grooming and tacking up. Casually compare these responses with those of your previous day. This vital observation helps you to notice any irregularities in health or soundness, the impact of your previous training session, and the current state of being of your horse.

If you enter the horse's living area in a clear state of mind, you are also doing yourself a favor, as this can be a form of meditation for you to begin your "horse life" time. Observing your horse during this time gives you vital input that will help prepare you to get the most out of the day's ride.

Seven phases of a training session
1. Clear your mind
2. Greet and observe your horse while preparing him for ride
3. Warm-up
4. Practice one to three training sets
5. Confirm
6. Review
7. Cool down and relax

WARM-UP

Warm-up, one of the most important aspects of each day's ride, allows you and your horse to loosen up and prepare for the day. It also gives you time to assess how you and your horse are feeling that particular day and to work out any stiffness or blocks. Comparing each day's warm-up from the previous day's warm-up and the last training set will help you to determine the appropriate training program for the day.

Warm-up Overview

√ Horse and rider are *focused* on each other
√ Rider checks *position*
√ Rider checks *horse's* responses
√ Rider compares horse's responses to yesterday's warm-up
√ Rider compares horse's responses to yesterday's training session
√ Rider decides what to include in first training set

Your warm-up will follow the same routine but the focus points depend upon the stage of riding you are in. If you are in Stage 1 or 2 your main focal points will be your position, alignment, relaxation, and spring. In Stage 3 your focus is a combination of factors concerning both you and your horse. By Stage 4 and 5 the main focus is the horse.

Warm-up Checklist for *All* Riders

Develop and follow a systematic checklist for your position and your horse's performance. Your personal position checklist should be the first check you make while you are walking the horse and letting him loosen up. Whatever shows itself as a problem during

Rider's Daily Horse Warm-up Checklist	
Leg	Prompt forward response to each leg
	Prompt response to move shoulder to opposite side
	Prompt response to move hindquarter
Rein	Soft, quick submission to rein aid
	Flex equally on both sides
	Equal response on each side
	Accepts elastic soft contact
Focus	Attentive to rider

IMPORTANT: Ride equally in both directions and frequently change directions (rule of thumb: not more than one time around the arena without a change of some sort). Compare the 'feeling' of the horse going in both directions.

this check is to be identified and, fixed as soon as possible. If it is not possible to fix it right away, the first portion of the training time should be dedicated to its repair.

Tales From the Trip

Mary

One day Mary arrived for her lesson unusually distracted. She soon shared the problem with her instructor: her son was ill and she was worried about him. Although Mary usually did not have a problem with her position that she had in the past—having her weight go down through her thigh—her worry and distraction on this day caused it to resurface. During the warm-up Mary identified the tightness she felt as "hard thighs." She practiced a few transitions with "softening the thighs" and then went forward with her program of working on a course of jumps. Her instructor's role was to remind Mary to include "soften my thigh" with each half halt (adjustment) she made between her fences.

Focus begins with a mood check. If your mood is fine, ideally you want to be focused on the task at hand, not allowing yourself to be distracted. The other challenge is to stay in the moment. *(See Chapter Experience the Moment—Personal Insights)*.

Warm Up Check List for Riders in Stage 3 and Up

Once you have gone through your personal checklist, it is time to move on to checking your horse. During the warm-up you feel the horse's rhythm and follow it. It is important that you also

Rider Personal Daily Warm-up Personal Checklist	
Position	
Alignment	Straight line ear-shoulder-hip-heel Straight line elbow-bit
Suppleness and Spring	Elastic, centered spring from head down through heel Equal spring in each ankle Relaxed, supple joint check
Relaxation	Freedom, looseness of body
Mental	
Focus	Balanced attention to horse and environment "Get on horse's page"
Effectiveness	Respond promptly to horse Expect prompt response from horse
Mood	Content, happy, attentive to horse and riding
Relaxation	Calmness and presence of mind

establish a mental connection with the horse, keeping the horse focused on the work being asked. In addition to having an acute awareness of the horse's natural rhythm, you must stay on a predetermined route. During this check you have some evaluations to make. Record the results in your mind from one warm-up to the next and from the end of one ride to the next. Pay particular attention to the comparisons of this warm-up to the previous day's warm-up, and the comparison of this warm-up to how the horse felt at the end of the previous day's training/schooling session. These important comparisons provide vital information on the progress of the training program.

Tales From the Trip
Tom and Night Air

Tom is very skillful in his warm-up. After he quickly executes his personal checklist, he takes Night Air, his event horse, through a warm-up program. Tom walks and trots in both directions, first asking Night to do a few transitions from walk to trot to test Night's response to Tom's leg aids. Satisfied, Tom then begins neck bending two inches, sometimes to the inside, and sometimes in counterbend. Tom is evaluating Night's response to his rein aids and his inside thigh as well as Night's suppleness. Intermixed with this work Tom does a few twenty-meter circles in both directions, evaluating Night's rhythm, relaxation, and straightness on this pattern. Night loves to canter, so within a few minutes Tom adds the canter with a few twenty-meter circles in both directions. Depending on how Night feels (compared to his previous warm-up and training session), Tom will decide how many transitions and ring figures he will do, as well as how much neck bending. He always does the transitions along the straight side of the arena, so he can more easily feel any resistances that might occur. When he is finished with his warm-up and evaluation, he decides where to begin his training session based on his intermediate plan.

Use exercises and evaluate the results as you follow your checklists. The following exercises are for use during warm-up to help evaluate the horse's responsiveness and flexibility. You can decide what order is best for your horse, starting with the easiest and moving to the most difficult.

Practice an effective warm-up. The correct warm-up influences each day's training sessions as well as the progress of the training program. When you use this consistently it will take only a few minutes of your riding time.

WARM-UP REVIEW

Part of each day's review is to recap the feelings of the overall performance, of your horse and of yourself. After warm-up while walking your horse, review the comparison from today's warm-up with the

> **Warm-up Exercises**
> - Transitions with light contact
> - Maintaining bend while changing directions
> - Changing bend when changing directions
> - Transitions with light contact and bend
> - Simple figures with specific over-bending of one to three inches.

warm-up of your previous ride. This important information will give you the feedback you need to know what to include in your first set. You can make a second comparison at the end of warm-up is to compare the warm-up of the day with the last set of the previous ride. This information gives you insights into your long-term training program.

TRAINING SETS

It is during these sets of training that you build upon your training program as well as practice the skills needed to advance toward your goal. Your warm-up will indicate if you need to do some remedial work, go on with your practice, or add a new skill.

A new skill for you or your horse should not be added until the most recent skill you are learning is confirmed and has become easy to perform consistently. To make the decision, ask yourself if the new skill is easy and if you can do it correctly without thinking about it.

Please note, that even when walking, the horse is asked to move forward with energy and you maintain the correct position.

You may have one to three training sets with walk breaks in between. Please note, that even when walking, the horse is asked to move forward with energy and you maintain the correct position.

 Especially when walking, the horse is asked to move forward with energy and you maintain the correct position.

CONFIRMING INSIGHTS

When a new skill begins to feel good, give yourself and your horse time to "feel" the results of your training program and commit it to your muscle memory. It takes several days of consistently riding with the same "feel" to turn it into a habit. You and your horse own the new skill when it can be performed from "feel."

 Ideally, once you get the feeling, spend about five minutes enjoying the new sought after feeling as simply as possible to allow it to 'sink' into your muscle memory.

REVIEW

The review sets the mental pathway to connect thoughts to feel, and commits them to memory to be retrieved at your next training session. When you have finished your lesson or ride, as you walk around the ring, you should review the three most important points of the lessons, bringing together the thought and the feeling. The three things can be focused on you, on your horse or on a combination of the two. Most important is to keep it simple, choosing three of the most important points and committing to memory the feelings as well as the facts.

COOL DOWN AND RELAX

Cool down for 15-20 minutes, enjoying the moment—the nature around you, the feeling of your relaxed, stretched body, your horse's elastic, flowing, and energetic walk. Return to your "real life" exhilarated and refreshed.

Tales From the Trip

Mary

Because Mary felt frazzled between the morning chaos and the church meeting she had to run that night, she decided to drive the long way to the stable and play some of her favorite music. As she drove, she allowed herself to calm down and then to review what she had to do to prepare for her evening meeting. Once she finished this, she reviewed her time line and plan for the remainder of the day one last time. She then allowed herself to enjoy the rest of the drive in the moment, without thinking about the past or the future.

Mary arrived at Tiger's stall and was rewarded with his happy whinny! This response always helped Mary feel welcome. Mary tacked up Tiger and noticed he was touchy when she groomed his loins. A quick review of her last training session drew Mary's attention to the fact that she might have worked him too long during that session, as he had felt so good. Mary's quick review also told her that she might be in too big a hurry to prepare for the upcoming show.

Alert to Tiger's touchy loin area and her tendency to be in a hurry, she began her warm up. Mary soon discovered that she was not as relaxed as on the last ride; she discovered tension in her shoulders and lower back. Tiger felt fine, almost as good in his warm-up as at the end of yesterday's training session. Mary decided to do a second warm-up set for herself, including some exercises to relax her lower back and shoulders. She kept this set short, doing shoulder rolls and chest-on-the-crest exercises.

As she walked, she decided that she would keep her next set short as soon as Tiger was correctly through. Instead of 30 minutes of work, she would do 20 minutes. Her program included short test pieces to prepare for her competition. Once she started this set, Mary discovered that Tiger was more distracted than usual. He wanted to look out the arena gate towards the barn and peer into the distance, which was unusual for him. Mary began to get frustrated, so she walked and reviewed both herself and Tiger. She did a quick mental check: how was her focus? She realized that when Tiger felt good she began to think ahead to her preparation for evening meeting. That was easy to fix, and she and Tiger remained focused on the training at hand for the remainder of the ride.

Since she did not do anything new or unusually, Mary decided to consider her whole ride as the confirming ride time because her whole ride was actually confirming what they did the previous day. What she learned was about her mind, and was not related to new muscle memory.

Her review revealed the need to remain focused and the feeling she had when she was able to draw her attention back to the task at hand. Second she was reviewed the effects of her focus on Tiger's responses. Third, she promised to do some stretching exercises for her shoulders and lower back before coming to the barn tomorrow. And fourth, she spent her first few moments of her cool down reviewing the wonderful feel she had when she and Tiger were moving together.

GOAL SETTING
by Tanya Boyd

You are enrolled in a full-time informal school called "life."
Each day in this school you will have the opportunity to
learn lessons. You may like the lessons or hate them, but
you have designed them as part of your curriculum.
—Cherie Carter-Scott Ph.D.

Making progress is important to humanity, especially in areas that are meaningful to each individual. Much of North American society, whether in business or pleasure, is built on striving towards those moments of success when we have won the class, or beat the other team, or "made it" in our chosen profession. Even advertisements focus on these moments of success to help sell products. We are inundated with images of success; the victory gallop and the celebration dinner are two examples. We are conditioned to think that every day, every ride, should be a victory. What is not apparent, however, are the long hours of practice, repetition, struggle, failures, and defeats that are a part of the road to success. All of us want to succeed, to reach for our dreams, to become masters in the sport that we love. The first step toward mastery is realizing that it is a journey, an ongoing process of lifelong learning, and not a series of uninterrupted victories. On the journey toward success in the equestrian world, it is important to know and keep an eye on the ultimate goal as well as incremental goals along the way, and also to learn to enjoy all the time spent practicing on the path between goals. This chapter will help you understand the path to mastery through incorporating goal setting into your riding, and also understanding the importance of the plateaus between the goals that make up the largest portion of your life.

(RM) THE ROAD MAP

Role of Goals

Setting Goals

Resistance to Change

Learning to Love the Plateau

Daily Goal Setting

Role of Goals

Goal setting is a step toward turning dreams into reality. Most people can name their dreams at a moment's notice; as an equestrian you may name riding in the Olympics, or competing at the top level of your discipline, or becoming the best rider you can be, or owning your own farm. Many people do not reach their dreams, and may become disillusioned or frustrated with lack of progress toward their goals. On a smaller scale, you may know of areas in your riding where you would like to improve, but have a hard time making any improvement. This can be frustrating if you feel that you are trying hard to make the change, but nothing noticeable is happening. While these frustrations are real, dreaming is an important part of the journey, and is to be encouraged when in conjunction with goal setting. Goal setting is the tool that allows you to see the progress you are making towards your dreams, and thus alleviates some of the potential frustration. Goal setting gives a structure to the journey, and helps you learn to enjoy the process of navigating the waters as you get closer to your dreams.

The first problem with this is that, in this sport, you can never be "perfect." Even a very good shoulder-in can always be better. Even if you get a "10" on your trot lengthening, or ride a clear round in the jump-off, the next time you ride you will not be guaranteed the same results. Riding is a sport of continual learning and always has the potential for improvement. If you are too focused on goals, you can easily become disillusioned or frustrated when you do not achieve them in quick succession or with consistency.

The second problem with being too focused on the end goal is that it takes some of your energy and focus away from where you spend most of your time—practicing the basics and the everyday riding that takes place in between meeting each goal. A first level rider whose goal is to ride Grand Prix will not ever get to the point where she will not have to work on the basics of walk, trot, and canter. You never really leave behind previously accomplished goals. Even Grand Prix riders spend most of their time simply improving the walk, trot, and canter, without pirouettes, passage, and piaffe.

The key to the journey of success is having dreams, making goals, looking ahead to where you want to go, and then learning to enjoy the process, including the times when you do not seem to be advancing, or maybe even feel like you are going backwards.

This is part of the learning curve for all activities and sports, but is more complex in equestrian sports due to the important partnership with the horse.

The danger of goal setting is that you can become too focused on goals.

Setting Goals

The Process

Goal setting itself is fairly simple. First, list everything you want to do, including things that you think are just dreams. Divide these into categories, such as riding goals, teaching goals, professional goals, relationship goals, etc. Within each category, group what you have written as dreams, long-term goals, and short-term goals. Hopefully you will see that your short-term goals lead you toward your long-term goals, which point to your dreams within each category. Then the daily work is determining daily goals from your short-term goals, and evaluating your progress regularly.

Characteristics of a good goal

- A good goal is performance-oriented rather than outcome-oriented. Your goals should be based on a task that you want to perform rather than an outcome that relies on the judgment of another person. Instead of writing, "I want to win my class at the horse show next month," write, "At the horse show next month I want to ride my dressage test with more consistent bend through the corners than I did at the last show."

- Write **S.M.A.R.T.** goals (as described by Larrie Rouillard)

  S. *Specific:* It is important to make your goals specific and simple. Instead of writing, "I want to ride a good shoulder-in," write, "I want to ride a balanced shoulder-in at the trot with the proper angle while maintaining forward energy." It is also important to make your goals specific to you and your horse.

  M. *Measurable:* Write goals that you can easily know when you have achieved—something that you or your instructor can see on a video, for example.

  A. *Action-oriented:* Use a verb when you write your goals. The only way to change something is to "do" something about it. "Doing" something can include visualization as well as physical movement.

R. *Realistic:* While your dreams do not have to be realistic, as you get closer to the present your goals need to get more realistic, so that you feel that each goal is achievable from the one before.

T. *Time- and resource-constrained:* Set a deadline for the goal. It is important to remain flexible if unforeseen difficulties or problems with resources needed arise, but setting a deadline gives you additional energy to work toward your goal.

Resistance to Change

In order to make progress in riding, as in anything else, you must be willing and able to change. Change is what learning is all about, and in order to make progress you must learn. However, change is exactly what your body is programmed against! Homeostasis is a physical phenomenon built into your body that you have to deal with whenever you want to learn or change or make progress. Homeostasis is what keeps your body the same temperature and regulates every function inside your body to make sure things stay the same and keep on working. If you make a change in your routine behavior or way of thinking, your body's first response will be to try to get you to come back to the way it was before. Yet it is possible to change, obviously, since you do it throughout your life. You need to be aware that change will be accompanied by anxiety, struggle, and uncertainty. Setting goals helps give structure to your change, so that you can see on paper the logical progress that is laid out. This gives you the material you need to talk to your "homeostat," telling it to relax, and that the change is planned out and will be done carefully over time.

Learning to Love the Plateau

North American culture teaches you throughout your life to do things in order to get something else. You study hard in high school so you can get into a good college. You graduate from a good college so that you can get a good job. You get a good job so that you can make lots of money to buy a house or a car or vacations. People are taught from a very young age to keep striving for those big moments, but most people are not taught to enjoy the in-between times. In riding, you begin at the walk to learn the basic position so that you will not fall off when you trot. Maybe you started on the lunge line for a little while until you felt secure enough to ride on your own. Most kids and adults cannot wait to

Even a bad day in the saddle is better than many things in life.

get off the lunge line. For many kids, walk, trot, and canter on the flat are tolerated only because they have to do that before they can jump. Many adults hurry through the basics so they can get to the "fun stuff;" the leg-yielding, the flying changes, piaffes, pirouettes. Instead of this intense focus on the "highs," you need to learn how to enjoy every day, every moment, in the journey. This is what will enable you to stick with it to the next high point. There is a bumper sticker, "Even a bad day on the golf course is better than a good day in the office." I think this applies to riding as well, and can be a reminder that even the tough days can be enjoyable.

As with any sport, every new movement is only new once; then it takes many repetitions to improve it and make it natural. During the first few repetitions of a new skill, you may feel an improvement each time you do the movement. In learning the sitting trot, you may feel a little more secure each time you do it for the first few days or lessons. But there will come a point where you can no longer feel the improvement. You practice each day, but it does not seem to change. This is the point at which impatience can often appear. Either you think that this is as good as it is going to get, or else you may get bored with waiting for more improvement and want something else new to try so that you can get back to feeling daily improvement again. This stage of the learning process is called the plateau, and the reality is that most of your life is lived on the plateau. Even after winning a gold medal in the Olympics, there is always tomorrow and tomorrow and tomorrow. A person who is completely goal-oriented will not stay in the sport of riding for the long term, because the majority of time is spent on the plateau, between goals; and unless one learns to enjoy the plateau, most of life will not be enjoyable.

Think about the role that riding plays in your life.

- As you drive out to the barn do the cares of the day begin to drift away, and as you walk into the barn and breathe in the sweet smell of hay and warm horses, do you relax and smile?

- Does the act of grooming your horse release any remaining stress from your body, and does his nicker at your approach make you laugh?
- When you ride, do you enjoy every moment, even when things are not going the way you hoped?
- Is even a "bad day at the barn better than the best day away from the barn"?

This is the master's path. It is not to say that you do not work hard, trying to improve with every ride. You definitely do work hard, striving for progress with every ride; but your real enjoyment comes from simply being with your horse, riding, even if visible improvements are not made every day. You recognize the role of the plateau—that learning is taking place even if you cannot feel it or see it—and you have learned to wait patiently for the next spurt of growth. Goals are definitely important, but are *only one part* of riding. Ultimately it is the person who enjoys the process of learning and growth that will stick with the sport and climb the highest.

Some have said that there is a "face of mastery;"—a look of calm concentration that shows both effort and enjoyment. You can see this in some professional photos taken at major sporting events, or even in your own family photo album. Watch the faces of the riders at the next competition you attend. Some riders' faces may show severe tension without enjoyment. These riders may be so goal-oriented at that particular moment (the outcome-oriented goal of winning the class being foremost in their minds at that moment) that any enjoyment of the sport or the moment is lost. Then there will be other riders whose faces are calm, serene, with a definite sense of enjoyment. You will know that they are working hard, but what shows outwardly is their enjoyment of being in that arena at that time, riding each movement. Goals are

George Leonard, in his book Mastery, says, "Practice, the path of mastery, exists only in the present. You can see it, hear it, smell it, feel it. To love the plateau is to love the eternal now, to enjoy the inevitable spurts of progress and the fruits of accomplishment, then serenely to accept the new plateau that waits just beyond them. To love the plateau is to love what is most essential and enduring in your life."

important, but they exist in the future, and we live in the present. We must have goals so we know which direction we are going, but we must learn to be fully aware of, and enjoy, the present.

A rider who can balance the strengths of goal setting with the love of the plateau, or an instructor who can help students find this balance, is on the path of mastery, the road to success.

Daily Goal Setting

The most important part of goal setting is the daily incorporation of goals into your riding and lessons.

As you groom your horse and tack him up for the day's ride, what do you think about?

- Your day at work?
- The dinner you have to cook when you get home?
- Just the pleasure of being at the barn with your horse?

These are all fine things to think about, but this is also a good time to review your last ride or lesson in your mind and think about what you want to work on during this ride. If you've had a hard day, maybe a good goal is to relax by going on a trail ride. If you had a breakthrough in your lesson the previous day, maybe you want to see how quickly you can recreate that feeling on your own, without your instructor's assistance. Before you get on your horse, have an idea in your mind of what you think you want to work on during that ride. Then you enter the arena and begin warming your horse up. Now is the time to ask yourself how you and your horse are feeling today. How does this warm-up compare with your previous warm-up? During the warm-up, reevaluate your goal for the day based on how you and your horse feel. This flexibility is very important; your goal is not an ultimatum that you *must* accomplish. Instead, it is a guideline to help you continue to move forward along your journey of learning.

Here is where one of the dangers of goal setting arises: If you come to the barn absolutely set on working on trot lengthenings, and you take your horse out of the stall and get him ready while visualizing your beautiful trot lengthenings, and then you get on him and feel in the warm-up that he is a little stiff in his back, but you still stick to your predetermined goal to *do* those lengthenings, you are not going to accomplish your goal. Your horse will probably just remain stiff and you will have to work extra hard to get any kind of increase in stride at all. You will probably finish that ride very frustrated or feeling defeated because you did not accomplish your goal. If, however, when you feel your horse's stiffness in the warm-up you are able to revise your goal at that point to help your horse loosen up in his back, and then proceed with your ride from there, you are much more likely to achieve that goal and feel successful. This is where the idea of the master's journey is important. Even though you may think that you are going backward because you had to work on stiffness in the back instead of trot lengthenings, if you are on the master's path you realize that you are still learning and your horse is still learning, and this is what matters. Just because you didn't get the trot lengthenings today doesn't mean you are a failure. Instead, you learned how to work your horse through a stiffness in his back, and this will help you in the future when you do get to work on trot lengthenings.

At the end of your ride, as you cool out your horse, you need to ask yourself whether you met the goal you set, thinking of the positive parts of the ride and also the parts that you would have wanted to be different. This is a good time to get an idea of what you would want to work on during your next ride.

Journal Notes

After your ride, it is very helpful to make short notes in your riding journal about your initial goal, how you modified it after the warm-up and why, whether you met that goal by the end of the ride and why or why not, the positive parts of the ride, and what you think you want to work on during your next ride. Writing this daily does not take much time, and can be a very powerful resource for you along your journey. Having a record of your goals and rides puts each day in perspective. If you have a particularly frustrating ride and feel like you are getting nowhere, it is nice to be able to go to your journal and look back a month or two to see the progress you really have made. It is also a good way to get the most out of your lessons. Before each lesson you can review your journal entries for the previous week or month for a clear, concise reminder of how your rides have gone since your previous lesson. This allows you and your instructor to get on the same page much faster and saves valuable time.

What if you don't accomplish your goal
during the lesson or training session?

This will happen from time to time, even with the planned reevaluation of goals following the warm-up. People have a tendency to feel frustrated or depressed if they do not meet a goal once they have set it, especially daily goals. It is important for you to see the progress that *was* made in the lesson, and to understand why you did not reach the goal that day, as well as what is still needed in order for you to reach the goal. If you leave a ride feeling like you did not meet your goal and you know why, you will be able to continue working toward this goal in your next training session. But if you do not meet your goals, yet you have a clear understanding of what you *did* accomplish, why you could not complete the whole goal, and what specific things you need to work on at home in order to make it possible to complete the goal, you can leave the lesson with energy and motivation to go and work on those things. If you have not met your goal after three rides it is time to reevaluate your goals.

Tales From the Trip

Julie

Julie is eleven years old, and has been riding since she was three. She rode saddleseat most of her life and just recently switched to dressage. She has a fourteen-year-old horse named Angel. When Julie came to her first lesson at camp, the instructor asked her what she would like to work on. She didn't really know and was very quiet. The instructor asked her what she usually did when she rode Angel, and what kinds of things she worked on in her lessons with her regular instructor. This helped her begin and she said that they usually used draw reins on Angel and were trying to get her to put her head down and stretch into Julie's hands. The instructor said that it sounded reasonable to work on getting Angel to stretch into her hands, so maybe that could be the goal. Julie didn't bring the draw reins to this first lesson, so the instructor asked her to warm Angel up. It was quickly apparent that Angel was very tense and nervous in the new place. Julie handled her very well, remaining calm with very quiet hands. Her position needed some work because her legs were quite far forward and not on the horse's sides.

Because of her age and the horse's tension, the instructor started talking to Julie as she was doing her warm-up, asking her how Angel felt, and what she usually did to relax Angel. They took a walk break and talked about how Angel felt that day compared to how she usually feels, and then decided that the goal for the day would be to get Angel to relax. They used ring figures to keep Angel's attention and help her relax. By the end of the lesson. Julie could feel a difference in Angel, and understood that she had accomplished the goal of getting Angel to relax. They decided that the next goal would be to get Angel more relaxed and stretching.

The next day, Angel was much less tense to begin with, so it did not take as long to get her to relax. Julie found that one of the exercises she had used to get Angel to relax also helped her begin to stretch into Julie's hands, so by the end of that lesson she was getting a couple strides of stretching. Julie caught on very quickly to the idea of goal setting, and was able to be very flexible with her goals based on how Angel felt each day. What was especially remarkable was how comfortable Julie was working on the same thing each day. While the other kids in the camp were asking to do new movements or "tricks" each lesson, Julie was content to get Angel a little more consistent in her stretching, or a little more responsive to her leg. She was exactly right about what Angel needed, but many kids would not have had the patience to see that need, accept it, and enjoy it. Julie was on the master's journey because she recognized that she and her horse were learning even while they were on an apparent plateau, not making great strides in level or movements. Julie enjoyed work on the basics, and that is another characteristic of a master. There is no doubt that Julie will progress towards her long-term goals and dreams, because she has the ability to enjoy the process and does not need constant success to motivate her.

Andrea

Andrea is fifteen years old and returned to the camp for a second year. Last year her horse had been new to her, and she had not had him on the bit at all. Her camp instructor was amazed to see the progress she had made over the year, not only in herself and her horse, but also in her maturity and ability to understand and use goals. She was introduced to goal setting the year before during camp, and this year when the instructor asked her during her first lesson what she wanted to work on, she spoke right up and said she wanted to work on balancing her horse in trot lengthenings. She spoke with clarity and simplicity. The instructor watched her warm-up, and all the pieces were there for working with trot lengthenings, so they were able to proceed with Andrea's stated goal that day.

Every day during the first week Andrea came with an appropriate goal, warmed her horse up well, and she and the instructor proceeded to work on the goals. She was really happy with her own progress and with her horse. The second week she wanted to work on canter lengthenings one day, but her horse was lethargic and lazy and leaning on her hands. The long, hot days of camp were getting to him. She and her instructor talked about how she and her horse felt that day (hot and tired), and modified the goal for the day to getting her horse responsive to her leg and then quitting early if he got it. They then talked about that decision to change the goal from a higher level movement (canter lengthenings) back to a basic exercise (getting the horse moving off her leg). Andrea admitted to feeling a little disappointed, and maybe a little like a failure; but she understood the need to modify the goal since she knew the canter lengthenings would not be a success if her horse was not moving off her leg. The instructor discussed how the exercise they used to get her horse moving off her leg could actually help in the canter lengthenings, and talked about the steps they would use the next day to balance her horse in the lengthenings if he was more responsive in her warm-up. It ended up being a positive experience for Andrea and her horse (who did respond to the leg and thus had a shortened lesson and an extended snooze in his stall), and gave her tools to handle other times when she might not be able to do exactly what she wanted to do during a ride.

Sarah

Sarah is nineteen years old and brought her older Arabian mare to camp. It was Sarah's first time at camp, and she was much older than the other campers. Sarah was quite hard on herself, and nothing was ever good enough for her at first. Her goals were to get Princess to be round and through her back and steady in Sarah's hand. On the first day Princess was so tense and nervous that Sarah could only walk her with little bits of trot. Princess's head was up in the air the whole time and she was not paying any attention to Sarah. Sarah and her camp instructor were finally able to get Princess's attention and get her to stay on route, but Sarah didn't feel like she was making progress towards her goals.

The next day Sarah got Princess's attention sooner, and was able to get Princess to relax in her back a little and stretch into Sarah's hands in the walk and trot. They progressed quickly, but Sarah could not see it. It was never good enough. Sarah felt Princess always should have been more consistent, or less heavy, or rounder, or holding it through every transition. The camp instructor used video to show Sarah Princess's progress, and that helped a little bit. At the end of every lesson the instructor had Sarah tell her the three good things that happened during the lesson (the instructor could think of fifteen right off the bat), and this was very hard for Sarah at first. Only after she named the three would her instructor let her say the one thing she would want to be different and wanted to work on the next day. By the end of the two weeks, Sarah was able to see her own and Princess's huge improvement from the first day, and she realized her own tendency towards perfection. Seeking perfection is not a bad thing, but she needed to learn to see the goals accomplished along the way and celebrate those with her horse.

Kelsey

Kelsey is a fourteen-year-old student who came to camp with a fairly fancy horse, riding in a double bridle even though she was riding only second level. The horse behaved better in the double, she said, and she had a hard time controlling him in the snaffle. Kelsey's original two-week goal was "to be able to ride a good second level test." Kelsey needed to feel that she was always improving. Each time she came to her lesson she wanted to ride a new movement at a higher level, even if she had not solidified the previous movements. If her horse made a mistake or misbehaved, she would jerk on his mouth and slap him, or hit him with the whip. He was either "good" or "bad" at the end of the lesson, and her journal entries expressed this without details describing what "good" or "bad" meant for that particular day. The only thing that brought her enjoyment was the thrill of doing something new that she could tell her friends about.

Over the course of the two weeks, Kelsey was told that she needed to move down a level in her showing because she and her horse were not ready for second level, and she was consistently told not to abuse her horse. Kelsey realized that she had an anger management problem, and discussed with her instructor ways to handle her anger that would not endanger her or her horse. The other campers helped her out by being available to take care of her horse for her if she was upset at the end of a ride or lesson.

The advice to move down a level in showing caused Kelsey a lot of grief. She was ready to sell her horse because he could not move up the levels as fast as she wanted to, but she also really did love him and wanted to work with him. She and her instructor talked about reevaluating her goals to make them more specific and realistic. By changing her two-week goal to "learning to help my horse relax his back in the canter," she then changed her focus from needing to have her horse in a second level frame at all times (even with his tight back) to working on a more basic skill that ultimately would help her reach her original goal of riding a good second level test (and would help her to state more clearly what a "good" test was). Her whole focus changed from what she and her horse looked like, to helping her horse make the internal change of relaxing his back. Ultimately, this affected how he looked to those watching as well.

At the end of camp, Kelsey still had a long way to go, but she had experienced at least a little bit of enjoyment being on the plateau, and had taken steps to work on her anger management problem.

Nicole

Nicole began riding hunt seat when she was ten, then switched to eventing when she joined Pony Club at age twelve. She advanced through the USPC levels to the "H-A" when she was seventeen, gaining teaching experience through instructing other Pony Club members. Adults admired how she rode horses and began to ask her to help them with their horses through a combination of riding and teaching, so she gained experience teaching all ages of riders, beginners through first level dressage and training level eventing.

Through her teenage years she supported her "horse habit" by giving riding lessons and Pony Club prep clinics and teaching at Pony Club camp. She chose not to go to an equestrian college, and gave up riding and teaching for several years as she focused first on a science and then on a humanities college curriculum. She found that her previous experiences working with and teaching adults riding helped her when giving presentations in college and in interacting with the professors.

After graduating from college she decided that she wanted to become a counselor, so she went to graduate school and earned a master's degree in counseling, while at the same time working as a college admissions counselor. Following completion of her degree she worked as a college admissions director for two years. While she enjoyed the academic world and had enjoyed studying psychology, she soon realized how much she missed being around horses and working with people and horses together. Unsure of exactly what her options were, especially since she had not ridden for five years, she applied for a working student position at a dressage barn. Being a part of the daily running of a barn reaffirmed her decision to reenter the horse world, and the high quality lessons and school horses allowed her to quickly gain back her feeling for riding and working with horses. During this year, she also took part in an instructor's program that emphasized "how" to teach: skills like communication, goal setting, and awareness/observation. This program was really exciting because it combined a lot of what she had learned in her psychology classes with the horse world and teaching in particular.

At the end of the year she had the opportunity to work as a groom for three months with a special program preparing stallions for a testing. While this was a fun and culturally expanding experience, it also reaffirmed Nicole's desire to work with *both* horses and people in an intellectually stimulating way, where each day's work was a little bit different from the last.

The next step was a little unclear at this point, so Nicole began working with a counselor who helped her examine all areas of her life to see what career path and specific opportunity would be the best fit. She was asked to write down her dream job as fully as possible, with no limits. This was a fun exercise, and it revealed some interesting dynamics in what she wanted in a career. Then she was asked to write down the three things that she *must* have in her career, as well as two things that *must not* be a part of that career. Once the counselor and Nicole figured out what kind of a career she wanted and how that would fit into the rest of her life and her relationships, she worked with an equestrian career consultant to develop a plan and begin putting it into effect.

Through this process she realized that her time spent working in the nonequestrian world had not been a waste. She had learned valuable communication skills through working with prospective college students and being part of a college staff where teamwork was an important part of making daily decisions. She learned organizational skills, problem-solving techniques, conflict management, and had the opportunity to practice writing by putting together several proposals for new courses at the college. All of these skills would be valuable to her as she moved into an equestrian career. She would be communicating with horses, owners, and riders; needed to be organized as far as scheduling her lessons and keeping track of the progress of her students; and would use conflict management and problem-solving techniques in each lesson to help the horses and riders make progress together on the "same page." Her writing skills and enjoyment of that task did not automatically fit into a riding instructor's job, but it was important enough to her that she looked for a way to include that skill in her future career in some form.

Nicole considered becoming a full time riding instructor at a local barn, but decided that even with the daily differences that horses and riders experience, this still did not provide enough variety for her. She considered becoming a freelance writer for some national equestrian publications, but realized that she would not have enough immediate contact with horses and people in that job. She considered getting further training overseas and becoming a horse trainer, specializing in starting young horses, but again realized that it was important for her to be working with people and horses. Additionally, this option would require a large output of funds and time that she could not afford. Yet she also realized how important continuing education was to her, so that characteristic was added to her list of necessary items for the ideal job.

Finally, after many months of questioning and trying out various possibilities in her mind, she found the right balance. Today she is a successful instructor for Pony Clubs and lower level adult amateurs who specializes in incorporating psychology into her teaching, and she writes articles for various equestrian publications about integrating traditionally nonequestrian subjects into riding and training horses. She lives in her favorite part of the country and also leads equestrian travel tours to various parts of the world.

COMMUNICATION SKILLS FOR RIDERS
by Kathy Kelly, Ph.D.

Listening is actively focusing on what messages you are receiving, both verbally and nonverbally."
—Cherie Carter-Scott, Ph.D.

WHAT IS COMMUNICATION?

Communication is a form of give and take. We give information to others, and we receive information from them as well. This means that in order to communicate successfully, we need to do two things well:

1. Talking skills: *Send out* information that is understandable to others.

2. Listening skills: Understand what is being *sent back* to us in return.

The most common difficulties that occur between people and horses are a result of *poor communication skills*. People tend to send out what they think are clear *A skilled communicator means being good at both talking and listening.* and easily understood communications (with people, this tends to be words, with horses, it tends to be aids), and then operate on the assumption that the receiver of our communications understands clearly what we are asking. While our communications seem very clear to us, they are not always that clear to others. This can be for several reasons:

- Your verbal and nonverbal messages contradict each other.
  Example: Your words say, "I would love to go for a trail ride," but your facial expression and body language say, "I am really scared to go on this trail ride."

- You don't realize that your message is misunderstood.
  Example: When talking to your instructor, you say, "I don't like to jump over three feet," and your instructor thinks that you want to build up your confidence for jumping higher fences. What you really mean is that you don't have any desire to jump higher than three feet, and want to concentrate on being good and confident at the lower height.

- **Your communications are vague, confusing, or unclear.**
  Example: You are riding your horse, and you ask for a canter. Although you think you gave the right aid for canter, and in your mind your intent is clear, in actuality, your aids were unclear to the horse, and because your horse is confused, he runs faster in trot, thinking that this is what you wanted.

USEFUL SKILLS FOR BETTER COMMUNICATIONS

The world of psychology offers us some fun and useful techniques that can improve our talking and listening skills. These techniques, if properly used, can make our efforts to communicate with people and horses less frustrating, and ultimately more effective.

Talking Skills

Before we talk about *how* to communicate, it helps to understand the *goal* of communication.

Communication Cycle

All good communication is completed in a cycle of give and take between speaker and listener:

- First, there is the speaker's statement or question → Then there is the listener's response → Finally the speaker acknowledges the listener's response.

Sounds simple, doesn't it? Then why does communication between people go so wrong? The answer lies in the *response* of the listener. Good communication is effective only if it helps the communicator get what they need. Therefore, it is important for us, as speakers, to get the response from our listeners that we are looking for. The response of the listener then sets the stage for either a positive communication cycle, in which both speaker and listener understand each other, or a problem communication cycle, in which speaker and listener are at odds. If you, as a speaker, get responses to your communications that make you feel heard and understood, and help you get what you need, you are most likely an effective and competent communicator. If, however, you find that people respond to your words or actions in less than ideal ways, there may be a need for you to hone your communication skills.

So, what goes into becoming a good speaker?
Speak Directly

This is not as simple as it sounds. Some of the more common reasons why people fail to speak directly include:

- Fear of exposure
- Not knowing their own wants and needs
- Feelings of shame or embarrassment
- Wanting others to "read their mind" as evidence of care and love
- Unsure of other people's response

Speaking directly minimizes confusion over what you want, feel, or need. Once people know what it is that you saying in clear terms, they are not left to try and guess or make assumptions about what you mean by your statements. When people guess or make assumptions, they can be correct, but often such efforts are way off target—leading to much confusion in the communication department.

Seek Out Possible Assumptions

When a listener's response is "off target," most people *react* by responding back immediately, with emotion. This serves only to escalate the problem. The following steps can help you to check for possible incorrect assumptions that your listener is making about you or what it is that you have said.

Check out what you think you heard. Sometimes we don't hear correctly. If you are aware of the assumption the listener is making, then state that. No matter what, adopt a curious stance, and try hard not to respond in a defensive or angry tone.

- *Examples:* "I'm hearing you say that . . . " or "Are you hearing me say... ?"

This step alone corrects many misunderstandings. If, however, the listener continues with a difficult response, then go to the second step.

State your feelings using "I statements." "I statements" show that you own your own emotional reactions, and are not laying blame on the listener for your feelings (no one can *make* anyone else feel anything).

- *Examples:* "Boy, that makes me feel sad," or "Gee, I am sort of feeling attacked right now..." or "Ouch! That hurts!" (a sense of humor is sometimes just what we need). Stay away from, "You make me feel . . ." "Your statements" put people on the defensive immediately.

Third, offer the listener an alternative to the message they are sending. Sometimes we all say things in anger or haste that we really don't mean. By stating what you think the listener is trying to say in a more positive way, you provide them with a face-saving 'out' that can defuse many difficult situations.

- *Examples:* "I wonder if you are trying to tell me. . . ?" or "Maybe what you are saying is. . ."

Call the Process

Sometimes the response you get from your listener is so off base or unusual that you have no idea what to say or do. In this situation, you might want to think about "calling the process." This simply means that you state clearly and briefly what you see or feel (or both) happening between you and the listener. Be cautious, as this strategy tends to bring up emotions fast and furious. It is a way to cut through a person's defensives and get right to the heart of the matter because you are describing concrete behavior that is not easily denied.

- *Examples:* "Gee, I can't help but notice that you seemed to shut down just now," or "Your tone of voice suggests that you are really angry with me" or "Gosh, I am really confused by your response. Can you help me try to understand?"

Remember, the goal of communicating is to get a response. What that response is can tell you much about how you communicated your information. It also can tell you a lot about the listening skills of the person you are talking to. Listening is the other half of the give-and-take equation of good communication skills, and is a vital part of the process.

Listening Skills

In order to be a good communicator, no skill is more important than being a good listener. In truth, this is probably the most important part of being a good communicator. Think about it...how many people do you know that really listen well? You probably find these folks enjoyable to talk to and be with. In fact, many good listeners are considered great conversationalists. Why is this? Not because they hold people sway with their witty conversational style, but because they are very good at getting *you* to talk about *you*. Most of us love to talk about ourselves—it is our favorite subject! And when we have an interested and receptive listener, we tend to think very highly of that person's communication abilities.

So, what goes into becoming a good listener?

The Goal of Good Listening— Getting on the Same Page"

Good listeners have the wonderful ability to grasp just what is being communicated to them. Once you understand, you can then respond appropriately. When

Most Important Point:
When listening, be interested! Lack of interest is usually obvious. Only the most self-focused, or desperately lonely talkers will continue communicating anything substantial if they feel that the listener is uninterested.

you respond appropriately, then the speaker can acknowledge your response, and you can enjoy the effects of a positive cycle of communication. This can be described as "getting on the same page" as someone else, because they realize that you have heard them clearly and correctly. This is such an important, but underemphasized skill! Research has actually found that the communication skill of being able to understand other people is one of the strongest predictors of job success and higher-than-average salary earnings. This fact alone is one good reason to develop one's listening skills!

Active Listening Skills

Good listening is not the passive activity that many people think it is. The techniques included in this section require *effort*, which is why they are called *active* listening skills. They may seem a bit awkward at first, but with practice, these skills will soon become more natural to you. Pay attention to how others respond to your use of these techniques. It is amazing to see how much people appreciate your efforts, and respond by sharing important information. Don't be surprised if you experience fewer communication misunderstandings and conflicts than you did before you started using these techniques.

Active listening has two steps:

Step One: You Need to Understand the Speaker

How do you do this? Ask questions! In order to get a sense of exactly what the speaker is trying to get across, you need to ask questions. Questions are a great way to keep a speaker talking. When listening actively, there are many reasons for asking a question.

- You are confused:
  "Help me with this..."
  "I don't think I am quite following you here ..."

- You need more information:
  "Can I ask you a question?"
  "I don't understand. Can you tell me more about . . . "

- You are curious:
  "Wow, this is interesting! I'd like to know more about . . ."
  "Okay, so now I am wondering . . ."

- You are feeling the speaker's emotion:
  "Boy, that sounds wonderful! What did it feel like?"
  "This sounds so stressful . . . how are you handling this all?"
  "You seem so sad when you talk about . . ."

Step Two: You Need to RESPOND Back to the Speaker

- *Repeat back to the listener a brief but succinct summary of all that you have heard—in your own words!* This is called paraphrasing. It is important that you don't repeat back exactly what you heard, or you risk sounding like a parrot—and

Another Important Point: Respond! A good listener gives feedback in some shape or form, and does not just sit there quietly waiting for the speaker to finish talking so they can start speaking themselves.

this is truly annoying to the speaker! Be sincere about trying to understand. You will come across as truly caring about the other person. People struggle the most with this step—not because they don't want to respond, but because they don't know *how* to respond. Here are some phrases that can help:

"So, what you're telling me is . . ."

"In other words . . ."

"If I get this right, you mean . . ."

And, the classic "therapist response" "What I hear you saying is . . ."

Once you have responded, the speaker may agree or disagree with your summary. If they agree *great!* Now is the time for you to formulate your communication back to the person *based on what you now know.* If the speaker doesn't agree, they will usually try to correct you, by saying, "No, that's not what I meant," or "Well, not exactly . . . what I am trying to say is," or something similar. Allow the speaker to clarify and correct, then respond back with a summary again. Do this until the speaker says something like "Yes, that's right!" or "Exactly!" You will know when you have it right—it is pretty clear from the feedback you get from the speaker.

GOOD COMMUNICATION INVOLVES BOTH TALKING AND LISTENING.

When you are the speaker, try to *be direct* about your wants and needs. If you receive a response back from your listener that is not what you were hoping for, you can *check for assumptions* or *call the process*. The goal is to clear up confusions so that your listener correctly grasps what it is that you are trying to say. Just because you say something that is clear to you does not mean that your listener understands it the same way.

When listening, *be active!* Ask questions to clarify, expand, or gather more information. *Respond* by giving feedback in the form of your own verbal summary of what you hear the speaker saying. If your summation is off-base, allow the listener to correct you and then summarize again. When paraphrasing, be original, and use your own words.

Practice these communication techniques and watch how many of your interpersonal problems become resolved. Communication is a skill, and therefore can be learned. With time and effort, anyone can improve their communication abilities. It just takes practice. Good luck!

MENTAL PRACTICE
by Jill K. Hassler-Scoop

*Dr. Charles Garfield's research shows that almost
all of the world-class athletes and other peak performers
use visualization. They see it, they feel it, and they
experience it before they actually do it.*

The road to becoming a good rider is filled with joy and success as well as with bumps, roadblocks, and challenges. As we covered in Personal Insights, our brain, our most powerful tool, is central to all areas of learning. Training our mind to practice mentally by using visualization and imagery has at least twelve benefits.

Mental practice means practicing a skill in your mind, without being physically involved; it is a mental rehearsal. Whether it involves watching and emulating the performance of another horse and rider or imagining your own performance, mental practice can be one of the most important tools for any athlete. We can train ourselves to create mental images that simulate the riding experience. If we learn to see it and feel it, it can have the same value as actually riding. Our body does not segregate the actual experience from the mental practice, therefore mental practice can be a perfect practice every time.

SHORT HISTORY
More than 2,500 years old, the art of mental imagery was part of the Buddhist and Taoist meditation practices. Eastern European and Russian athletes used it in their sports training it the early 1960s. It was first introduced into American sports in the games of tennis and golf and is now used regularly by athletes of most nations. The German's have included mental training in their system for many years.

WHY MENTAL PRACTICE WORKS
"By doing lots of mental practice," says Dr. Steven Ungerleider, "we are setting the stage for movement to become quite automatic and easy to recall." You can perform a mental workout any time, in any place. It saves wear and tear on you and your horse, creating important muscle memory for you. However, it cannot replace the training time your horse needs or the conditioning time you need to have the correct muscle tone. (*See Chapter—Fitness for the Rider—Fact Insights*).

If you want to practice mental visualization of a training session, it is important to include how you felt and/or looked during a specific practice session. Viewing the positive aspects is essential. When you correctly visualize something, your body responds as if you were actually riding. You will discover that when you get back in the saddle your reactions will be exactly as you ex-

12 Benefits of Mental Practice
1. Develop effective habits
2. Replace ineffective habits
3. Reduce performance anxieity
4. Learn a new skill
5. Practice at times you cannot ride
6. Overcome or manage fear
7. Replace a negative experience with a positive experience
8. Prepare for competition
9. Problem solving in day-to-day riding
10. Anchor a successful feel to memory
11. Effectively learn a pattern
12. Effectively riding a course

perienced them in your mental practice. You can begin by recalling a ride or movement you want to practice and then review it in your mind repeatedly, feeling it as you do your mental review, or you can watch your own performance and recall the feeling as you watch the performance. The important point is that you do a positive review that includes feeling. If your performance is not as you wish it, it is better to review the perfect performance, as you want it to look and feel. All review is learning, so it is important to have positive images as you practice.

HOW TO USE MENTAL PRACTICE
Learning a New Skill

Your mind does not care whether you are imagining it or doing it. Your muscles can learn new skills during mental practice. Each mental practice can be perfect; thus we can learn more quickly. Before we can learn the correct feel it is ideal to feel it. The best way is to have a lesson on a horse who responds correctly to you, so you can feel it happen. If you are lucky enough to do this, it is important that you walk around quietly as quickly as possible after the "feel" and commit it to memory, for future recall. If you do not have the opportunity to actually feel it, the next best thing is to watch a video of the skill being performed correctly and

"By doing lots of mental practice," says Dr. Steven Ungerleider, "we are setting the stage for movement to become quite automatic and easy to recall."

imagine you are riding it with the rider. Imagine what it feels like as you watch it. Feel it as you watch it. In all cases the mental repetition of the feeling is vital to the process of learning.

Suggested Steps

There are many ways to practice this. Some of you will discover that you do this automatically, others will discover that you have not received full benefit because you are missing a step, and a few of you will discover a new very positive skill to help you between riding sessions.

- Review what you want to practice
- Clear your mind
- Relax using your favorite method
- Bring forward what you want to practice
- Review it in your mind as you feel it
- Repeat your review

Important Points

- Think positively
- Spend 5-15 minutes at a time

Tales From the Trip

Terri

Terri spent six months trying to learn the shoulder-in during her weekly lessons. It was not going well, so she did not practice at home when she rode alone. Frustrated and feeling very down on herself, she researched additional ways to practice. Mental practice seemed the best solution. First she watched a video of a rider performing a shoulder-in. As she watched, she imagined that she was that rider, feeling the horse move under her as she used the aids she had been taught. She then sat quietly, emptied her mind, and visualized the shoulder in as she understood it to work. She discovered that she had difficulty matching her aids to the feeling. She practiced faithfully two times a day; three days later she felt that her aids were effective and her body relaxed. Once she felt good, she tried it on her horse. Terri was amazed—she had struggled for so long, and in one week using mental practice she had successfully gained the skill. She was anxious to show her new skill to her instructor, who could not believe the change.

LEARNING A PATTERN FOR COMPETITION

Whether you are learning a pattern at the last minute, such as a show jumping course, or in advance, such as a dressage test, mental practice fosters the best results once you are in the actual competition. Many riders fail to train for the performance test. Preparing to compete is very different from a typical training session to advance you or your horse's skills. Two points must be considered; First, the route itself must be learned so well that you do not need to think about the pattern or route, and second, you must have the effective communications with your horse to get timely responses. This enables you to prepare your horse to do the pattern accurately, not when your horse feels ready as you often do during training sessions. Ideally, competitive riders should spend a few minutes in each training session practicing the skill of preparing the horse for a movement rather than doing a movement when the horse feels ready. This consistent daily practice will help prepare for the competition performance.

The riding pattern needs to be committed to memory so well that your competition focus can be dedicated to the communications needed to ride your horse effectively. If you must think of your route instead of doing just riding it, you are losing valuable mental freedom for the most effective "feel" for the adjustments needed in the show ring. Competitive riders need to develop an effective method of learning patterns. The most effective method includes taking the time for mental practice off of the horse.

Steps to learning a pattern

1. Clear your mind.
2. Bring forward what you want to learn.
3. Start with the entrance to the ring, and go through the pattern as it would feel and exactly as you want to ride it.
4. Repeat it until you can feel the route without thinking about it.
5. Once you can do this, review the pattern with the preparations for all turns, movements, or obstacles.
6. Review again as though you are actually riding with all your preparatory half halts.
7. Repeat this until you can do it quickly and feel and see yourself performing.

Important Points

- Practice this as often as possible prior to the performance.
- Visual learners can watch a performance, imagining they are riding, or can draw it on paper and review feeling as follow the route.

PREPARING FOR THE ACTUAL PERFORMANCE

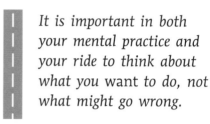

It is important in both your mental practice and your ride to think about what you want *to do, not what might go wrong.*

Preparing for a competition takes more than knowing the pattern you need to ride, it takes a quiet, confident mind that is in the present. Distractions of all kinds can only interfere with the communication needed between you and your horse. You need to work with your coach to find out how best to balance your need for input with your need to be in the moment with your horse. Some of your best coaches are there, in case you need them, but are quiet and wait for you to ask for help or wait to affirm that you are correct. Competition performances are to show off the skills you and your horse have acquired. The following steps have proven to be the most effective for preparing for a competition performance successfully.

Steps to Prepare

1. Acquaint yourself with the competition area, including the warm-up area.
2. Acquaint your horse with the area and be careful to consider the factors that might influence how he feels: trip stress, noise, activity, and footing. If you think the conditions of the competition site will effect your horse, do a mental practice that includes the "feel" of what you expect with the appropriate changes in your riding to adjust for the needs of the site. Important in both your mental practice and your ride to think about what you want to do, not what might go wrong.
3. Five minutes prior to the performance prepare yourself and your horse.
4. *Talk to* no one.
5. Bring forward your quiet mind.
6. Review the pattern you are going to ride.
7. Do your final preparation to enter the arena.
8. *Have fun.*

After Competition

For continued training benefits of your performance, your review is vital. However, this review should not take place immediately; you need a few minutes to process the points before discussing them with anyone.

- Take a few minutes to recall the *good* points.
- Take a few minutes to recall the performance problems.
- Commit the good points to your memory to discuss and review later, and discuss the problems and solutions on how to improve the next time, but *do not* commit these to memory.

Tales From the Trip

Sue

A respected jumping trainer insisted that Sue practice three different fences in sequence during each training session, and a full course of 6-10 jumps once a week. Before each course practice Sue had to spend a few minutes visualizing her route and riding her balanced horse on the pattern. After her practice she reviewed how it actually felt compared to her visualization. After several months of this practice, Sue discovered that her mental practice and actual courses matched; even better, she was meeting almost ninety percent of her spots correctly into the fences.

Allen

Allen is an event rider who loves to compete. His jumping rounds were almost always clean and fast. If he was lucky his dressage performance was always in the middle of the class, but more often he was near the bottom, always costing him his sought-after ribbon. His attitude was that the dressage was a waste, and his instructor did nothing but tell him to just do it. At one of his events, he met Karen, who was new to eventing and they struck up a friendship. They watched each other ride and discussed performances. Karen had a few rails down in show jumping but did well in dressage. They discussed their performance results, which included their "problems." Allen decided to take a few lessons with Karen's instructor and began working on his dressage. He learned that it was not his riding that was a problem, but his lack of practice. He learned to use mental practice and committed to it. His next competition six weeks later, moved him to the top third after dressage and he won his first ribbon. He discovered two important points in this practice: First, he had been restricting his horse while trying to stay on the dressage pattern, and second, he had been going into the ring with a negative attitude. Allen's goal included mental practice for his dressage work for five minutes a day. Allen helped Karen add boldness and power to her jumping, so both were very happy in their sport and in their new found friendship.

For learning a new skill, perfecting your performance, or learning a competition, mental practice is a valuable tool to use. The most important aspect of this practice is to "feel" it as you ride it. Feel your route and feel your body communicating with your horse as you ride the route with balanced turns and consistent rhythm, with your own body in the appropriate balanced position.

RIDER'S TOOLBOX
by Jill K. Hassler-Scoop

All you need to do is look, listen, and trust.
—Cherie Carter-Scott, *If Life is a Game,*
These Are the Rules

The fundamental learning skills of awareness, training framework, goal setting, communications, and mental practice have all been given their separate chapters. They are essential learning tools. In this chapter you will find a few additional skills that can be very helpful for you to consider as a rider. These are: positive attitude, simplicity in learning, consistency, appropriate concentration and focus, patience, and trust.

POSITIVE ATTITUDE

Your attitude is your innermost point of view toward yourself, your horse, and the world. Having a positive attitude about life is the first step toward a successful journey. We can all learn to have a positive attitude. —Jill K. Hassler, *In Search of Your Image.*

Six Important Tools for Better Learning
▪ Positive attitude
▪ Keep it simple
▪ Consistency
▪ Concentration and focus
▪ Patience
▪ Trust

What exactly is attitude? According to the dictionary it is "manner of acting, feeling, or thinking that shows in one's disposition." We can go one step further: it shows in our communications and in how we view life experiences. Have you had a negative thought such as, "I don't like that jump into the water, I am afraid my horse will stop," and then experienced exactly what you thought? Attitude can be reflected in actual experience.

Your horse is a perfect mirror of your attitude. If he is misbehaving or not performing up to par, take an honest look at how you feel mentally and physically. Once you recognize the problem, do your best to fix it. If you feel you can't fix it, don't ride seriously that day. If you spend too many days in this state of mind, it is a good idea to seek professional advice.

In most cases you can choose to be either upbeat, positive, and open-minded, or discouraged, pessimistic, and negative. Often we don't realize what our attitude is, as we don't take the time to listen to ourselves. It is very tempting to blame the weather, our horse, or the environment instead of looking inward to see if our attitude might be affecting the outcome. If you find yourself with a negative attitude, ask yourself a few questions:

- Am I in the "right" environment for me, including but not limited to lighting, openness, noise, and cleanliness?
- Do I enjoy the people I am around? If not, why?
- Am I tired or depressed? If so, what can I do about it? Am I attracted to the negative side of thoughts and words? If so, how can I become more positive?

No matter what, train yourself to have a positive attitude, positive thoughts, and positive self-talk. View misunderstandings and roadblocks as opportunities to learn, rather than as failures.

KEEP IT SIMPLE

You can process several pieces of information at one time, but you can learn only one thing at a time. Most riders want to focus on too many details and thus interfere with the "feel" and the ability to train muscle memory. While training muscle memory, you need to keep it simple and give yourself enough time and repetitions to do the task without thinking. Taking this time to learn one thing at a time can actually speed up your learning process. There are several key points to consider: keep the number of words to a minimum, use clear descriptive words, and when practicing keep no more than three points in the forefront of your mind. Practice these points until you are bored and can do them without thinking about them.

The mind is like a fertile garden . . . It will grow anything you wish to plant—beautiful flowers or weeds. And so it is with successful, healthy thoughts or negative ones that will, like weeds, strangle and crowd the others. Do not allow negative thoughts to enter your mind for they are the weeds that strangle confidence.

—Joe Hyams,
Zen in the Martial Arts

Tales From the Trip

Amy

Amy rode very well until I asked her to go into the corners. As soon as I asked for this, her horse began to lose his rhythm. After I convinced her of the importance, we set out to begin the learning process. Our goal was to get to the point at which Amy could ride around the ring, going correctly into the corners without thinking about it. Once this happens, it will be committed to her muscle memory. To keep it simple, the first step was to ride around the perimeter of the ring. This was not easy, as Amy was in the habit of cutting the corners. Breaking this habit took several weeks of practice. The second step was to get a counter overbend as she kept the same rhythm going into the corners. The challenge here was that her horse wanted to slow down and not keep moving. The third step was to go around through the corner with an inside bend. The challenge here was that when she used her inside hand to bend, he wanted to move to the inside, so he had to learn to respond to her inside leg more effectively. The last step was to go into the corner and be able to give with the inside rein in the middle of the corner. By the time Amy got to this step, she had little trouble with it. Each step had to be confirmed before she could go to the next step. It took ten lessons to achieve this goal. Several months later Amy thanked me for insisting that she learn to ride the corners correctly. Now she recognizes how much better her ring figures ride, but even more importantly how much more supple and relaxed her horse is performing.

CONSISTENCY

Horses insist upon consistency. You need to learn to be consistent for their sake—consistent in your training plan, consistent with your aids, consistent with your expectations, and consistent with your reference feel. More than anything else, consistency takes mental discipline. A successful training program is grounded on consistency to help create natural actions of the mind and body that are the foundation of your ability to respond to your horse.

- Horses are more comfortable and better trained if ridden with consistent aids.
- Horses have more muscle and fitness with a consistent work schedule.

- You will become more consistent in performance if you,
  - follow a training plan
  - maintain a consistent reference feel
  - remain consistently aware

CONCENTRATION AND FOCUS

Sally Swift says it best: "Ride with soft eyes." This is easier said than done. The environment, your horse's lack of attention, or your own thoughts can distract you, but you do need to deal with the distractions. It is not fair to your horse or safe to ride while distracted. You can also be too focused, but, ideally you can find a happy middle ground. Like all the other mental skills you can learn to be appropriately focused but it may take attention and practice. Distracted horses need focused riders, and distracted riders will create distracted horses. Either way in the partnership, focus is your responsibility. Understanding the four basic types of focus that you need to use when riding will help you.

Four Types of focus
Broad external

You observe what is going on around you. If riding in a ring with obstacles or other riders, it is this focus that allows you to avoid collisions and to get your own work done. No matter what you are doing broad external focus is required for safety.

Broad internal

This is the bigger picture of your knowledge base, both mental and muscular. It is also the information you build on when you are learning a new skill or practicing an old skill. Using our example of practicing the half-seat position over jumps, your broad internal focus is used to understand what your mind and body need to do to perform the exercise. It is the concrete knowledge that is combined with your knowledge that you gained in your warm-up to best perform your exercise. (You also used the broad internal focus as you go through your warm-up checklist each day *(See Chapter—Training Framework)*.

Narrow external

When you learn a new skill and practice it, it requires that you put narrow external focus into action. Let's say you are practicing your half-seat position over a few jumps. Your narrow external focus is on the outcome of maintaining the half-seat position as you do these jumps.

Narrow internal

While organizing to practice the jumps you move to a narrow internal focus to make a simple plan to put into action. Narrow internal focus is on the detail that goes into executing the skill. It is the mental organization, simple and concise, without "why" plan to practice.

In doing the exercises above you use all four of the focuses as needed. If you are stuck in only one, you will not do your exercise very effectively. This is how all four types of focuses are automatically used while you are performing the few fences in the half-seat.

> *It is a big job for your body to coordinate your mind and spirit. You were not born on a horse. You do not instinctively communicate with your legs while your hands remain quiet. Your natural movements must be tailored to coincide with the needs of your horse. You have much to learn about how to influence a horse tactfully and consistently, and it is no easy job to put your mind into his. Acquiring the appropriate attitudes and goals for yourself and your horsemanship may take years of self-analysis and work. Sometimes it is difficult to accept the need for patience with our own being.*
>
> —Jill K. Hassler,
> *Beyond the Mirrors.*

- Broad External—awareness of where the jumps are and where the other riders are.
- Broad Internal—listening to your mental and muscle memory to perform the exercise.
- Narrow External—focusing on the intended outcome of the exercise.
- Narrow Internal—making a simple plan to put the exercise into action.

PATIENCE

It takes more than a decision to be patient. Patience is a result of being knowledgeable, understanding, and accepting that the process takes time. It takes knowing as much as possible about yourself, the sport, and the process of learning. Once you collect the information, you evaluate the realistic time and effort it will take and then enjoy the process.

Tales From the Trip
Tina

Tina enjoyed event riding, and tried to keep up the grueling schedule of preparing for the competitions, taking care of her six children, and being the wife of a professional. Her riding was losing its enjoyment. She realized that she had been frustrated for several years because she was not making the progress she expected. She did a self-evaluation. She decided that she loved to jump and loved the speed of the cross-country, but did not have the time to keep her horse properly conditioned. Tina made a difficult choice in the form of a deal with herself. She would spend the next five years doing jumper shows and taking dressage lessons, so that when her youngest child turned twelve she would begin eventing again. Once Tina made the decision, her rides became fun again. She was able to be patient because she reduced the demands and settled on more realistic expectations and a more realistic time frame.

TRUST

Trust is built by reliable, consistent, decisive, and loving actions over a period of time. You should not ride a horse you do not trust, as this is not safe. All relationships should begin with a basic trust, and as time goes on this trust is cemented into a partnership. To get a satisfying performance or to develop a progressive learning and training program, you must trust the horse you are riding. How do you do that? A suggested formula to develop trust:

- Learn as much as possible about your horse and the subject you are studying.

- Verify the information by investigating it.

- Begin with conditional trust; that is, you trust but you remain open and aware. If you are making progress, you can trust the process and keep moving. If you are not making progress, you need to reevaluate your situation.

- Either follow your plan or create a new one, but keep looking for trust.

Tales From the Trip

Andy and Star War

Andy's horse was stiff and hollow, their performance looked like a war between two creatures! We worked on relaxing Andy and overbending Star War, his horse. Finally Star War relaxed but Andy kept holding. It did not take Star War much time to return to his stiffness. With some hesitation, finally Andy gave Star War a pat while in an overbend. To Andy's delight Star War relaxed into the non-bending hand. This feeling was all it took for Andy to be convinced that he needed to learn to trust Star War. This did not fix the problem, but it gave Andy a tool to work with, and after some practice his rides had a beautiful forward, relaxed motion, with no indication of discord, only harmony seventy-five percent of the time.

COMPARING TERMS

The mental skills that are discussed in Learning Insights are part of both the German and American systems. Different terms are sometimes used. Use the following chart to help you integrate what you read.

German terms	American terms	Action of term
Relaxation	Relaxation—included in Supplementary Learning Insights	Creates optimal conditions for your body to function—appropriate mental relaxation and physical body tone
Body-feel	Muscle memory—included throughout the book, especially in Technical Insights	Develop clear sense of each body part and be able to use it quickly and independently
Conceptualize movement	Visualization, mental practice—Learning Insights	Think about and feel movement or action when not on the horse
Concentration	Experience the present—Personal Insights	Attention to the present, which allows you to act quickly and effectively
Positive outlook	Positive attitude	Positive thinking and talking, helps you get what you want.

TECHNICAL INSIGHTS

The road map of technical skills provides riders with the order in which riding skills are ideally learned. We encourage riders to go back and forth to develop the skills as described in the following chapters outlining The Stages of Rider Education

A book cannot teach you how to ride. To learn to ride, you need a suitable horse and a qualified instructor. What a book can do is expose you to the many paths that lead to accomplished riding. This section, "Technical Insights" is designed to guide you through the specific learning process than develops *correctly educated riders*. Not all riding is the same, and we want to make it clear that we are focusing on the basic balanced position. This position leads to the development of an educated and independent rider who has the skills and abilities to ride horses forward, round, and honestly "through," no matter what the specific riding discipline is. We begin with **The Purpose of a Training Plan** written by German trainer, Stephan Kiesewetter to give you the overview of the "Ideal Route."

Along the way, this book will explain and (hopefully!) clarify some of the common points of confusion, such as "what is forward?" and "what is the half halt?" Throughout the stages, we emphasize the importance of developing muscle memory and feel. While we cannot actually teach you these critical skills in a book, we do give you the important facts and ideal order of learning that lead to mastering these abilities.

 No book can teach you how to ride. What this book wants to do is be your guide along the road to classically correct riding. . .giving you insights, explanations, and helpful hints along the way.

If you are a new rider, you will find these stages to be an important outline for you to follow as you begin your wonderful journey towards becoming "a rider." *If you are currently riding*, we suggest that you read through all five of the stages to determine where your current level of skill and education places you. Sharing the stages with your instructor can help you a lot, as they can offer valuable insights and feedback about your riding. While most of you will recognize "your stage", don't be surprised if you feel that you span two or three of the stages! This is because the process of learning to ride is circular in nature. Every rider has a foot, so to speak, in other stages as they progress into the next stage while continuing to confirm the skills from earlier stages. Horses don't know stage one from five either, so riders may find that their horse issues force them back to an earlier stage as well. If you discover you and/or your horse have some "holes in the road," it helps to identify what they are, get help to "fill them in," and continue moving forward.

The issues of rider position and level of horse control, at all levels, acts in a circular fashion. Correct position leads to better control and better control allows students to feel safe, so they can relax and improve their positions!

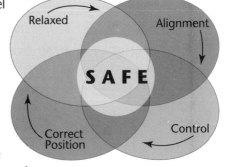

Vital to all learning is to first understand *what* it is that you are going to learn. Therefore, we open each stage with the **BIG PICTURE** which includes an **Overview**, and a **Road Map** outlining the steps needed to master the skills of each stage. The Road Maps will be further developed in each following step. This book is focused on classical riding so included in the Big Picture section of each chapter we have described our **Ideal Route.** It is based upon the German riding system, which has a long history of producing highly skilled, classically correct riders. Because the United States does not have such a "system" of riding as they do in Europe, the Ideal Route is very rare in America. However, knowing the "ideal" can help you seek out and select what is best for you given your individual learning circumstances. What is unique about the Stages of Rider Education is that although they are grounded upon solid, proven principles, they address and acknowledge the differences between learning to ride overseas and here in the United States. Under **Alternative Route,** we discuss some of these differences between Germany and the United States, and talk about different ways Americans can try to reach the same end, but perhaps along a different path than the one outlined in the German system.

The **ROAD MAP** is developed in the sub-chapters. There you will find the **Destination/Goal** of each step as well as the development of the **questions** found listed in the **Big Picture** section under Road Map, which explains the theory important to that step. This is done in the form of answers to common questions that come up at that stage. Knowing the theory behind what you are doing is important to learning. We tried to keep the theory as simple as possible so that it stays helpful and practical, and does not end up confusing you! There are also ⓟ **Points of Interest** along the way, and these are a mix of tips, facts, and general "interesting to know" points we think are important. ⓞ **Observation Points** is a unique section, designed to help you develop your "eye." Watching other riders can be of enormous learning benefit, but how many times have you wondered just what is it that you are supposed to be looking at? In this section we offer practical and concrete guidelines for what to watch for when observing other riders, in the hope that this will further your learning process. Matching the facts with your eye and converting it to your "feel" is an excellent learning opportunity.

The last chapter in each stage, **Putting It All Together**, includes a review of each stage, outlines **Suggested Order for Learning**, and finishes with a section called **Roadblocks**. Roadblocks are problems that prevent you from getting the performance results you want during a ride. We have included check points to help you determine your roadblocks as well supplementary training suggestions to help overcome the roadblock. Because all causes of roadblocks stem from the same potential three sources, we list them here in the introduction so that we don't have to repeat this information in each stage.

CAUSES OF ROADBLOCKS
Roadblocks have three basic causes:
1. Rider's position: relaxation, elasticity, alignment, and/or fitness
   - Relaxation: Body is stiff—any or all parts
   - Elasticity: Joints lost elasticity
   - Alignment: Body is not in center or level, thus is out of balance
   - Fitness: Body is weak, cannot hold position with ease
2. Rider lacks knowledge or support
   - Unclear idea of what to do—limited education or understanding of the technical skills
   - Not enjoying the feel—thinking too much
   - Frustrated from lack of progress—lacking a daily plan
   - Confusion—trying to learn too much too fast
   - Unaware of feel of individual body parts—unclear or cluttered focus

- Uptight or fearful—feeling out of control or other safety issues

3. The horse is not suitable for a variety of reasons
    - Lack of training (young, green, spoiled)
    - Stiffness
    - Not appropriate for your level
        - Nervous, scared, or high-strung
        - Extremely lazy and unresponsive

When you suspect that you have a roadblock, you can follow the thinking process in chart below:

Thought process for problem solving your roadblocks

1. Check your position; alignment, spring in joints and relaxation
    If you find a problem work on it and continue
    If you feel fine...

2. Check your horse's response to your leg and rein aids and relaxation
    If you find a problem work on it and continue
    If you feel fine...

3. Return to the previous step you learned successfully, confirm that you feel good in it
    If you have not solved your problem...

4. It is time to turn to your instructor to help you identify the cause (s) of the roadblock so that you can progress with your learning experience.

At the end of Roadblocks, there are charts that can be used as diagnostic tools as well as supplementary learning options that we have found to be particularly suited for helping riders through some of the more common riding problems associated with that specific stage.

Threaded through the stages, you will see Tales of the Trip. Here you are introduced to riders who are working in this current stage and have agreed to share their stories with you. Sometimes it is fun to learn from reading about the paths others have taken!

Enjoy your trip!

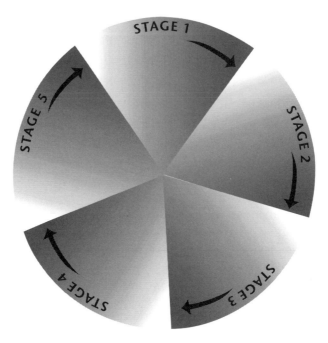

*Throughout this section you will notice five illustrations which
summarize the important skills learned at each stage and how
these elements intertwine to create a circular flow of riding skills.
The skills for each stage are listed in the chart below.*

Stage	Skills
Stage 1- Position and Elementary Control	▪ POSITION; aligned, deep, balanced ▪ Relaxation; understanding of role and begin to put into practice ▪ Control; elementary ▪ Route and rate; basic understanding
Stage 2 – Use of Aids for More Advanced Control	▪ Rein aids; learn use with correct response from horse ▪ Leg aids; learn use with correct response from horse ▪ Route and rate; put them consistently into practice ▪ Basic straightness; understanding of role and begin to put into practice ▪ Flexion, bend and overbending
Stage 3 – Aids in Action	▪ Energy; introduction, understanding and put into practice forward and rhythm ▪ Reference Feel ▪ Half Halt
Stage 4 – Rider Education and Horse Education Meet	▪ The German System; understanding ▪ Rhythm ▪ Looseness ▪ Throughness and contact
Stage 5 – True Partnership Development	▪ Impulsion ▪ Straightness and balance ▪ Collection

THE PURPOSE OF A TRAINING PLAN
by Stephan Kiesewetter

*Respecting the correct basic principles ensures that the horse
receives a training appropriate to its equine nature, and
enables the rider to enjoy his sport and practice it safely.*
—The Principles of Riding

The goal of all training, whether for horse or human, is to
develop a special ability to its full capacity. The Scale of Education
for the horse, developed in Germany centuries ago, has the same
goal. It is a training system meant to bring out the full capacity
of the horse's natural capabilities, and is valid for all equestrian
disciplines. This training system is not focused on one specific
discipline, but rather provides a foundation that is a starting point
for developing in the advanced training any special abilities in
certain disciplines that an individual horse may have. The rider's
responsibility in the advanced training is to follow the preferences
and abilities of the horse. Riders whose horse's interests and abilities do not match their own must consider a change of horse rather
than force a horse to do what is difficult and not enjoyable for
him. In the same light, riders who are buying horses need to consider
their own long-term interests, as well as current level of education
and skill, before purchasing a horse.

The Scale of Education is a holistic training system. It develops
the horse's physical attributes (condition, flexibility, strength,
coordination, etc.) as well as psychological characteristics (mental
strength, concentration, cognitive skills, behavior, etc.). The horse
that is carefully educated by a sensitive and analytically thinking
rider through this training system will gain physical strength,
balance, self-confidence, and beauty. Additionally, a systematic
training program is a prerequisite for performance. A successful
athlete, whether horse or human, results from a systematic, consistent training program that produces the physical condition
necessary for a stellar performance. Without this solid foundation
the athlete would be physically over challenged, which can also
cause mental overload and stress.

It is the ethical responsibility of the rider as a human being to
provide for the needs of the horse through engaging in a systematic and consistent training plan. This plan has to consider the

short-term, mid-term, and long-term aspects of the training and development of the horse. The Scale of Education provides the framework for the horse's physical and mental education. It is the responsibility of all serious riders to understand this system.

The overall goal of the Scale of Education is "throughness" (Durchlässigkeit, "letting the aids through"). This is the essence and the culmination of all the steps and stages. In Durchlässigkeit the horse is in the physical and mental state to be able to react to the "whistling aids" of the rider, and thus is a pleasure to ride.

The overall goal of the Scale of Education is "throughness" (Durchlässigkeit, "letting the aids through"). This is the essence and the culmination of all the steps and stages. In Durchlässigkeit the horse is in the physical and mental state to be able to react to the "whistling aids" of the rider, and thus is a pleasure to ride.

None of the six steps in the Scale of Education can be considered apart from the relationship they each have to the others. They are developed in a certain order in the daily training program and the long-term training plan, while always kept in the context of the overall goal. Progress in the training of the horse is determined by the horse's consistent response during each phase. When a rider is deciding how fast to progress a horse's education through the steps, she must consider the horse's conformation, his individual physical development, and his mental outlook.

A certain standard of quality needs to be developed in each step of the Scale of Education before progressing to the next step. Once this quality is consistently achieved at a certain step, the horse and rider can work towards achieving this quality in the next step. By following this plan, the training progresses up the scale and also results in each lower step improving along the way. When a certain quality of rhythm is achieved, the horse and rider move on to work on looseness. When a certain quality of looseness is achieved, the horse and rider progress to contact, and will also realize that an even better quality of rhythm has been attained through the process. With this better rhythm will come better looseness, and so on and so on! The overall Scale of Education is like an elevator: once you push the initial button to get it started, you just have to stay on it and not get off until you reach your destination.

GERMAN SCALE OF EDUCATION CHART

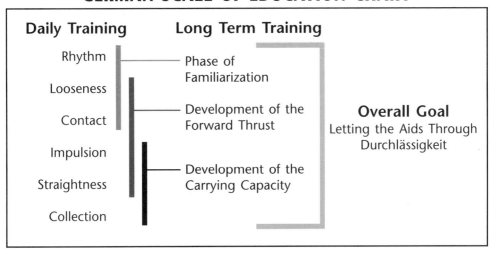

The Scale of Education offers riders a daily training plan. Within this training plan riders must develop each step in the right order. Each day is a new day and riders must start again to find a good rhythm, looseness, etc , progressing each day through the stages as far as the horse's level of education allows. As this daily work is done, the rider is also always moving toward a long-term training plan.

The process of education is continual for the horse. With a young horse, the rider must initially get him used to the tack, the rider, the rider's weight, and finally, the rider's aids. The rider must familiarize the horse with all these things in such a way that the horse associates a positive feeling with each new experience. During the Phase of Familiarization the rider must have the patience to build confidence in the horse. A bad experience during this phase might destroy the basic confidence of the horse. By the same token, the rider must also be very clear and determined in what she is asking for or else the horse will be confused and will not understand what is being asked. During this time, the hierarchy between horse and rider needs to be clarified. In a herd of horses there is always an alpha horse and a beta horse, and that is what allows

The daily training program gives the rider the opportunity to develop each step in the right order and thus begin advancing toward the long term training plan.

The basic confidence between horse and rider should never be destroyed. peace to reign in herds. If the alpha/beta relationship between the horse and rider is not made clear, the relationship will always be stressful to both parties, and may even become dangerous. Clarifying the hierarchy does not mean punishing; it means making clear, strong, positive connections when the horse responds correctly. The basic confidence between horse and rider should never be destroyed. Mistakes made during this time will result in a long-term, ongoing struggle between horse and rider over the course of the horse's education. Therefore, only advanced, well-experienced and well-balanced riders with a correct seat should be allowed to ride young horses.

During the development of forward thrust, we increase the energy within the horse. The horse becomes stronger and better balanced. As the horse gains flexibility and understanding of the aids, he will let the aids work through his body. The big joints of the hindquarters become more able to bend. Also within this phase, the topline will become rounder and more muscular. The horse learns to use his whole body for the work, and instead of just putting up with the rider's weight, the horse works *with* the rider's weight. If the rider works carefully and properly through this stage, the rider and horse will become one harmoniously forward swinging unit. In this phase the rider now adds energy, impulsion, balance, strength, flexibility, the ability to bend the joints, and expression to the characteristics developed in the phase of familiarization.

If the rider does not train the horse correctly during this phase, it will become obvious as soon as the rider tries to collect the horse. Instead of transforming part of the forward thrust into carrying capacity, the rider will only receive tension and a reduction in energy.

As in the phase of familiarization, everything that has been done well makes the following steps easier. Each problem needs to be fixed as it arises, before the rider progresses the horse's education. If this is not done, problems will become accentuated in each subsequent step.

During the development of carrying capacity, the rider begins to ask the horse to transfer part of the forward energy into carrying power. The overall energy within the horse is not reduced, but rather goes in a different direction. It changes from a purely forward thrust into a forward, *upward* power. By this time the horse is developing the strength to carry his torso more towards the hindquarters and to keep his hind legs more underneath the center of gravity. Through this process, the area used to support the horse's body becomes smaller as the hind legs are carried closer to the front legs. In order to maintain balance in this new body carriage, the horse must pay attention and respond to each little weight and leg aid of the rider. This is what we call "throughness."

Each horse has a certain natural balance, and in the process of the horse's education, the rider adds lateral balance (straightness) and later on ridden balance (longitudinal balance). Therefore, well-trained and schooled horses are very well-balanced, and these are the horses that are most suitable for unbalanced riders (beginners). The best balanced rider is needed for an unbalanced horse, which means that young horses should be ridden by advanced riders; and the best balanced horses are needed for unbalanced riders, which means that beginner riders should start on well-schooled, balanced horses. Unfortunately, this rarely happens in the real world! Some riders say, "I would like to learn together with my horse!" This sounds cozy and happy, but can be disastrous for both horse and rider. It is the rider's ethical responsibility to provide the best situation for the horse, since the horse cannot choose. The philosophy behind the Scale of Education does not allow for novice riders and novice horses to be partnered. It is the responsibility of instructors and trainers to explain the importance of this to their students, and to help provide appropriately schooled horses for beginner riders.

During the development of forward thrust, we increase the energy within the horse by the use of exercises.

The Scale of Education, properly followed, along with the prerequisites, is at the heart of creating a sound, happy, well-performing horse!

 Stephan Kiesewetter's chapter, The Purpose of a Training Plan, talks about the importance of following a systematic, logical, holistic program when training horses and riders.

The evidence in support of this approach is easily found at the international levels of competition, where German horses and riders dominate the medal stands.

His main point: Inexperienced riders need to be mounted on educated horses, and inexperienced horses need to ridden by educated riders.

This is absolutely the *ideal* approach to training. However, in the United States, we often do not have access to the quality horses or trainers that are needed to make this approach work. Some riders do not have access to educated trainers and many riders do not have access to educated horses! Education is expensive and time-consuming; therefore the trainers and horses that have advanced training are often busy, located in high-density areas, and expensive! But there are alternative routes to Rome, as they say. Our *American Stages of Rider Education* is designed to provide the American rider (who is such an eager learner!) with one such alternative route. By modifying the European system to fit the reality of riding education in the United States, our goal is to provide American riders with an understanding and knowledge of the basic steps associated with the correct training of the rider. A correct seat is the cornerstone of all good riding, and many American riders lack this basic skill. Our *American Stages of Rider Education* also address the issue of an inexperienced rider on a less-than-ideally educated horse—a fact of life in the United States. Therefore, the focus of our approach is twofold: 1) we teach riders "how to sit correctly" on a horse, which allows them to develop an educated, independent seat as they progress in their riding; and 2) we pay special attention to "the basics of horse control," so that riders can relax enough mentally to focus on their body position. When the rider has mastered the core fundamentals of how to sit and how to communicate through the aids, the horse, whom we all agree is our most valued teacher, can better understand what the inexperienced rider is asking. While this approach is, and always will be, fraught with difficulties and frustrations, under a careful program of education and training, with good supervision, riders and horses can learn how to work correctly together, which leads to many years of enjoyment of the rider and horse partnership.

STAGE 1—POSITION and ELEMENTARY CONTROL

Big Picture

OVERVIEW

The main goal of all riding instruction is to develop riders with an independent seat. In order to do this, you first need to learn the "classically correct" basic, balanced position, which requires you to master two difficult tasks: 1) to learn how to sit correctly on a horse (which initially feels quite awkward) and, 2) to *unlearn* normal human responses such as gripping, tension, stiffness, and holding. Once you learn how to sit correctly on a horse, and relax in this position, you are ready for the next step in riding, which is to develop coordination in the use and timing of the natural aids used to influence the horse. Your goal should be the development of a truly independent seat. An independent seat is a seat that is educated enough so that your pelvis can follow the motion of the horse at all three gaits without the need to resort to gripping anywhere (especially with thighs or arms) to stay balanced or still. This allows your hands and legs to be under your voluntary control. You can then apply the aids for such important tasks as influencing the horse's direction/route and speed. If you wish to become a true partner with the horse, your seat needs to be classically correct and educated enough to move "as one" with the horse.

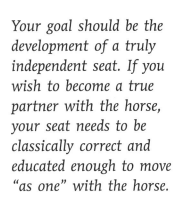

Your goal should be the development of a truly independent seat. If you wish to become a true partner with the horse, your seat needs to be classically correct and educated enough to move "as one" with the horse.

ROAD MAP

The Correct Position on the Flat and Over Fences

What is a correct position on the flat and over fences?

Why is it so hard for riders to keep the correct position on the flat and over fences?

Why is a good seat so important?

What is a "good" seat?

Why is relaxation so important when learning?

Elementary Control
Why is elementary control dealt with in Stage 1?
What are the natural aids?
What is the basic function of the legs?
What is the basic function of the hands?
What is the best way to communicate with the hands?
What are route and rate and why are they so important?

Putting It All Together

THE IDEAL ROUTE
In the ideal world, riders learn in two stages: 1) initially they are put on a lunge line to learn basics of how to sit and balance on a moving horse, and 2) they graduate to a quiet, dependable school horse to learn basics of control.

On the Lunge Line
A properly conducted lunge lesson is the safest way for new riders to begin learning. Riders started on the lunge line learn correct position faster because they are able to work on the control of their own bodies and their balance without worrying about controlling the horse. It is the ideal opportunity for riders to develop seat and position without the complication of what to do with their hands.

Off the Lunge Line
Once riders have gained control of their body and have a correct position at the walk and posting trot without using their hands for balance, it is time to add lessons off the lunge line. Because the lunge line allowed the riders to first learn basic body control and balance, off the lunge line riders may pick up the reins and begin to learn how to control the horse by telling him to stop, go, turn, and move on.

Benefits of the Ideal Learning Process
It gives riders time to develop balance before they pick up the reins and possibly use them for balance.

It helps riders to develop the correct position and early "feel" that prepares them to recognize when they move together with their horse. This feeling eventually leads to soft, sensitive hands and the development of a flexible and secure seat.

Riders will learn to use their legs before their hands—a wonderful and correct habit that will forever be important in their riding career!

Once control is introduced; the position of many riders takes a temporary step backwards, but only for a short while! This is because you are learning to coordinate what your brain is telling your body to do with what your limbs actually are able to do. *Be patient* with yourself through this process! If your position has been committed to muscle memory from proper practice, with awareness, it will return once you feel the coordination of the aids for control (unless safety issues become a problem).

ALTERNATIVE ROUTES

In the United States, new riders are often faced with the challenge of learning correct riding under two "less than ideal" scenarios: 1) How to learn position when lunging isn't available and, 2) How to learn on a horse that may not be the most appropriate for the beginner in terms of control issues.

When lunging isn't available

Instructors may not be able to provide lunge lessons for a variety of reasons:

- They don't have a horse that is well trained on the lunge line.
- They don't have the space or a safe place to lunge.
- They are not comfortable lunging students.
- They don't offer private sessions; all lessons are done in groups.

If, for whatever reason, lunging is not available, some alternatives are available:

- Take a private lesson on a well-schooled horse in an enclosed arena where the instructor is always close to the horse.
- Have the instructor or assistant lead the horse during the lesson
- Take a group lesson on a quiet, predictable school horse that politely follows the other horses around the ring.

A Word About Group Lessons

There are pros and cons about the group lesson format. On the plus side, you can learn from watching the other riders and listening to the instructor's comments. On the minus side, you may not get the kind of individual attention you need at this level. Minor position faults may go unnoticed or be left uncorrected when there is a group of riders all at once in the ring. These "minor" faults add up and lead to bigger position problems later on. If the school horses are not well trained, they may actually encourage riders to learn the "wrong feel and response" from the beginning. A good school horse will be a willing but quiet and steady mount, who stops when properly asked, and moves forward without either too much energy or a complete lack of it. If, however, you have to choose between a horse that is too forward versus a horse that is too slow, choose the "too slow" horse. Quick horses teach new riders to pull on the reins, get tight in their arms, and tense all over their bodies, all of which become much more difficult to correct later on in one's riding education. *(See Chapter—The Right Horse Through the Stages—Horse Insights)*

When the beginner's horse is not the most appropriate in terms of control

Sometimes new riders find themselves in lesson programs that mount them on horses that for one reason or another are less than ideal for the beginner rider. These horses may either be young or untrained, lazy and unresponsive, nervous, scared, high-strung, or fine-tuned for upper-level competition and therefore too sensitive to the aids for the beginner rider. Under these conditions, riders would do well to consider searching for a lesson program that does not use such inappropriate mounts for their beginner riders. If, however, you *own* one of these more difficult horses, you will want to search for an instructor that has experience in helping riders work through this challenging situation. Some of the approaches you can expect an instructor to take when faced with this challenge include:

- Put the horse in training while you take lessons on another horse.

- Give a lesson in a small, safe part of an arena where the instructor can stay close to the horse and work with him from the ground while you are mounted.

- Teach you the elements of *control* before position, so that safety is addressed.

 New riders are encouraged to take the time to seek out the *best* lesson program they can find for their initial training, even if they must make sacrifices, such as traveling a longer distance to get there or taking fewer lessons per month. *The most important time to have appropriate instruction and horses to learn on is during Stage 1.*

The Correct Position on the Flat and Over Fences

There is little disagreement throughout the world over what constitutes the "correct" way for a rider to sit on a horse. It is the "basic, balanced position," which is the position that minimizes the stress and strain on the horse from carrying a rider.

GOAL/DESTINATION

To understand what the correct position, is, and why it is important to maintain it *when the horse is moving* on the flat and over fences.

⬇ ROAD MAP

What is the correct position?

On the flat

The "correct" position is when you sit over the horse's center of balance. Once in the saddle, classically correct riders rest comfortably in the middle

No matter what discipline you are learning, the best instructors will teach you to first learn the basic, balanced position, as this is the foundation for most of the riding disciplines.

of the seat—not too far forward or too far back—with the legs dropping softly against the horse's side. In this correct position, there is no tension or gripping on the part of the rider. Your legs have a soft and steady feel against your horse's barrel, and your upper body is relaxed, yet straight. Your arms are supple and without tension, hanging down from the shoulder. Your elbows are

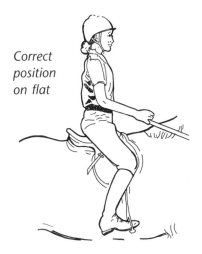

Correct position on flat

Correct half-seat

gently bent, slightly in front of the waist. Your hands are positioned just above the withers, slightly apart, holding a soft, steady contact through the rein with the horse's mouth. The position is not unlike that of standing on the ground. Perhaps the greatest hallmark of the classically correct position is having your body aligned in such a way that you can draw a straight line from your ear, through their your shoulder, down to your hip, and ending up at your heel. If this straight line is not in place, you are not in alignment and thus not correct.

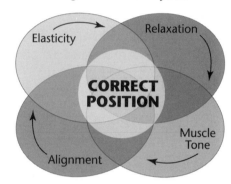

A rider's position is composed of four elements:

Elasticity   Relaxation
Muscle tone   Alignment

All 4 of these elements are linked to balance and positive muscle memory!

Over fences

The correct position over fences is called the "half-seat," "two-point," or "jumping" position (sometimes people refer to this as the "galloping position," but that is not truly correct. The galloping position is a position designed for galloping at speed). When jumping, the horse's center of gravity shifts forward, and he needs to use his back to the fullest degree when thrusting his body over the fence. Around the turn of the century, the jumping position evolved from riders sitting

behind the motion to riders shifting their center of gravity slightly forward and lift their seats slightly out of the saddle in order to match the horse's changed center of balance. It is important that for every inch you lift your seat out of the saddle, you allow an equal amount of weight to fall into your heels, which serves to keep you balanced in this more vulnerable position. Importantly, in jumping position you need to maintain *equal contact throughout your thigh, inner knee, and calf,* with a straight line from hip to heel. A common mistake new riders make is to grip too much with the thigh and knee in an effort to feel more secure. It is important that you shorten your stirrups for the half-seat, as this makes it easier to get your seat out of the saddle and allows your weight to fall into your heels. Similar to the basic, balanced position on the flat, in the jumping position your hips need to move with the motion of the horse in the same way they do when you are sitting in the saddle. Ideally, the lower leg and upper body stay quiet and balanced over the horse's center of gravity, and the pelvis takes on the responsibility of moving with the horse.

When horses jump, their center of gravity changes rapidly—from behind the withers as they sink on their haunches in preparation for takeoff, to the front of the withers as they take off (in a rear-like position), to the center of the withers in the air over the jump, and back to the front of the withers upon landing. Therefore, your upper body needs to be flexible enough to stay upright during preparation and takeoff, slightly forward in the air, and slightly back upon landing (so as to not add extra weight to the horse's front end on landing, when his balance is already very forward). In order to be able to move your upper body around properly when jumping, your lower leg must be strongly and securely anchored at the girth, under your hip. If not you will lose your balance!

Most importantly work to develop the downward spring or sinking of weight as you go up in the post or jumping position.

Why is it hard to maintain the correct position on the flat and over fences?

Most riders will agree that it is not very difficult to hold the basic, balanced position at the halt, or even the walk. The difficultly arises when you try to keep the basic, balanced position when the horse is *moving*. That is, a horse doesn't just stand still; he trots, canters, gallops, and jumps, to say nothing of shying, bucking, and bolting! When a horse moves, he creates a tremendous amount of energy, and this energy goes in many different directions. In order to learn how to maintain the correct position on a moving horse, you will find that you must allow your body to move with the energy of the horse, all without tension or gripping. It takes time to learn *balance* on a horse. Adding to the challenge is allowing your body to *move* with the horse while it remains in the basic, balanced position. The natural human reactions of gripping and using strength are not helpful in learning to ride; these reactions actually hinder the process! The struggle for riders learning to stay in the basic, balanced position during movement is twofold:

- Riders are learning to find their own balance on a moving animal. This is hard to do, and the human instinct is to get tense, grip up, and hold on when their balance is threatened.
- Riders need to simultaneously learn not only how to stay on and stay with the horse's moving energy, but also how to *control* the horse at the same time.

A horse has a mind of his own, and riders need to feel in control over where the horse is going, and how fast he is getting there. So, in Stage 1, riders need to feel a sense of elementary control, or they become focused on safety issues (and may even resort to force or artificial aids to stay in control) and thus are unable to relax and learn the natural state of balance so necessary to the correct position.

No wonder learning to ride correctly is so difficult!

Why is a good seat important?

A good seat is important because it allows your energy to move with the energy of the horse. Without a good seat, a horse's energy becomes "stuck," creating tension in both you and your horse, and a host of other problems in riding. As your riding progresses a good seat becomes "independent" and then can be used as an aid for directing and controlling a horse's energy.

What is a good "seat"?

To answer this question, it helps to know a little about the human pelvis, which actually makes up what we call your "seat." The bones of the pelvis and the sacrum are fused together to make one big joint that must learn to move with the horse's back in order to keep you safely and comfortably in the saddle. The bottom of the pelvis (i.e., your seat bones) can be described as similar to the runners of a rocking chair, with the front and back parts of the pelvis lifting up slightly in a gentle curve. A good seat is one that sits in the "neutral" position, in the center of the runners. This allows the pelvis to move not only back and forth gently with the motion

Correct position includes the following basic truths:

There is a straight line perpendicular to the ground from the rider's ear to shoulder to hip to heel.

The rider's seat gives the appearance of being "deep" by having the rider's weight going down from the head through the body core and flowing out from the insides of the heels, with the heel being the lowest point of the foot.

The rider has flexible, elastic joints that act as shock absorbers, especially for the lower back, hips, knees, and ankles.

The rider's weight is balanced evenly on both sides of the horse.

The rider can follow the motion of the horse with his or her seat in the correct "centered" position.

of the horse's back, but side to side as well. Your legs hang naturally down from the pelvis, with your body weight falls softly into your heels. No grip is needed because you stay on by using the balancing motion of the pelvis, which will move with the motion of the horse's back. Your upper body remains centered and tall with your legs on either side of the saddle acting as counterweights for your pelvis. This prevents you from sliding off the saddle. As you can imagine, this takes some time to learn and perfect. Hence, the importance of a good school horse at this stage!

Why is relaxation so important when learning?

If you could ask horses what they most want their riders to work on, many would probably say something like, "Get this person to relax, would you? My back is killing me!!" Seriously, relaxation is a critical and often overlooked component of your education.

IMPORTANT FACTS ABOUT THE SEAT!

- Riders need to learn how to sit in the neutral spot of their pelvis so that their seat can move with the energy of the horse.

- Improving the seat is an ongoing process, culminating in the development of an independent seat by Stage 3.

- A correctly moving seat will be developed into an important aid as you advance, and it becomes a vital part of your aids in stage 4.

There are two kinds of relaxation: mental and physical. In the ideal state of mental relaxation, your mind is on the subject at hand, free of clutter, able to enjoy the present. Body relaxation is a physical state in which your joints move free of tension and your muscles are toned to be used as effectively as needed. Because relaxation is a state of body and mind, the influence of relaxation is circular.

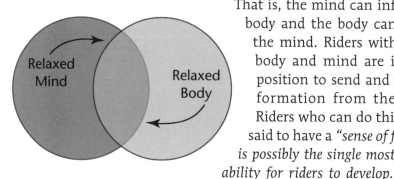

That is, the mind can influence the body and the body can influence the mind. Riders with a relaxed body and mind are in a better position to send and receive information from their horses. Riders who can do this are often said to have a *"sense of feel"*, which *is possibly the single most important ability for riders to develop.*

 The most important ability for you to develop is a sense of "feel." If you have a relaxed body and mind you are in a better position to develop this elusive sense of "feel" because you are better able to send and receive information from your horse.

ⓟ POINTS OF INTEREST

- The use of a good school horse is critical for new riders' sense of safety, comfort, and balance, because he will not create undue fear or worry for his riders.

- Once riders develop the feeling of correct body alignment, they can practice relaxing in this position and will develop the proper muscle tone needed to maintain the correct position. This requires a lot of practice riding in the proper position while relaxed.

- New, fearful, or worried riders naturally grip to stay on and must be taught by a good instructor not to do so.

- Instruction is important in the early stages of riding so that riders don't fall into bad habits early on, which are harder to correct later on.

- In order for the riders' body, especially their seat, to follow the movement of the horse, riders need the following: a clear understanding of the basic, balanced position, relaxation, a correct position, a degree of fitness (appropriate muscle tone), a sense of feel, and a clear mind.

 When you take the time to learn the correct position, you will find that you feel much more balanced, secure, and comfortable when riding.

O OBSERVATION POINTS

- Watch many different riders, both experts and novices. When watching, see if you can pick out those riders who ride, or are attempting to ride, in the correct position, with a straight back, a perpendicular line from ear to heel, relaxed joints, a flexible seat that moves with the horse, etc. Also notice those riders who are not riding in the correct position. Can you see a difference in the rider's effectiveness, and balance, and in the horse's comfort level?

- Take a video of your own riding and watch it in real time and in slow motion. Compare what you see with what you feel. Can you see relaxation? Is there spring in your joints? Do you have a straight line from ear to shoulder to hip to heel? Does what you see match what you feel?

- Observe or visualize a rider you admire, and try to "feel" as if you were that rider when you are on your horse (*See Chapter—Mental Practice—Learning Insights.*)

All learning involves understanding the theory and the technical skill, and transferring this learning to muscle memory through lots of proper practice. Intellectual learning cannot make up for feel, and lots of natural feel needs to be followed by an intellectual understanding. Riders need both sets of skills!

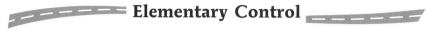

Elementary Control

*Position and control are linked! Being in control
allows a rider to relax, and a relaxed rider can
learn the correct way to sit on a horse!*

GOAL/DESTINATION

To help riders understand elementary control and why learning elementary control is part of Stage 1.

ROAD MAP

Why is elementary control dealt with in Stage 1?

Learning to ride in the United States differs in many ways from learning to ride in Europe. Two of the most important differences occur at the early stages of rider education. In Europe, beginners start out: 1) on well-trained horses and 2) on the lunge line until they can walk, trot, and canter in the basic, balanced position. In the United States, beginners often: 1) start out on old, lazy, young, untrained, spoiled, or even scared or hot horses and, 2) begin riding solo around the ring, directing the horse. These differences are *huge* when it comes to learning to ride. That is, beginners in Europe are not asked to control the horse until they have established their basic balance on the horse. Often the beginner in America must learn how to control the horse at the same time that they are learning their basic balance on the horse. For this reason, we are including the concepts of elementary control in Stage 1 of our Rider Education System for American Riders.

What are the natural aids?

NATURAL AIDS CHART

Aid	How Aid is Communicated	Function of Aid
Hand	Reins	Direction and Speed
Leg	Used on and behind the girth	Creates power and energy
Seat	Motion of the rider's pelvis (hips)	Allows forward energy by following the horse's motion
Voice	Tone of voice	Assists leg and hand

What is the basic function of the legs?

In the beginning, your legs simply ask the horse to move. As you advance in your riding education, your legs' role includes generating the right amount of energy and directing the horse's body to move in certain ways. In the early stages of riding, your legs should be quiet and relaxed on the horse's barrel. A small squeeze should bring about a desire and willingness on the horse's part to move forward. If your legs are constantly working, or you use them to grip, your horse will overreact by going too fast or ignoring your legs altogether. Neither response is a good one! To maintain the correct leg position, your body weight will go down through your center and the inside of your legs to your heel. This deep, elastic seat will encourage you to let your legs hang in a relaxed fashion on your horse's side. This is good because you then will be able to use your legs in a way that maximizes communication with your horse.

What is the basic function of the hands?

Your hands (along with your legs, seat, and mind) guide and direct the energy created by the horse when moving. Your hands, because they are connected to the horse's sensitive mouth, have a responsibility to be sensitive, flexible, relaxed, receiving, responsive and following, so as to not injure, hurt, restrict, or confuse the horse as he makes natural movements with his head and neck. A horse uses his head and neck as a balancing aid, similar to the way you use your arms. If a horse is prevented from using his neck naturally for balance, he tends to become anxious, strong, and fast, as he is trying not to fall down. Imagine being asked to walk across a balance beam with your hands tied behind your back! This is what it is like when a horse is asked to move with his head held or tied down. Your ability to follow the motion of the horse's head with your arms, without restricting the horse's natural movement, is critical to a correct riding education.

A horse's head and neck are used for balance in the following ways:

Walk: long back and forth motion

Trot: almost no movement (subtle back and forth motion)

Canter: slight up, out, down, and back and forth motion

A restrictive, tight hand not only limits the horse's balance, but also limits how much the horse can swing his hind legs underneath his body. This is important because it is the ability of the horse to "engage" his hind legs that allows him to balance and carry himself and the rider safely. Although each horse may react to restriction by riders' hands differently (some slow down, others get nervous or panicky, still others speed up), all horses respond to the holding of the rein by taking shorter steps with their hind legs. In some disciplines this may be the answer you are looking for in your performance, but not in dressage and basic training of the horse.

What is the best way to communicate with the horse?

When communicating with a horse it is helpful to understand these few points:

- Horses naturally seek a pressure-free and pain-free state.
- Horses have a simple (but not dumb) mind.
- Horses are innately lazy.
- Horses gain comfort and security through routine.

So, horses like things to be kept simple and they want to avoid pressure and pain. Therefore, the following cycle of communication has been found to work best for horses because it is simple, straightforward, and can be done consistently:

PARR (Prepare, Ask, Respond, Reward)

- The rider *prepares* the horse for a question.
- The rider *asks* the horse the question.
- The horse *responds*.
- The rider *rewards* the horse's proper response.

In sum, the rider applies pressure, the horse yields, and the rider releases the pressure—simple!

What are route and rate and why are they so important?

Route refers to direction, or where a horse's hooves go when in motion. Rate refers to the speed or pace the horse is going. The ability to stay "on route" and control the "rate"

For want of control, relaxation is lost. For want of relaxation, position is lost. And for want of position, all is lost!

gives beginning riders the confidence associated with being in control. That is, new riders tend to feel safer, more secure, and better balanced when they are able to control the route and rate of the horse they are riding. This means that new riders need to not only develop the elementary control skills that will help them steer their horses, but also get into the habit of always knowing where they want to go. This is not as easy as it sounds! Many riders (not just beginners) fall into the trap of just riding around, without a real plan or sense of direction. This is comparable to getting into a car, starting the engine, and beginning to drive without giving any thought as to where to go!

Route and rate (rhythm/speed) are related to your relaxation and position:

- If *you can stay on route (the intended path)*
- And *you can maintain rate (the desired pace)*
- Then *you can become relaxed (no muscle stiffness)*
- Which *ultimately leads you to being able to maintain the correct position in balance!*

Route and rate are controlled by you, the rider, using a clear mind and your natural aids.

Control leads to safe, confident riders who can relax and maintain a correct position. Until you feel some semblance of control, learning will take a back seat to survival. This is simply human nature.

Position and control act in a circular fashion. Control allows you to improve your position, and correct position leads to better control.

℗ POINTS OF INTEREST

- It is important that the horse that you use while learning the use of aids *already* accepts the aids. Young, or green, horses are themselves unsure of the correct response to the aids, so they will not help new riders understand the proper feel and response to the aids.

- When you feel in control you are better able to relax, and when relaxed your mind is free to think about improving your position.

- Under all conditions the horse must go "on the route" you ask. First you must know where you want to go. During Stage 1, the route should stay simple and easy to follow. As your balance and relaxation improve you will feel that you are in control. In turn, controlling direction will help to improve your balance.

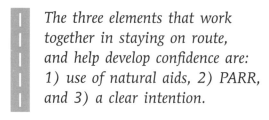 OBSERVATION POINTS

- Watch riders control-
ling their horses around
the ring. Which riders
seem to be directing the
route and which riders
seem to wander around,
letting the horse decide? Which horses seem more content and
happy in their work? More relaxed? How about the riders?

The three elements that work together in staying on route, and help develop confidence are: 1) use of natural aids, 2) PARR, and 3) a clear intention.

- Observe how often riders will put their horses on a circle, and
how long they will stay on a circle. Does circling seem to help
these riders control their horses or does the circling seem to
make the pair even more unbalanced?

- What are some of the aids you see riders using to control their
horses? Do you see artificial aids used? Harsh bits? With what
results? What is the action of different riders' hands when controlling the horse? Are the reins used sensitively or harshly? Is
there a backward pull on the reins? If so, can you see the size
of steps the horse is making with his hind legs? Are they shorter
when the rider pulls backward or holds on the reins?

- Watch videos in slow motion in order to see clearly the subtle
interplay between rider's hands and horse;s ability to use his
hind legs.

- Watch a horse and rider at your level and one step ahead of
you and try to match what you see with how it feels. Between
rides take a few minutes and visualize what you saw and felt.

 Be patient with the learning process! Even in the ideal world,
adding the natural aids to your "tool kit" often causes you
to feel awkward, as if you are learning to ride all over again.
As route and rate are introduced, you can expect to feel
that you are taking a step backwards in your riding. You
are facing new challenges to your relaxation and position.
This is part of the *normal learning process*. When you learn
a new skill, an old skill slips; you reclaim the old skill and
then practice the new and old skill together.

Putting It All Together

Trip Review and planning

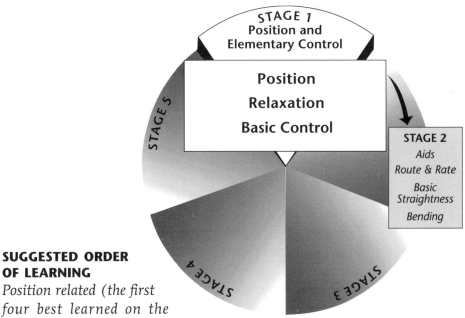

SUGGESTED ORDER OF LEARNING

Position related (the first four best learned on the lunge line):

1. Walk with relaxed, centered, and correct position

2. Posting trot with rhythm of horse

3. Half-seat or two-point seat with rhythm and with deep, stretched heels, elastic ankles while centered

4. Sitting trot with a following seat while maintaining a relaxed, centered, and correct position

Control-related:

1. Learn the basic use of aids to control a horse at walk, then at trot.

2. Walk around the perimeter of the arena, making certain your horse walks where you want to walk.

3. While maintaining position, walk around the ring, stay on route, and practice a few simple exercises. To do this you will take your reins in one hand and do simple exercises like touching your toes, the horse's ears, etc.

A body that knows from experience what to do (rather than simply a brain that thinks it knows) is what makes good riders good, and great riders better. This is a result of creating correct muscle memory.

4. Practice figures at the walk—turns, diagonals, large circles, figure eights and serpentines.

5. Trot around the arena with your hands remaining still

6. Perform walk – trot – walk transitions.

 As you go through each step in the suggested order of learning, ask yourself, "Can I maintain the correct position with elastic joints, weight going down through my heels, steady hands, and an even pace while completing the exercises?" If "Yes," then continue with the sequence.

Once you have learned the points in position and control, you can begin here:

1. Trot without stirrups, maintaining centered, relaxed position

2. Walk—trot transitions with and without stirrups, maintaining centered, relaxed position.

3. Trot in half-seat position, maintaining centered, relaxed position.

4. Walk and trot over ground poles, maintaining centered, relaxed position.

5. Learn canter in two-point position while staying balanced and centered.

6. Jump small fences at the trot.

7. Learn to sit the canter while maintaining a following seat and correct, centered position.

8. Trot over small jumps, possibly landing in canter, maintaining centered, relaxed position.

ROADBLOCKS

Everyone experiences roadblocks during the learning process. This section is designed to help you when these blocks occur. At this level the most common roadblocks occur when you try to learn too much too fast. Each step takes time to practice.

Check Points

You can use the Check Point questions below to help you uncover your roadblocks. Once you determine a roadblock, you can begin to work on fixing it, or get help from your instructor if you are unsure of how to fix the problem. The fundamental skills of *awareness* and *communication* are key to uncovering your road-blocks. If, in answering the following questions, you discover a roadblock, refer to the Roadblock chart to help you figure out the source of the problem so that you can work towards fixing it. You can gain additional help by referring to the Supplementary Training chart.

Thought process for problem solving your roadblocks

1. Check your position; alignment, spring in joints and relaxation
   If you find a problem work on it and continue
   If you feel fine...

2. Check your horse's response to your leg and rein aids and relaxation
   If you find a problem work on it and continue
   If you feel fine...

3. Return to the previous step you learned successfully, confirm that you feel good in it
   If you have not solved your problem...

4. It is time to turn to your instructor to help you identify the cause (s) of the roadblock so that you can progress with your learning experience.

Awareness

Awareness refers to your ability to be present to the "here and now" of the riding process. This section focuses on "feeling" questions.

- Do you feel spring in your ankle?
- Do you feel your ear, shoulder, hip, and heel in a line perpendicular to the ground?
- Can you move your body, not using hands for your balance?
- Do you feel all of your joints to be elastic?
- Can you follow your horse's head and neck movement with light contact?
- Do you feel in control of your horse without your body changing positions?
- Can you feel your leg softly on the side of your horse free of tension?
- Do you feel you can maintain a correct, well-balanced position when riding all three gaits and jumping low fences?

What do you think is the cause of your Roadblock?

ROAD BLOCKS Stage 1	RIDER BLOCKS					HORSE BLOCKS			
	ALIGNMENT	ELASTICITY	RELAXATION	FITNESS	EDUCATION	RESPONSE TO LEG	RESPONSE TO REIN	BASIC STRAIGHTNESS	RELAXATION
Why am I gripping with knees?									
Why am I gripping with calves?									
Why am I balancing on horse's mouth?									
Why do I feel I have tight joints?									
Why does my horse not stay on route?									
Why am I perched forward?									
Why am I sitting too far back?									
Why am I getting tired while riding?									
Why am I afraid of falling off?									
Why is my horse going too fast?									
Why is my horse not slowing down when I ask?									

• Can you feel the motion of your seat follow the motion of the horse while keeping your legs on your horse's side and your upper body tall?

• Do you feel comfortable, confident, and relaxed while riding?

Communication

Communication refers to your ability to use effective communication skills. *(See Chapter—Communication Skills—Learning Insights)* This section focuses on "skill" questions.

- Can you attach a feel word to each part of your body?
- Do you praise yourself in a few words for success?
- Can you acknowledge a mistake and plan to fix it in a short time?
- Do you use a complete communication cycle in conversations with people?
- Do you see, hear, and feel positives responses and communications before negatives?
- Do you have a clear understanding of what you want your body to do?
- Do you recognize what you do well and feel good about it?
- Are you able to make corrections thinking about what you want to happen, rather than what did not happen?
- Are you using the communication cycle effectively on your horse?
- Do you feel you can control the route (direction) and rate (speed) of your horse while maintaining your correct, relaxed position?
- Can you ride around the ring, enjoying your horse as well as your surroundings?

Supplementary Training

You can overcome roadblock with the assistance of unmounted training. This will speed up the learning process when mounted on your horse. This is to the advantage of the horse, who is more comfortable and better able to perform for you if your body and mind are working at maximum capacity.

One way you can help yourself in the learning process is to pick one word to describe how your body feels when balanced and relaxed. A few examples we have heard from riders are: springy, elastic, loose, soft, jelly-like. Most people will try to describe their feelings in a sentence or more; train yourself to use only one word if possible. Once the word is established, you can use it as a quick reminder connected to the feeling you are learning.

STAGE 1 – SUPPLEMENTARY TRAINING FOR RIDERS		
Roadblock	Supplementary Training	Where to look for more information
Limited understanding of what to do	Read the entire stage and identify where you are	The Order of Learning
Thinking too much Cluttered focus	Learn to empty your mind and focus on task at hand Practice visualizing what you want to feel, see it and feel it	Supplementary Learning Insights The Relaxed Rider Learning Insights Mental Practice
Lack of a daily plan	Create a plan	Learning Insights Goal Setting
Learn too much too fast	Review the steps	
Uptight or fearful	Relaxation Identify fear	Supplementary Learning Insights The Relaxed Rider Personal Insights Worry, Anxiety and Fear
Stiff body Lack of coordination	Relaxation Physical exercises	Supplementary Learning Insights The Relaxed Rider Pilates for Equestrians Yoga for Equestrians T'ai Chi for Equestrians
Horse issues	Get qualified help with your training program	Find a qualified instructor

Tales From the Trip

Penny and Sunflower

I am forty and *love* horses. I rode as a child, then gave up riding for boys after competing in local shows in pleasure classes, both English and Western. A year ago I bought Sunflower, a ten-year-old Arabian, my first horse in twenty-five years. I bought her out of a field of fifty horses, and her history is somewhat sketchy.

My children are still my first priority in terms of my time, so I am lucky if I can ride two or three times a week. After riding for two months on my own, I decided I needed instruction because I wanted to prepare for a local horse show in six months.

I went for an evaluation with Ms. Bailey. She explained that I needed to work on my position by bringing my legs under me, developing a deeper seat, and relaxing. She did not feel it was realistic to be ready to show successfully in six months, as both Sunflower and I had some foundation skills to put in order. If we moved too fast, we could create problems in our future riding goals and progress. Even though I was disappointed, I agreed and we set up a regular lesson schedule, two times a month.

Lesson 1

After the evaluation we got started. First she had me adjust my leg and seat so that my legs were in the correct position. I learned to relax my legs and let my body weight travel from my head through my body and out my heels. After trying to help me feel this with the "trip" through my body three times, she sensed my frustration; I just could not get it! So she asked me to close my eyes and feel the springing in my ankles during the walk, first one and then the other. First, I discovered that my thigh and knee were very tight; I could not feel past them. We did a few exercises and I tried again, this time I felt my thigh relax, but I had to do it with my eyes closed.

She allowed me to practice this for fifteen minutes, then we began the trot. Sunflower immediately cut her corners. Ms. Bailey explained that I was concentrating so hard on my position that I forgot to control Sunflower. In reality, I did not even realize that we were cutting corners, but I did not tell this to Ms. Bailey! After a few more times of cutting corners, Ms. Bailey stopped me and explained the role of controlling Sunflower so that I could focus on continuing to allow my weight to go down through my legs and out my relaxed ankles. I questioned this information, but decided to pay attention and see if it helped. It did. When Ms. Bailey saw my leg working properly in the corrected position, she asked me for one word to describe the feeling. I felt silly, but decided to give my word: "skwishy"! To my surprise throughout the rest of the lesson, Ms. Bailey would ask me if my legs felt 'skwishy! As soon as she asked I was surprised to discover that I knew if I had it or not. If my answer was no, she would ask, "Where does it feel tight?" This helped me identify my problem and be aware of it. We continued to focus on this feel at the walk and trot around the outside of the ring.

During the review, Ms. Bailey asked, "What do you feel are the most important points you learned in this lesson?" I replied, "I learned two things; first, I need to fix my seat, and second, I need to ride on the outside of the ring." She then asked, "What do you need to fix in your position?" "Make my leg feel skwishy." "Yes, I agree, but first you need to adjust your position, aligning your leg under your seat." Ms. Bailey then reminded me to ask myself periodically how my leg felt to make certain I could maintain the "skwishy" feeling. Since I ride only a few days a week, she suggested that I practice the feeling using visualization.

Lesson 2

Two weeks later, I was proud to show Ms. Bailey the improvement in my leg position and relaxation. She was very pleased with my progress; this really made me feel good. Since I was doing so well, she decided to add some ring figures to our work. To my astonishment and concern, as soon as I left the track I noticed that I tipped forward and lost my skwishy feeling. I guess Ms. Bailey noticed my frustration and offered me an explanation: Many people resort to their old issues when the figures get more complicated. She helped me prepare Sunflower for the circle and then explained how I had to think around the circle, reminding myself to feel my "skwishy" feeling before I started the circle and again when I was about to leave the circle. After practicing this for fifteen minutes, I felt good and was smiling. Ms. Bailey decided to let me try a serpentine—I went to pot again, losing my smile along with my "skwishy" feeling and my route! Ms. Bailey suggested we wait to add this, and work on confirming circles and crossing the diagonal. My assignment for the next two weeks is to practice corners, circles, and diagonals at walk and trot, and canter on circles only. During these exercises I am to ask myself three questions: Am I on route? Do I have my "skwishy" feeling? Am I enjoying my feeling? I can't wait for my third lesson!

STAGE 2—USE OF AIDS
for More ADVANCED CONTROL

Big Picture

OVERVIEW

In Stage 1 you learned about the classically correct position, called the basic, balanced position. You also learned about the importance of elementary control when first learning to ride. Stage 2 introduces you to the use of the rein and leg aids, and develops you further as a rider in two important ways: 1) By paying attention to the way your horse responds to your aids, you are developing the all-important first step of "feel," and 2) When you practice using your aids *properly*, you are developing a sense of "muscle memory." Key to this learning process is your attention to your horse's route, degree of straightness, and speed.

 ROAD MAP

Rein and Leg Aids

How is the rein aid applied and what is the horse's correct response?
How is the leg aid applied and what is the horse's correct response?
Why is route so important for Stage 2 riders?
What is basic straightness and why is it important in Stage 2?
What is the difference between flexion, bend, and overbending?

Putting It All Together

 Many riders find it helpful to understand "why" they are doing something in a certain way. When you learn the basic, underlying principles (theory) behind what it is you are doing, the aids make more sense, so you learn faster.

"If a rider initially learns the wrong things concerning the feeling of the aids or the horse's body (or if an instructor teaches the wrong things at this stage), it will become necessary to correct such problems later in the rider's education, where it can be frustrating and time consuming for both riders and instructors."

—Stephan Kiesewetter

THE IDEAL ROUTE

To best learn the proper "feel" of a horse's response to the rein and leg aids, as well as continue to develop and solidify the proper "muscle memory," Stage 2 riders would have access to the following ideal conditions.

The horse is a major part of every rider's learning process—for good and for bad. If the horse is properly trained, he acts as a "teacher" in that he responds to correctly applied rein and leg aids, giving new riders a chance to learn the correct "feel" immediately. If riders learn on untrained or improperly schooled horses, they do learn, but unfortunately they learn incorrect habits, techniques, and skills—all of which will have to be unlearned later on, at great effort and expense!

- Enter Stage 2 with some degree of proper, basic body balance and elementary horse control.

- Are able to ride a horse that is a "school master" in that he knows more than you do, and has been ridden correctly in the past. Such a horse is likely to respond immediately to all of your appropriately applied aids, yet also let you know when your aids are incorrectly applied.

- Will have the time to both practice and take lessons in the same week. This is important, so that they can learn to think on their own, and work things out through trial and error between lessons.

- Will have access to an instructor who has classical riding and training experience as well as a positive and encouraging teaching style.

ALTERNATIVE ROUTES

You may find that you learned to ride under less than the ideal conditions described above. Here in the United States, riders are not always able to follow the ideal route, for many reasons. These include a lack of trained horses, a dearth of qualified instructors, and school and work schedules that limit the time spent riding. Yet, true to the American spirit, riders have found ways around these problems, and have learned to ride, and ride well, despite the obstacles in their path. However, each "alternative route" offers its own unique set of challenges to work through. As you read through the following obstacles that require an alternative route, see if any of them apply to you. If they do, you may find that you simply need to "correct" an old habit that developed early on in your riding because of this obstacle. Corrections tend to fall into one of three categories: 1) spending more time in the saddle, 2) getting proper instruction, or 3) readjusting your goals to fit more realistically into your schedule and life demands. *(See obstacle chart next page.)*

> You may notice that we are not including the seat as one of the natural aids taught in Stage 2. At this stage of riding, riders are first taught how to keep the seat in a "neutral" position, meaning that it stays centered, relaxed and can follow the motion of the horse's movement. Later on, the seat becomes an "active" aid, but only after riders have become independent with their seat, legs, and hands.

  ## Rein and Leg Aids

The first step in horse and rider communication

GOAL/DESTINATION

Stage 2 has three major goals for riders: 1) to learn the correct use of the rein and leg aids, 2) to feel the horse's correct response to the rein and leg aids, and 3) through practice, to develop the proper muscle memory associated with the individual rein and leg aids.

 ### ROAD MAP

How is the rein aid applied and what is the horse's correct response?

You use the rein by gently squeezing your last three fingers on the rein, as if you are gently squeezing water from a sponge. The horse should respond to this small squeeze of the fingers by "softening" (yielding) his jaw in the direction of the pressure. There should be no turning of the horse's head and neck by this simple rein aid. All the response should be in the horse's jaw. Initially you will learn to use the rein aids with light contact. As your training advances, the contact may become stronger, but will always remain relaxed and flexible.

OBSTACLE CHART		
Obstacle	**Associated Problems**	**Alternate Routes**
Lack of Qualified Instruction	_ Lack of a correct basic, balanced position _ Uncorrected bad habits, such as pinching with knee or calf, or leaning in on turns _ The use of odd, or "unique" aids to get a horse to go, such as "kissing" the horse to ask for canter _ Using artificial aids incorrectly, usually to "control" the horse in some way	_ Read a book and get an understanding of what you need, and then ask a friend of family member to be eyes from the ground. _ Get a video of your level and watch it with a friend or family member and then ask them to watch you. _ Attend a clinic either to watch and learn or to ride. Take a friend or family member with you to watch and help you when you return home. _ Take an independent study course with video lessons and evaluations.
Learning on an Inappropriate Horse	_ Stiff, tight, body, especially shoulders and arms resulting from stiff or unschooled horse _ Backward use of rein—always pulling, not trusting enough to "give" because of the horse's lack of response. _ Too strong use of aids, not knowing when horse softens or responds _ High levels of frustration when the horse doesn't respond _ Fear response on part of rider—doesn't trust the horse _ Stiff, inflexible seat—rider isn't relaxed, so hips don't follow horse's movement	_ Learn how to lunge and teach your horse to lunge, and then ask a friend or family member to lunge you. _ Save money and travel to the nearest training center for some lessons to get the feel of what you want to learn on your horse _ See if you can get someone who is more experienced than you and has some success, like an 'B' Pony Clubber to help you by riding your horse, so that your horse becomes better educated. _ Find a working student position where you can ride a trained horse and get the "feel."
Lack of Time	_ Feeling "stuck" in progress—not making a lot of headway _ Moving on to more difficult skills before the acquried skills are confirmed _ Stiff seat and hands, and lack of body balance due to not having enough "in the saddle" time _ Tension, irritability, and short temper from too much time pressure _ Feelings of guilt over not riding more often _ Lack of rider "fitness"—muscles get sore and stiff after every ride	_ Make a plan that is realistic that matches your goals and your time, then stick to the plan. _ Research ideas to gain fitness during your regular day, be innovative.

Your fingers may be doing the squeezing, but it is the rider's arm that dictates whether the rein aid is soft and flexible or hard and rigid. Ideally your arm hangs down in a relaxed way from the shoulder, with a slight bend at the elbow. Your fingers are around the rein are firm yet soft, no stiffness or strength should be seen or observed when the rein aids are used. To prevent the reins from slipping you can hold the rein firmly between your thumb and first finger without creating any tension in your wrist or elbow joints.

The key to getting the correct response to your rein aid is to make certain you have elastic joints and you are using a steady hand, with only the fingers providing the pressure on the reins, while the wrist, elbow, and shoulder remain relaxed.

How is the leg aid applied and what is the horse's correct response?

Your leg can be either "passive" or "active." A passive leg hangs softly against the horse's barrel, in the same way that your skin is in contact with the leather of your boot. An active leg applies pressure to the horse's side, without tightening or gripping upwards with the leg. The order of applying a leg aid is always the same: passive leg, to active leg, returning to a passive leg. The horse's response to the leg aid depends on what is being asked, but in all cases the horse should *react.* This may mean moving forward or to moving laterally, but when the horse feels the increased pressure of the leg aid, the horse should move.

When talking about leg aids, two terms are frequently confused: "driving" and "pushing." Instructors may tell their students to "drive, drive, drive," or "push on," which often results in the rider leaning back, driving their seat down into the saddle, with their legs pushing harder against the horse's side. However, using stronger leg and seat aids does not properly drive or push a horse forward. In actuality, this action only encourages a horse to become "hollow" in his back. Rather, driving a horse forward is an advanced technique requiring the rider to use a combination of seat and leg, with the leg using only the normal pressure against the horse's side, not increased pressure.

ONE-TWO-THREE RULE
How to Get Your Horse to Respond
immediately to Your Leg

1. Apply a leg aid with a light squeeze of the calf
    (no gripping upwards with leg!).

2. If the horse does not respond by moving forward
    immediately, you give a quick kick with the leg.

3. If the horse still does not respond,
    then your deliver a quick, firm tap with the whip
    or crop *behind your leg* at the same time that
    the leg is used.

This last combination should be firm enough to make the horse
really jump forward. Reward your horse when he responds (even if
he goes forward more than you originally wanted) by going back
to your light leg connection.

Why is route so important for Stage 2 riders?

In Stage 1, staying on route was basic to helping you remain in balance and as relaxed as possible. In Stage 2, two important lessons become obvious when you stay on route. First, directing a horse along a specific path—which typically includes corners, specific ring figures, or turns—teaches you that you must prepare the horse so he is balanced and ready to move his body in the direction you ask. If he is not prepared, he can very easily lose his balance, causing him to speed up or shift his body in an awkward position to accommodate your request. Second, staying on route lets you know whether you are really in control over your horse's straightness, and thus balance. Do you ever find yourself wanting to ride a circle to help your horse feel better? Many times riders will let their horse move off a specific route (usually to go on a circle) in order to avoid having him speed up, slow down, or change his body position. In reality, he is losing his balance and the circle becomes a masking figure for you. It hides the fact that you are not in control of your horse's straightness, or balance. In order to keep your horse on route, you will discover that you need to give your horse clear and uncomplicated directions as well as use your leg and/or rein aids to maintain the same rate on your desired route. As you advance, staying "on route" becomes the foundation for knowing

when to adjust rhythm and
straightness by "feel." Thus route is the
first and foremost factor to indicate whether
you are really riding your horse or just being a
passenger on him.

What is basic straightness and why is it important in Stage 2?

"Straightness" in its classical definition means that *the horse must travel in such a way that the hind feet follow in the tracks of the front feet, no matter what shape or figure he is making.* That is, if a horse is traveling on a straight-away, such as down the long side of the ring, the horse's head, neck, shoulders, back, and hindquarters should all be in a straight line because his hooves are in a straight line. If the horse is traveling on a circle, the horse has to "bend" his body slightly in a curve to make sure that that his hind feet step in the tracks of his front feet. Doing so also keeps the horse's head, neck, shoulders, back, and hindquarters straight because no one part of the horse is allowed to drift out (typically the hindquarters) or fall in (typically the shoulder). When a horse does this, it is said to be traveling straight. This definition is the reason why, in riding arenas everywhere, instructors are telling their students to ride their horses "straight on a circle," much to the confusion of newcomers and spectators alike!

Hooves falling on straight line on straightaway and in corner

Horses don't find it easy to travel straight. People don't naturally travel very straight either. Do the following exercise and you will be more understanding of how hard it is for your horse to travel straight, especially on a circle.

1. Fill up two buckets of water,
2. Walk down the middle of your barn aisle carrying the two buckets of water.
3. Next, draw a straight line down the middle of the barn aisle, and again walk straight down the middle of that line while carrying the water buckets.

What was the difference between your two walk attempts? Most people find that when walking "normally" the weight of the buckets pulled them side-to-side as they walk. That is, they do not travel very "straight." When trying to follow the line (route), people find that walking with the buckets becomes more difficult. In order to travel straight with those buckets, you are forced to shift (distribute) your weight *equally* from side to side as you walk. In other words, you had to exert effort to "balance" yourself when walking with those buckets, just as a horse must exert effort to "balance" himself when traveling straight on a line or route.

What is the difference between flexion, bend, and overbending?

Bend and flexion are two terms that are confused with each other. The following definitions are based on the classical approach to riding:

Flexion

Flexion deals with the position of the horse's head only, not his neck. Flexion happens when the horse relaxes his jaw and gives a slight turn of the eye in the direction of the asking rein. The rider, in glancing down, can see the "inside" eye and edge of the "inside" nostril. Thus, flexion can be thought of as the positioning of the horse's jaw. A horse can turn his jaw side to side, or drop it down towards his chest (this is referred to as too much flexion—sometimes called "over-flexing").

Bend

Bend is a term with numerous meanings. In classical terms, bend refers to the position of the horse's body, not his head. To be "bent" means that the horse is supple enough when walking, trotting, or cantering to step up under his body with his inside hind leg. This causes a gentle curve in his body, which stretches the outside of his body on the line of travel. A correctly bent horse with an engaged inside hind leg is often described as supple. In the classical definitions, bent and supple are interchangeable words.

 The word "bend" has many connotations in the horse world. People use this word to describe the suppleness of the horse's body (as in the above definition), the bending of the head and neck (as described in overbending below), and the degree of flexion (as described above).

 By learning the rein and leg responses systematically, through "feel," you will find that you can quickly commit the correct feeling associated with bending and flexion to your muscle memories.

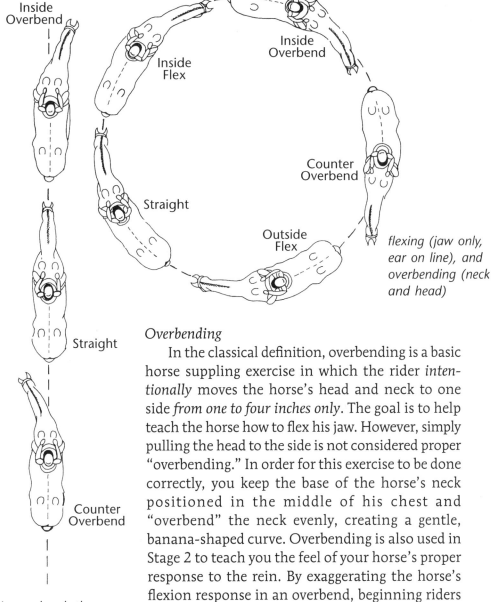

Inside Overbend

Inside Flex

Inside Overbend

Counter Overbend

Straight

Outside Flex

flexing (jaw only, ear on line), and overbending (neck and head)

Straight

Counter Overbend

In overbend, the base of the neck remains in the center of chest and the neck overbends not more than 4 inches

Overbending

In the classical definition, overbending is a basic horse suppling exercise in which the rider *intentionally* moves the horse's head and neck to one side *from one to four inches only*. The goal is to help teach the horse how to flex his jaw. However, simply pulling the head to the side is not considered proper "overbending." In order for this exercise to be done correctly, you keep the base of the horse's neck positioned in the middle of his chest and "overbend" the neck evenly, creating a gentle, banana-shaped curve. Overbending is also used in Stage 2 to teach you the feel of your horse's proper response to the rein. By exaggerating the horse's flexion response in an overbend, beginning riders quickly learn to associate the use of their fingers on the rein with the horse yielding in his head and neck. As riders become more familiar with the rein aid, they can begin to ask for the subtler flexion response. (*See illustration describing the differences.*)

When overbending your horse, it is important to also use your leg aid at the girth so that the horse is encouraged to yield in his shoulder. If the horse is allowed to move his body into or away from the overbend, he is avoiding responding correctly.

🅿 POINTS OF INTEREST

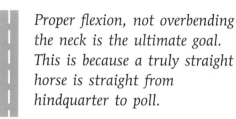

Proper flexion, not overbending the neck is the ultimate goal. This is because a truly straight horse is straight from hindquarter to poll.

- Educated horses are best for teaching about rein and leg aids because they help you learn how a horse is *supposed* to respond. When educated horses are used to teach the rein and leg aids, it is beneficial in that it prevents you from making the common mistake of overusing your hands and legs when the horse doesn't respond, or responds inappropriately.

- In correct riding, only 5 percent of your aids are given by the hand, with 95 percent of the aids given with the seat and leg. Therefore, it is important that you use the rein aids properly and that the horse responds correctly.

- When you are using the aids to flex, bend, or overbend, nothing else in the horse's body is supposed to change, including his straightness, route, or rate. If any of these other changes takes place, either the horse has found a way to avoid answering properly or you have not applied the aid properly.

- The hands play the role of directing the energy. A good way to think of your hands, as receiving energy and then directing it. Your goal as you move through the stages is to create hands that are independent from your seat.

Actions of rider's hand and effect on the horse		
Action	Horse Part	Communication effect
Fingers	Jaw, poll, and neck	Route/Direction, Rate (Speed/rhythm) Flexion Roundness
Outside hand	Outside jaw & poll	Degree of roundness Rate (Rhythm/speed) Receiver of energy
Inside hand	Inside jaw & poll	Neck flexion

- Your leg aid is light and effective, used to communicate without pushing or forcing it.

- You need to consistently keep your leg softly on your horse's sides at all times. After the leg is used, leg aid is released back to light contact on the horse's barrel. An active leg always returns to a passive leg as soon as the horse responds correctly.

Actions of rider's legs and the effect on the horse		
Left leg behind girth	Left hind leg	Move forward or over
Right leg behind girth	Right hind leg	Move forward or over

- The horse is the power source, and if you are unable to initiate a response with as little effort as one uses to turn the key in the ignition of a car, the horse is not responding properly, and the end result is an unresponsive, dull horse and a frustrated rider.

Basic Balanced Position Reminder

It is important for you to keep the leg in the correct position before, during, and after the use of the leg aid. When using an active leg, either at the girth or slightly back from it's normal position (1 – 2 "), be sure to return it to the passive state, in the correct position, which is under your hip.

- Riders who initially learn to use their aids one-at-a-time develop the proper feel of the aids in their individual body parts, which ultimately leads to the development of independent use of the aids. This critical skill is essential in order to advance and to train horses.

- Staying on route is essential during the bending process—as it is during all of riding—as this is the basis of both rider and horse balance. If the horse is allowed to deviate from your desired route, it can create havoc with your balance. Likewise, if you do not keep the horse on route when bending, it becomes difficult for the horse to stay balanced.

O OBSERVATION POINTS

Watch riders and observe how they are using their hands. Ask yourself:

- Is the rider allowing the horse's energy to come forward, toward the horse's head, or is the rider restricting the energy by bringing the hand back toward the horse's withers?

- What is the contact like? Is it steady and flexible, or tense and rigid?

- Develop your "eye for energy" by watching the horse's walk and trot. Can you see the horse take equal-sized steps with both front and hind legs? If so, at the trot you will see the horse make two equal-sized triangles between the front and hind legs. If not, you will see smaller steps being taken behind when compared to the size of the steps taken in front. Also, can you see the horse's hind hoof prints fall into or in front of the front hoof prints?

- Does the rider have a following arm that has a break in the elbow and a soft movement in the shoulder? This kind of arm makes a connection to the horse's mouth that allows the energy of the horse created by the hind legs to come forward through the back and into the rider's hands.

- In the trot and canter do you see quiet, giving hands, or hands that bounce or stay too still by being frozen or pushed into the horse's neck?

- When the rider is doing downward transitions, do his/her hands remain forward to receive the energy that is still coming forward from the horse? Or, do you see hands that get tight, stiff, and backward in their action?

Watch riders and observe how they are using their legs. Ask yourself:

- Do you see the rider keeping an even pace at all times? Or, does the horse slow down, speed up, or in general seem to dictate the pace to the rider?

- Does the horse respond to the rider's leg aids immediately with energy, or does the rider have to kick, poke, cluck ,or use the whip?

- Do you see a horse who is enjoying moving forward with ears up and tail swinging, or one who appears tense, unhappy, or bored?

Putting it all together
Trip Review and Planning

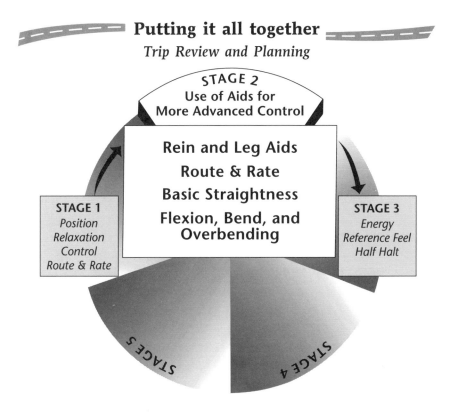

 Basic rules of Stage 2:
- Use only one aid at a time.
- Expect an immediate response to any request made with hand or leg.
- Expect quality to response: light, consistent responses to all aids.
- In time, with correct practice your aids will be used in the correct timing and coordination

SUGGESTED ORDER OF LEARNING

We encourage all riders to learn how to jump as it improves many areas of your riding; however, some riders may feel as though they prefer to ignore last three points.

- Learn to establish a light contact with a following hand.
- Ask your horse to move forward off your leg from a light squeeze.
- Learn to use the "outside rein aid" by overbending your horse to the outside.

- Learn to use the "inside rein aid" by overbending your horse to the inside.

- Ride your horse with proper bend in each direction.

- Ride your horse with "counter" (outside) overbend in transitions.

- Ride your horse with an inside overbend in transitions.

- Turn on forehand to learn to move one of his hindlegs to side.

- Trot to canter transitions with overbend.

- Practice cavaletti with and without small jumps.

- Practice small jumps on comfortable curves.

- Practice small jumps with transitions between the fences.

ROADBLOCKS

Roadblocks at this level occur because you begin to challenge your coordination by adding control, thus affecting your ability to maintain a correct position. You may find that while you are learning to use the correct aids and get the appropriate response from your horse, roadblocks develop in your position. This is normal—rather like the infamous two steps forward, one step back. Remember, this is still forward progress!

The most common causes of Rider Roadblocks left over from Stage 1:

- You are unclear of what to do or what to expect with your rein and leg aids, either through limited education or lack of understanding of the aid sequence or response.

- Your horse is unsteady or inconsistent. This occurs when you move from one step to the next before one step is confirmed.

- Your communications are late, usually because you are thinking too much at one time, are focusing too hard, or are distracted.

- Your body stiffens up when you ask, and your horse does not respond immediately.

Check Points

You can use the Check Point questions below to help you uncover your roadblocks. Once you determine a roadblock, you can begin to work on fixing it, or get help from your instructor if you are unsure of how to fix the problem. The fundamental skills of *awareness* and *communication* are key to uncovering your road-blocks. If, in answering the following questions, you discover a roadblock, refer to the Roadblock chart to help you figure out the source of the problem so that you can work toward fixing it. You can gain additional help by referring to the Supplementary Training chart.

Awareness

- Can your attention go to your fingers, calf, or thigh separate from the rest of your body?
- Do you feel elastic joints and a steady hand, with only the fingers providing the pressure on the reins, while the wrist, elbow, and shoulder remain relaxed?
- Are you aware of changes in the horse's response to your fingers?
- Whenever you use your hands do you use your legs to help get the response from the rein?
- Does your horse respond with equal lightness and number of inches of bend on each side?
- Is your leg lying softly on the side of the horse, as gently as a boot touches the leg it covers?
- Is your body weight traveling down the inside of the leg and out the heel to ensure a firm, deep leg?
- Are you aware of the position of your leg during and after you use it as an aid?
- Are you aware of your energy and weight as it travels from the center of your body through your seat and out the inside of your heels, while your seat follows the motion of energy that begins in the hind leg and travels through the back of the horse?

Communication

- Do you know the response you are supposed to get before you give a rein or leg aid?
- Can you speak up when you are confused in a lesson?
- Do you ever praise yourself (silently) when you do something right?

- Do you have a clear plan of what you are trying to achieve in each day's ride?

- When you get an unintended response, what do you do?

- Do you consistently use the 1-2-3 rule (a small squeeze, a sharp kick, the whip)?

- Can you ride and talk to a friend or enjoy the view while atomically piloting your horse and you are doing what you want to do?

Thought process for problem solving your roadblocks

1. Check your position; alignment, spring in joints and relaxation
   If you find a problem work on it and continue
   If you feel fine...

2. Check your horse's response to your leg and rein aids and relaxation
   If you find a problem work on it and continue
   If you feel fine...

3. Return to the previous step you learned successfully, confirm that you feel good in it
   If you have not solved your problem...

4. It is time to turn to your instructor to help you identify the cause (s) of the roadblock so that you can progress with your learning experience.

Roadblock chart

What is at the root of my roadblock? For each problem identified, use the chart to determine if this problem is due to one or more of the rider and/or horse factors. *(See chart on page 259.)*

Supplementary Training

You can overcome roadblock with the assistance of unmounted training. This will speed up the learning process when mounted on your horse. This is to the advantage of the horse, who is more comfortable and better able to perform for you if your body and mind are working at maximum capacity. *(See Stage 2—Supplemental Training for Rider on page 260.)*

ROAD BLOCKS
Stage 2

What do you think is the cause of your Roadblock?

	RIDER BLOCKS					HORSE BLOCKS			
	ALIGNMENT	ELASTICITY	RELAXATION	FITNESS	EDUCATION	RESPONSE TO LEG	RESPONSE TO REIN	BASIC STRAIGHTNESS	RELAXATION
Why am I gripping with knees?									
Why am I gripping with calves?									
Why am I balancing on horse's mouth?									
Why do I feel I have tight joints?									
Why does my horse not stay on route?									
Why am I perched forward?									
Why am I sitting too far back?									
Why am I getting tired while riding?									
Why am I afraid of falling off?									
Why is my horse going too fast?									
Why is my horse not slowing down when I ask?									

Stage 2 – Supplementary Training for Riders		
Roadbock	Supplementary training	Where to look for more information
Tight body when aids used	Visualization _ Correct feeling of leg response _ Riding a corner of figure that might be challenging you during your rides. _ Confirming a good feeling you gained during a ride. Relaxation Physical exercise—yoga, T'ai Chi, Pilates	Learning Insights Mental Practice Supplementary Learning Insights The Relaxed Rider Pilates for Equestrians Yoga for Equestrians T'ai Chi for Equestrians
Holding with hands	Visualization _ Correct feeling of rein response _ Feel of correct position elbow to bit with bend in elbow and relaxed shoulders and wrists. _ Squeezing fingers while joints stay soft and relaxed Physical exercise	Learning Insights Mental Practice Supplementary Learning Insights The Relaxed Rider Pilates for Equestrians Yoga for Equestrians T'ai Chi for Equestrians
Getting tired when riding	Relaxation Fitness	Fact Insights Fitness for Riders Supplementary Learning Insights The Relaxed Rider Pilates for Equestrians Yoga for Equestrians T'ai Chi for Equestrians
Limited understanding of what to do	Reread previous stage Read the entire stage and identify where you are	The Order of Learning
Thinking too much Cluttered focus	Learn to empty your mind and focus on task at hand Practice visualizing what you want to feel, see it and feel it.	Learning Insights Mental Practice
Lack a daily plan	Create a plan	Learning Insights Training Framework Goal Setting
Learn too much too fast	Review the steps in the stage	
Uptight or fearful	Relaxation Identify fear	Supplementary Learning Insights The Relaxed Rider Personal Insights Worry, Anxiety & Fear Chapter
Stiff body	Relaxation Physical exercises	Supplementary Learning Insights The Relaxed Rider
Horse issues	Get qualified help with your training program	Find a qualified instructor

Tales From the Trip

Taxi and Blockbuster

My name is Taxi. I am a twenty-five-year-old woman and have been riding since I was fourteen. I have been riding at local stables for eleven years, averaging four days a week. My current horse, Blockbuster, is my fifth horse. My instructor encouraged me to buy this five-year-old half-bred Percheron so we could learn together and I would have a "good" horse. But after six months passed, all I could do was walk and trot, and even then I felt that I did not have much control over his speed.

I registered in a clinic because my instructor insisted that I needed to improve my position so that I could gain control of Blockbuster. Despite my nervousness, I took the leap, saved my money, and went to the clinic. After watching us for a few minutes, Ms. Smith, the clinician, asked a few questions. She knew that I wanted to work on my position, and she explained to me that my position was OK, and could not be improved until I could control Blockbuster. The first thing that she explained was that I had to stay on the outside of the ring and not allow Blockbuster to change direction. Second, I had to control his speed to maintain a steady rhythm. The first day of the clinic I learned to overbend Blockbuster to the outside of the arena, and to insist that he stay on the rail. I walked for the entire lesson, with overbend to outside, patting Blockbuster when he stayed in the three-inch overbend.

To my surprise, on day two of the clinic Blockbuster immediately responded to my counterbend aids. I was so excited! We added overbending three inches to the inside today. At first I had a lot of trouble. Ms. Smith asked me to relax my joints. Secretly, I thought she was nuts, with Blockbuster pulling on me with what felt like fifty pounds of force and moving to the inside of the ring. After a few minutes, Ms. Smith stopped me and felt my arm joints, and showed me how to relax them. She also explained to me how to hold with my fingers and make my leg active on the girth. After I made a few attempts while Blockbuster continued to ignore me, she told me to change directions and return to the overbend to the outside. He listened immediately, so I changed direction and tried the inside overbend again. He moved to the inside of the arena as soon as I used my inside fingers. Ms. Smith then gave me a whip to use on his shoulder as I used my leg. He began to listen and we continued to practice in each direction. Finally I was able to walk with an inside overbend and give on my inside rein. Even though I walked the entire forty-five minutes, I felt I had made a big step in gaining control of Blockbuster. I asked Ms. Smith why this was so difficult—was I doing something wrong? She explained that his short, stocky conformation, combined with his strong will and inexperience were giving me the hard time. She assured me that if I was consistent and patient, he would let go of his stubbornness and give me the overbend as soon as I asked for it.

Thank goodness this was a three-day clinic! On the last day, we started with counter bend, then went to inside bend, and Blockbuster *listened* to my aids. Next step was to do walk-halt with over counterbend, making certain that his body stayed straight along the wall and only his neck and head bent. I was so pleased—we were able to do this in both directions. We then added walk to trot with counter overbend. That, too, went well.

I asked Ms. Smith if I could get on her monthly clinic list. She agreed to take me on, so we discussed realistic assignments for the next month. I need to have a plan for my ride, and I need to be consistent with the amount of bend and my response to Block- busters obedience or lack of it. This is the foundation of my con- trol. It most probably will take a few weeks of practice to commit this to both of our muscle memories. I was given a list of increas- ingly difficult exercises to add to our program. Each new addition is to be added once Blockbuster is consistently listening to my aids for at least five days. Whenever a problem crops up, I am to return to the earlier step, reinforce it, and then move on again. Ms. Smith agreed that I have a problem with my position—namely, my upper body posture—and when Blockbuster is listening, I can remind myself to fix it. In the meantime, she gave me an unmounted exercises to practice off the horse to improve my position.

My exercises while riding, beginning with the first one on my list and not proceeding to the next one unless I am consistent with the first one.

Homework priority list

- Walk-trot-walk transitions maintaining counter overbend, and, straightness, poll to tail while staying on route

- Check if I can ride Blockbuster without a bend and feel like I am in control and able to trust him. If he begins to run or leave the route, I return to my overbend exercise.

- Cross the diagonal, maintaining the overbend I started with, staying on route

- Circles with either inside or outside overbend

**Remember to use the overbending in my warm-up each day to check Blockbuster's response and suppleness. Also remember to use it to prepare for figures and corners.

Unmounted exercises

- Shoulder roles ten times a day.

- Practice walking with correct posture, chest tall, stomach in, and head tall.

- Touch opposite toes four times a day.

I felt so good after this clinic. I had a plan and I was in control of Blockbuster. I did not mind the slow work because I felt so much better. I couldn't wait for my next ride!

STAGE 3—AIDS IN ACTION:
Advanced Communication Skills

BIG PICTURE

OVERVIEW

In Stage 3 you are introduced to the more advanced skills used to communicate with your horse. In order to do this, you need to understand and relate to the three major concepts associated with correct riding: 1) energy, 2) reference feel, and 3) the half halt.

(RM) ROAD MAP
Energy

What is energy?
Why is energy so important to riders?
What is "forward" and how does it relate to energy?
What is rhythm and how does it relate to energy?
What is an "independent seat" and how does it influence a horse's energy?

Reference Feel

What is reference feel?
What is roundness and how does it relate to reference feel?
What is consistency and how does it relate to reference feel?

The Half halt

What is a half halt?

Putting It All Together

THE IDEAL ROUTE

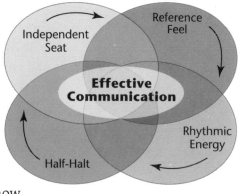

In an ideal world, you would enter Stage 3 having gone through Stages 1 and 2 on a well-schooled horse under qualified instruction. You would know how to use your individual rein and leg aids correctly and would now be working on developing the coordination to use them all together. At this point, because your position and use of aids for control are now firmly established in your muscle memory, you can now focus on developing a sense of "feel" for what a "round" and balanced horse feels like. Riding responsive

264

and trained horses, your lessons will now focus on learning to use the half halt (adjustment) to get back to that correct feeling when it is lost. Although your initial efforts to learn the half halt may be awkward and slow, a well-trained horse is sensitive enough to respond correctly to your efforts, which speeds up your learning process.

 By now you may recognize that you missed some important steps in Stage 1 or 2. Do not become discouraged; instead seek help to fill in the "gaps" as you continue learning.

ALTERNATE ROUTE

Riders are encouraged to find a qualified instructor who will help you develop the skills in Stage 1 – 3 in a way that you can enjoy the process and feel the progression. You will continue to progress while meeting the needs of you and your horse to create fill in the missing skills. You can explore various combinations offered on the obstacle chart in Stage 2.

Energy

"No engine, no ride," as the saying goes.

GOAL/DESTINATION

To understand what energy is for both rider and horse and 2) to understand the role of the horse's forward energy and rhythm when riding.

 **ROAD MAP**

What is energy?

Simply put, energy is movement. As such, energy is the foundation for everything we do when riding horses, from hacking on a trail ride to riding a grand prix dressage test and everything in between. When talking about energy, we need to address both the horse's and your energy, as both members of the team bring their own forms of energy to the partnership:

Horse

- Forward energy: This energy begins with the push/movement of the horse's hind legs and continues through the top line of the horse, ending in the hands of the rider to designate in direction, speed, and roundness. *(See Chapter—Stage 2—Role of hands and What is forward, below.)*

Forward energy
of horse and rider

• Lateral Energy: The movement of the horse sideways, which is used for flexing, bending, and lateral movements.

Rider

• Vertical Energy: This energy goes from the top of the head through the center of the body and toward the ground through the heel.

• Seat Energy: This energy works when the hip follows the forward energy of the horse that flows through the motion of the horse's back.

• Horizontal Energy: This energy flows from the elastic, energetic connection from elbow to bit, this is the receiving energy that is directed by the rider's hands via fingers and mental intent.

The energy of the horse in motion starts in the driving hind leg, moves forward through the back under the rider's following, elastic, balanced seat, moves on to the horse's light shoulder (the one about to bear the weight), into a soft neck and jaw, and finally to the bit. Riders then feel the energy in their hands as they maintain a steady contact with the reins to the bit.

Why is energy so important to riders?

When you ride a horse, it is energy that you are really riding, not a static horse. Therefore you need to understand energy in all its forms so that you can learn how to *receive, direct, and control* this energy when riding. That is, your goal is to direct your horse's energy, no matter how much or how little is available at any given moment. How to do this? First, in Stage 2, you learn to respond to what the horse is doing moment-to-moment, with clear and correct aids. Then, in Stage 3, you learn to be effective at directing a horse's energy by having clarity of purpose and making good decisions on a moment-to-moment basis. During this stage, you learn to use energy and continue energy's development in the horse through the stages to produce the more advanced qualities such as engagement, impulsion and collection.

What is 'forward' and how does it relate to energy?

Forward is the direction of energy. However, many riders misunderstand the word "forward" as used in riding. Forward from this perspective refers to energy that takes into consideration how the horse is moving (not just that the horse is moving). So, to be moving freely forward correctly, horses must meet two critical criteria: 1) they must be moving with activity and enthusiasm, and 2) they must be taking active steps with their hind legs, swinging them up toward their active front feet. Horses are *not forward* when they increase their energy by taking quicker, shorter steps with their hind legs. Correct forward energy has increased activity in the joints of the hind legs.

A "forward" horse needs to meet two criteria. He must move with:

Energy is movement

1. Energy, which means activity and enthusiasm, and
2. Engagement, which means the ability of the horse to bring his hind legs far up towards the front of his body with energy.

What is rhythm and how does it relate to energy?

Rhythm is the regularity of the horse's stride within each gait. That is, rhythmic horses will take steps that cover equal distances, with equal duration of time between steps. Due to the uniqueness of each horse's conformation and stride, each horse has his own unique rhythm. So, what is rhythm's role in energy? Well, rhythm describes a certain quality of energy, much like forward describes the quality of the horse's movement. Horses that move with a regular rhythm are a pleasure to watch, as they are using their energy efficiently. Being able to work in rhythm is the foundation of a horse's training in the correct system *(See Chapter—Stage 4)*. Once you learn to ride with rhythm, it is important that you recognize the horse's natural rhythm in the warm-up and follow it throughout the ride. In this way, you can "get on the horse's page." Ideally you should be aware of rhythm through the beginning, middle, and final phase of every ride, and be constantly aware of how the current rhythm compares to what was felt in the last ride. A horse's rhythm can be influenced by three factors: 1) his focus of attention (a flighty or distracted horse is seldom in rhythm!), 2) the degree to which he is kept "on route" by the rider, and 3) the ability of the rider to stay centered over the horse's balance by maintaining correct body position. A rider's rhythm can be influenced by four factors: 1) his focus and attention, 2) elasticity and alignment of position, 3) relaxation, and 4) feel.

A "forward" horse needs to meet two criteria. He must move with:

1. Energy, which means activity and enthusiasm, and

2. Engagement, which means the ability of the horse to bring his hind legs far up towards the front of his body with energy.

What is an "independent seat" and how does it influence a horse's energy?

An independent seat is a seat that is educated enough so that the your pelvis can follow the motion of the horse at all three gaits without you having to resort to gripping anywhere (especially with thighs or arms) to stay balanced and still. An independent seat is directly connected to your ability to use your aids effectively. When your seat is independent, this allows your hands and legs to be under your voluntary control. You are then in a good position to use your aids at the right time, in the right situation, and to apply them correctly in a split second. This level of coordination and timing is necessary for the more advanced aids to work.

An independent seat is necessary if you want to create energy and then guide and direct that energy correctly. If your seat is not independent, then some part of your body will be tight, tense, or gripping in some fashion in order to maintain your balance. Any tightness or tension on your part prevents the horse's energy from coming through, creating confusion and misunderstandings, which will interfere with your intended performance results.

℗ POINTS OF INTEREST

- The goal of correct riding is to create, direct, and control a horse's energy.
- Forward and rhythmic describe the quality of a horse's energy.
- The ideal movement of a horse is when his energy feels like *power* that is traveling throughout his whole body.
- The ideal movement of a horse also contains a feeling of elasticity, fluidity, and smoothness.

- A forward horse moves actively by taking as long a step with his hind leg as possible, not by speeding up, jigging, or changing gait.

⊙ OBSERVATION POINTS

- Watch horses and riders and evaluate what you see in terms of energy. Can you tell the difference between forward and fast? Pay attention to the length of stride being taken by the horse's hind legs. Are the front legs taking the length of stride equal to that of the hind legs?

- Watch horses and observe the rhythm of their movements. Can you mentally count out the beats of the gait in a steady rhythm? What does it look like when there is a lack of rhythm?

- When observing other riders, focus on those that you admire, and try feeling what you are seeing. When riding your own horse, try to recapture that feeling.

- Watch a video of you riding and see if it looks rhythmic and controlled, and compare this with what you feel.

 It can be difficult to tell the difference between forward and fast. Ask lots of questions, as this will develop your eye. Be patient, as this is a difficult concept to feel and practice.

 **Reference Feel**

A change in your consistent reference feel
is a key indication to activate a half halt!

GOAL/DESTINATION

The purpose of reference feel is to: 1) develop an awareness of the correct reference feel appropriate for you and your horse's level of training, 2) recognize its disappearance, and 3) understand the role of consistency in developing and maintaining your reference feel.

 Reference feel is the medium we use to determine the change in energy and balance gaining the information needed to do an appropriate half halt

 ROAD MAP

What is reference feel?

Reference feel is that wonderful feeling that you get between you and your horse when he is moving correctly forward and in rhythm and is straight, supple, and balanced. Importantly, the horse is traveling "round" *(See next section)*. This "good" feeling is felt in three places: a) in your hand from the rein contact (on a curve of any kind, the horse should feel solid and elastic on the outside rein, soft and light on the inside rein, so that you could soften the inside rein if you wanted to); b) in the soft, elastic connection of your leg with the barrel of your horse; and, c) in the fluid, flowing feel of your seat as it follows the movement of the horse's back. Once you experience the correct reference feel, the *absence* of such a feel signals the need for a half halt (which acts as an adjustment). Any deviation from the reference feel alerts you to action. The sooner you feel the change and respond, the fewer aids are necessary, and the more easily the horse understands what is being asked. *For this reason it is important that you learn the reference feel on educated horses, if possible, so that you can learn to distinguish correct feel from incorrect feel early on in your education.* When the half halt is asked for and responded to, the return of the reference feel rewards both horse and rider. It is a reward for the horse because you no longer need to "bother" the horse by asking for something, and it is a reward for you because the horse is moving comfortably in front of the your legs and the energy is freely moving forward to your hand.

REFERENCE FEEL

A good feeling in three places:

- in your hand from the rein contact (on a curve of any kind, the horse should feel solid and elastic on the outside rein, soft and light on the inside rein, so that you could soften the inside rein if you wanted to);

- in the soft, elastic connection of your leg with the barrel of your horse;

- in the fluid, flowing feel of your seat as it follows the movement of the horse's back.

Once you experience the correct reference feel, the absence of such a feel signals the need for a half halt (which acts as an adjustment).

A change in reference feel and/or rhythm alerts you to the need for an adjustment. It is your consistent awareness of the presence and *absence* of this ideal, desired feeling in the hands, seat, and legs that gives you the cue that a half halt (adjustment) is needed.

What is roundness and how does it relate to reference feel?

A round horse is the cornerstone of the reference feel. "Round" refers to horses that are using their muscles in their backs properly when moving. A correctly ridden horse, when moving in rhythm, forward, and straight, will have to stretch and elongate his back muscles as he propels his hind legs underneath his body, which makes the muscles take on a slightly convex or "round" shape. If a horse's back muscles are working correctly, then the energy created by the horse's hind end can travel across the back, under the saddle, and come into your hands. If a horse's back muscles are not working, the back is said to be "flat," or even "hollow" (when the back drops under the rider, taking on a slightly concave shape). A flat or hollow back prevents the horse from engaging his hind legs very far under his body, so the energy of the horse cannot come through to your hands. Therefore, no reference feel is correct unless the horse is "round." You can see a horse's back muscles moving by watching behind the saddle (in the loin area) and seeing if there is a side-to-side movement of the muscles. As you develop an educated seat, you can also begin to feel the movement of the horse's back underneath you.

What is consistency and how does it relate to reference feel?

Consistency is the backbone of any successful training program, be it for people or animals. Consistency includes the discipline of developing good habits, having clear expectations, being attentive to the horse, and responding immediately with appropriate corrections, and doing all this with a compassionate heart. Consistency starts with Stage 1 and develops throughout the learning process. In Stage 3, consistency of the reference feel is your central focus, particularly as it relates to both your contact and rhythm. As in all areas of

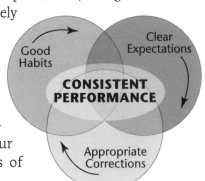

riding, consistency improves performance and performance improves consistency!

ⓟ POINTS OF INTEREST

- The reference feel is considered to be "home base"—the origination point for the changing dynamics between horse and rider.
- The reference feel needs to be identified individually in the three major parts of your body: legs, hands, and seat.
- When the reference feel changes, you use the half halt to return to the good reference feel.

ⓞ OBSERVATION POINTS

Watch horse and rider teams.

- Can you "feel" the energy you are seeing?
- Observe horse's backs when they are being ridden. Can you see the muscles behind the saddle move in a slight swinging motion, side to side?
- Can you see horses that are moving with backs that are "flat" or "hollow"? What is the difference between the length of strides that these horses take compared to horses that are traveling "round"?
- Can you see the energy of a round horse traveling from the hind end forward into the rider's hands? How does this differ from the energy being created in horses whose backs are flat?
- When watching other riders, can you tell if the horse responds immediately to the rider? If he does, can you see why? If not, can you see why not?

Watch different levels of riders.

- Can you tell the difference between Stage 1 and 2 riders, who are learning the aids, and Stage 3 and more advanced riders? What is the difference in how quick the rider applies the aids and how the horse responds to these aids? Where do you see yourself and your horse along this continuum?
- Can you pick out the riders who work their horses in a consistent manner versus the riders who don't? What aspects of a consistent program do you like? Can you develop a consistent sequence of practice in your rides?
- Listen to riders describe the feeling they are seeking or receiving from their horses. Do you hear riders who are both able and unable to accurately describe what is going on underneath them?

- Watch different lessons for different styles of instruction. Do you hear instructors who ask the rider a lot of "feeling" questions? Do you also hear instructors who talk constantly to the student, telling them what to do and when? Which riders are developing a sense of feel and the confidence to trust it?

 **The Half Halt**

*An adjustment that is the main form
of rider to horse communication*

GOAL/DESTINATION

To understand what a half halt is, what it is used for, and how it is done.

 ROAD MAP

What is a half halt?

The half halt is a combination of aids that asks a horse to make an adjustment in how he is using his body. It is composed

> *The main purpose of the half halt is to control and direct the ever changing flow of energy between rider and horse.*

of three simple steps: 1) You send the horse forward (increase his engagement), 2) hold the increased energy in your hands, back, and/or seat (the seat is used as an aid only after Stage 4), and 3) release the hold to the reference feel. Depending on the needs of the moment, the order of these steps can change, but all half halts end with a release that says "thank you" to the horse. The release also allows you to feel the horse's response to the half halt, as the horse can only respond after the aid is released. While the steps are simple and straightforward, the application, especially the timing, of the aids is more difficult. Similar to any of the more advanced aids, such as the leg-yield or shoulder-in, the half halt requires you to coordinate your leg and hand aids—a skill that is not ready to be developed until riders have completed Stages 1 and 2. The main purpose of the half halt is to control and direct the ever changing flow of energy between rider and horse.

Looking at the half halt as an "adjustment" makes it easier to understand when and why this aid would be used while riding. The following list contains some common situations that call for the use of a half halt:

- The rider is asking the horse to do something, like a circle, change of direction, or going in or out of a corner. This is called the "preparation half halt"
- The horse is getting ready to perform a demanding movement and needs more "oomph." This is often called the "engaging half halt."
- The horse becomes crooked, and needs to get his body back on the line of travel. This is called the "straightening half halt."

One or a combination of the three basic types of half halts are used for the following: The idea is to feel the loss of your reference feel and make the adjustment you "feel" is necessary to get it back.

- The horse becomes unbalanced for some reason, usually coming out of a movement, or entering into one.
- The rider wants to slow the horse down or speed the horse up.
- The rider wants to steady the horse's rhythm or tempo.
- The horse is leaning too heavy on one of his shoulders.
- The horse is traveling with one or both hind legs out behind him.

All of these scenarios require the rider to recognize what is happening (or about to happen), use the correct combination of *hand and leg* aids to "fix" the problem, and finish with a release of the aids to see if the horse returns to the reference feel the rider is seeking to maintain. As riders and horses work together, they become better and better at communicating with each other, and the half halt becomes more and more effective. Gaining this level of rider-to-horse communication is one of the main pre-requisites for a true rider-horse partnership.

Half Halt (adjustment) --- 3 Steps and 4 Basic Uses Timing, specific rein and leg aids vary depending upon need	
Push – hold – release	To prepare a horse for a change in direction or gait To create more engagement To straighten
Hold – push – release	For horses who get too strong in the hand

 The half halt is an adjustment a rider makes to control or direct the horse's energy.

As with many of the riding skills, the skills within Stage 3 work in a circular fashion. For example, the establishment of rhythm and reference feel are prerequisites of the half halt, but the ability to half halt improves the rhythm and reference feel.

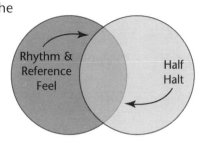

℗ POINTS OF INTEREST

- The half halt is the mode of *communication* between you and your horse. For example: Your horse is beginning to lean into his inside shoulder as you prepare to ask him for canter. You would half halt to help him straighten out, to gently tell him, "don't do that." Likewise, your horse begins to speed up at the trot; you half halt to say, "Please don't, let's stay at this speed, with this rhythm." Whenever you use your aids to help the horse get back into the "zone" (reference feel), you are communicating with him, and as often as not, this communication takes the form of some kind of half halt.

- The horse has a role in the communication process, which means that he may or may not respond. There is no guarantee that the half halt will work, *even if correctly applied,* just because you ask. That is, the horse can choose to answer or not. If the horse does not respond, it can be due to a number of factors, such as incorrect aids, position issues getting in the way, or because the horse is distracted, or green, or does not "hear" or understand you, or there is some physical limitation on the part of the horse (soreness, stiffness, lameness, etc.).

- A half halt is used for many reasons: such as when the horse gets heavy against your hand or leg, leaves the route, or speeds up. It is also used to prepare for *all* movements, figures, corners or transitions.

 In all the phases of training, rhythm is a major reason why riders would use a half halt. When the horse loses his rhythm, the rider uses the half halt to regain it.

 Rhythm needs to be maintained during transitions, movements, turns and straight lines.

- Riding is an activity that is constantly changing, moment-by-moment. Therefore, the half halt is used for continual adjustment, not just once in awhile.

- The rider must always be establishing the prerequisites for the half halt to work. These are: response to aids, relaxation, and forward energy.

- Half halts should take less than a second. Therefore many half halts (20, 30, 40, or more) are given in a single training ride.

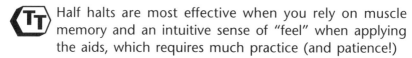 Half halts are most effective when you rely on muscle memory and an intuitive sense of "feel" when applying the aids, which requires much practice (and patience!)

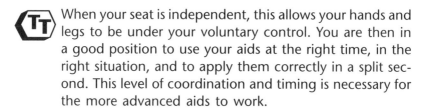 When your seat is independent, this allows your hands and legs to be under your voluntary control. You are then in a good position to use your aids at the right time, in the right situation, and to apply them correctly in a split second. This level of coordination and timing is necessary for the more advanced aids to work.

O OBSERVATION POINTS

- Watch and listen to riders taking lessons. How is the half halt taught? Is it used forcefully? Do riders pull backwards on the reins? Is it made clear that the rider's hands must be coming forward, even in half halt? That their legs must be active?

- Watch when a rider is asked to use the half halt. What is the rider trying to achieve by half halting?

- While watching can you see the rider giving the half halt? Ideally, you will not easily notice the half halt being given. Do you see the horse's corresponding response? You will recognize a half halt more in the horse's response as he makes an adjustment somewhere in his body.

- When watching other riders, can you see a connection between horses that travel in rhythm and go round?

- What does a round horse look like when he is not traveling in rhythm? Does the rider have to use a lot of rein to maintain the "head position"?

Putting it All Together

Trip review and planning

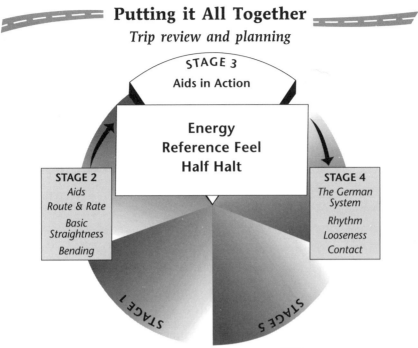

SUGGESTED ORDER OF LEARNING
Reference Feel

To practice *feeling energy* do transitions and notice the following:

- Pay attention to the feel of your horse's energy as his hind legs are coming forward to fill out your reins.

Getting to the end of Stage 3 means that you have developed a combination of your thinking mind and your feeling body.

- Pay attention to the feel of your horse's energy as your leg lies softly against your horse's side, using both active and passive leg.

- Pay attention to the feel of your horse's energy as it comes through your seat, allowing your seat to move with the motion of your horse's back at all gaits.

To practice *feeling rhythm* consider the following questions to help you feel if your horse has a regular rhythm at the walk and trot and walk to trot transitions:

- Is the rhythm regular?

- Does the rhythm have energy?

- Does your horse have more energy after the transition?

- Do you feel the same reference feel?

Half Halt

To practice the *engaging half halt* do transitions on the long sides and circles. As you do this, consider the following questions to help you feel if the half halt is "going through":

All half halts are used as needed based on muscle memory.

- Does your horse stay on route?
- Do you feel your horse fill out the outside hand with a lively energy?
- Do you feel the hind legs actively moving forward with energy in both up and down transitions?
- Does your horse respond promptly?
- Does your horse remain steady in your hand?
- Does your horse respond promptly to your leg?
- Does your horse feel more energetic after the transition?

To practice the *preparatory half halt* ride corners and circles. As you do this, consider the following questions:

- Can you feel what is happening underneath you? Consider your horse's rhythm, energy (degree of forward), straightness, and bend (suppleness), and use a combination of rein and leg aids to keep all these qualities through the movement (with a following seat).
- Does your horse stay on route?
- Does your horse maintain the same reference feel as before your preparatory half halt? Ideally, the horse should become light on your inside rein, so that you can give with inside rein if you want to.

The preparatory half halt prepares the horse so he will not lose his balance, energy, straightness, or rhythm, this half halt is done before and after a movement, as you are returning to a new line.

To practice the *straightening half halt* ride transitions with slight inside and/or outside overbend. This will help you develop a feel for keeping your horse on route and the horse's energy coming through from the hind leg to your hand. As you ride the transitions, consider the following questions:

- Does your horse move his shoulder into you inside leg? If so, overbend more and actively use inside leg on girth to move inside shoulder to outside hand.

- Does your horse "pop" his outside shoulder to the outside so that his hooves are no longer traveling in a straight line? If so, use your outside leg on the girth to move his shoulder back in line.

- Does your horse try to swing his hindquarters to the outside so that his hind hoof prints no longer track in line with the front hoof prints? If so, use your outside leg behind the girth to bring the hindquarter back in line.

- Does your horse try to swing his hindquarters to the inside, by coming against your inside leg? If so, use your inside leg behind the girth (you might need to use a tap of the whip to encourage the horse to move *away* from your leg, not into it) to bring the hindquarters back in line.

Once you have practiced the three types of half halts doing simple exercises to commit the "feeling" to muscle memory, make the figures and exercises more complex. Add serpentines, smaller circles, and lateral work. As you add difficulty, your goal is to be able to notice

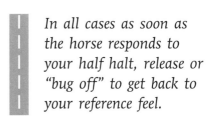

In all cases as soon as the horse responds to your half halt, release or "bug off" to get back to your reference feel.

any adjustments you need to make, *and make them,* to keep the horse in balance during the movement, automatically employing the engaging, preparatory or straightening half halt.

 As you practice, your goal is to begin to feel the appropriate aids you need *before* something goes wrong and your horse goes off route.

 Throughout all movements, try to keep the front of the horse lined up with the rear of the horse whether on the flat or over fences, and at all times maintaining a steady rhythm and consistent contact.

ROADBLOCKS

Roadblocks at this level occur when you begin to focus on consistent reference feel. You may discover that you are trying to think what you feel. This is impossible; it is better to learn this with your eyes closed. Thinking too much may cause your position to tighten. Reference feel combined with energy adds a new dimension to riding causing many riders to feel "out of control" in a new way. You will feel more energy and need to be quicker with the aids. You may discover that thinking about the half halt as an adjustment slows your reaction time. There is no time to think, as the half halt re-

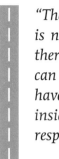

"The correct use of the inside hand is necessary, because without flexion there is no outside hand. Before I can ride with my outside aids, I have to come through with my inside aids and the horse has to respond to them."

—Stephan Kiesewetter

quires not only well-developed feel, but independence and more advanced coordination. When your body has more demands from your mind, roadblocks are likely to develop.

Check Points

You can use the Check Point questions to help you uncover your roadblocks. Once you determine a roadblock, you can begin to work on fixing it, or get help from your instructor if you are unsure of how to fix the problem. The fundamental learning skills of *awareness* and *communication* are key to uncovering your roadblocks. If, in answering the following questions, you discover a roadblock, refer to the Roadblock chart to help you figure out the source of the problem so that you can work towards fixing it. You can gain additional help by referring to the Supplementary Training chart.

Thought process for problem solving your roadblocks

1. Check your position; alignment, spring in joints and relaxation
   If you find a problem work on it and continue
   If you feel fine…

2. Check your horse's response to your leg and rein aids and relaxation
   If you find a problem work on it and continue
   If you feel fine…

3. Return to the previous step you learned successfully, confirm that you feel good in it
   If you have not solved your problem…

4. It is time to turn to your instructor to help you identify the cause (s) of the roadblock so that you can progress with your learning experience.

Awareness

- Are you fully aware of your challenges at this stage?
- Can you feel the horse respond to your leg aids, feeling the energy go forward and receiving it in your hands?
- Can you feel your horse's back moving underneath you? Can you tell when your horse has stopped using his back?
- Are you aware of your horse's rhythm? Or when you lose your rhythm?
- Does your horse give you quick, light, accurate responses, rather than slow, heavy, misguided reactions?
- Does your horse remain steady and quiet between half halts?
- Can you feel if your horse is parallel with the straight wall?
- Can you do transitions with flexion or while overbent a specific number of inches to one side or the other whenever you wish?
- Can you ride into corners with inside bend and giving with inside rein?

Communication

- Do you recognize and reward small changes for both you and your horse?
- How do you describe and feel energy?
- Is your seat able to move with your horse's movements at all three gaits? Or does it interfere with communications?
- Are your legs and hands becoming independent from your seat?
- What words would you use to describe your reference feel in hands, seat, and legs?
- Can you feel when your horse deviates from the reference feel?
- Do you consistently apply the correct half halt (preparatory, engaging, or straightening) to fix the problem?
- Do you return to your reference feel by "bugging off" as soon as your horse responds?

Roadblock chart

What is at the root of my roadblock? For each problem identified, use the chart to determine if this problem is due to one or more of the rider and/or horse factors. The problems that occur during Stage 2 often manifest themselves in Stage 3. Before you move on to Stage 4, Stage 2 and 3 roadblocks need to be addressed in your daily riding program. *(See page 282.)*

What do you think is the cause of your Roadblock?

ROAD BLOCKS Stage 3	RIDER BLOCKS					HORSE BLOCKS			
	ALIGNMENT	ELASTICITY	RELAXATION	FITNESS	EDUCATION	RESPONSE TO LEG	RESPONSE TO REIN	BASIC STRAIGHTNESS	RELAXATION
Why am I gripping with knees?									
Why am I gripping with calves?									
Why am I balancing on horse's mouth?									
Why do I feel I have tight joints?									
Why does my horse not stay on route?									
Why am I perched forward?									
Why am I sitting too far back?									
Why am I getting tired while riding?									
Why am I afraid of falling off?									
Why is my horse going too fast?									
Why is my horse not slowing down when I ask?									

Supplementary Training

You can overcome roadblock with the assistance of unmounted training. This will speed up the learning process when mounted on your horse. This is to the advantage of the horse, who is more comfortable and better able to perform for you if your body and mind are working at maximum capacity. *(See page 284.)*

Tales From the Trip
Sue with Applejack and T.J.

I am a 22-year-old high school graduate with extensive success as a hunter rider with many championships to be proud of. My horse, Applejack, a ten year old, well-mannered, obedient warmblood is my long-term partner. After I graduated, I tried several jobs so I could continue to ride, but finally I decided that I wanted to become a professional horsewoman. Before I could decide how to pursue my education, I decided I needed an evaluation. A well-respected clinician was coming into the area, so I contacted the organizer and requested an evaluation.

The clinician discussed with me my strengths and weaknesses, and helped me to develop a plan to turn my weaknesses into strengths. She said I lacked knowledge to match my talent. Specifically, I was holding tight to the reins and pushing like mad to get Applejack into a frame to do his movements. He had *no forward energy* but was obedient to my aids and had an excellent rhythm. While I rode Applejack straight, I was not careful about using the corners and ring figures accurately. My first set of goals: I need to relax, develop receiving hands and following seat, and use transitions and exercises to get Applejack forward. I discovered I had many "holes" in my education, but was confident after talking to the clinician that I could fix these problems and move forward. The plan we developed and practiced together:

Lesson 1

The point of my first lesson after my evaluation was to understand straightness, and overbending, energy and route/direction. We reviewed the role of my hand to receive energy, not hold it. We practiced the outside overbend, while staying on route and riding into the corners. Once I was able to overbend with Applejack responding correctly, Ms. Jones introduced the concept of energy.

Stage 3 Supplementary Training for Riders		
Roadblock	Supplementary training	Where to look for more information

Tight body when aids used	Visualization
	Relaxation
	Physical exercise—yoga, T'ai Chi, Pilates
		Learning Insights
		   Mental Practice
		Supplementary Learning Insights
		   The Relaxed Rider
		   Pilates for Equestrians
		   Yoga for Equestrians
		   T'ai Chi for Equestrians

Holding with hands	Visualization
	Physical exercise
		Learning Insights
		   Mental Practice
		Supplementary Learning Insights
		   The Relaxed Rider
		   Pilates for Equestrians
		   Yoga for Equestrians
		   T'ai Chi for Equestrians

Getting tired when riding	Relaxation
	Fitness
		Fact Insights
		   Fitness for Riders
		Supplementary Learning Insights
		   The Relaxed Rider
		   Pilates for Equestrians
		   Yoga for Equestrians
		   T'ai Chi for Equestrians

Limited understanding of what to do	Reread previous stage Read the entire stage and identify where you are	The Order of Learning

Thinking too much cluttered focus	Learn to empty your mind and focus on task at hand
	Practice visualizing what you want to feel, see it and feel it
		Supplementary Learning Insights
		   The Relaxed Rider
		Learning Insights
		   Mental Practice
		   Communication

Lack of a daily plan	Create a plan	Learning Insights
		   Training Framework
		   Goal Setting

Learn too much too fast	Review the steps	

Uptight or fearful	Relaxation
	Identify fear
		Supplementary Learning Insights
		   The Relaxed Rider
		Personal Insights
		   Worry, Anxiety & Fear

Stiff body	Relaxation
	Physical exercises
		Supplementary Learning Insights
		   The Relaxed Rider
		   Pilates for Equestrians
		   Yoga for Equestrians
		   T'ai Chi for Equestrians

Horse issues	Get qualified help with your training program	Find a qualified instructor

To practice this I did walk trot transitions with the overbend using a light active leg, expecting Applejack to respond immediately. Ms. Jones reminded me to relax as much as possible. At the end of the lesson she suggested a couple of books for me to read in addition to my riding homework.

Lesson 2

My overbending was excellent to inside and outside, so we added doing transitions between all gaits while staying on route. Ms. Jones felt I needed to understand the concept of reference feel, so we introduced this with the transitions. I found it easier to keep a steady contact with my reins after she held the reins as if she were the horse. I decided I wanted to ride Applejack with six ounces of rein contact. Leg contact was much more difficult because I discovered that I was constantly holding with my legs and pushing. We concluded that because Applejack did not respond immediately or willingly, I had developed a habit of holding in my legs. Ms. Jones explained that to get the correct reference feel in the leg we were going to do transitions with Applejack to get him off my leg. Once he was going forward, she asked me to give her a verbal description of the feeling I had in my leg. I thought for a moment about how it felt, and answered, "I don't know." Ms. Jones then asked me to do another transition, and then close my eyes and give her the answer. Wow, I thought, I can really feel with my eyes closed! "Bouncy" was the word that came to mind. During the rest of the lesson, Ms. Jones would ask me if he feels "bouncy," soon I connected the loss of the feeling with the need to lighten my leg and do a transition.

Lesson 3

We added more transitions, with periods of straightness between the overbends. By now I am committed to a planned route (I am a quick learner and am now dedicated to the process). I admitted that I had never insisted upon a specific route, and I often used a circle because my horse felt better than he did using the wall.

We also added the sitting trot—something that I had avoided like poison!

Lesson 4

Shoulder-fore was added. Ms. Jones caught me just doing the shoulder-fore so she explained the preparatory half halt. I had to be careful to keep Applejack in a slight overbend as one of the preparatory steps. I finally understood that I had been doing half halts in order to stay on route and do transitions, and in bending. We discussed the release step of the half halt as Applejack's reward for responding to my half halt. Ms. Jones was careful to remind me that the release was a return to my reference feel with the appropriate elasticity.

Lesson 5

All was going super, Applejack worked like a new horse, so we added transitions within the trot and in shoulder-fore. This exercise helped to get him suppler laterally and longitudinally.

Lesson 6

We continued to practice the same skills. Applejack needs to maintain this program as he strengthens his body.

NOTE: Sue was able to move quickly through the first few lessons of Stage 3 because she is talented and understands what she wants to do. Her problem was her lack of knowledge of the steps that were needed to direct the horse's forward energy. The rate of progress varies with the horse and rider combination. Applejack will move forward as quickly as his body gets suppler and stronger from the use of energy.

Crossroad 1

What do you want to do with your riding future?

OVERVIEW

The time has come for you, as a rider who has reached the end of Stage 3, to take a moment and think about your goals for riding. Horses, being the time-consuming and expensive proposition that they are, play a variety of roles in people's lives. Some riders dream of the Olympics; others wish to compete locally. Some riders choose to make horses their profession; others keep it as their hobby. Riding plans span the spectrum from occasional pleasure riding to international competition, and everything in between! So, what is the role of horses in your life? As we approach this riding review, we will ask you to consider many factors, including your interests, time, skill level, and financial situation—all of which will affect what your goals are and how you pursue them.

ROAD MAP

Do you know your destination?
What is realistic for you?
Consider your goals and interests.
Make a plan.
Investigate your plan.
Put your plan into action.

THE IDEAL ROUTE

In Europe, riders reach this Crossroad stage after Stage 5, not Stage 3. The reason is that Stage 5 riders' skills are highly developed and fine-tuned, with well-established basics underlying excellent technical skills. With these qualifications firmly in place, Stage 5 riders are ready to pursue a career in the horse training profession where excellence is expected on a daily basis. Perhaps the biggest difference between Europe and the United States in terms of equestrian education is that the Europeans have a "system" in place that the majority of horse professionals adhere to. With professionals all teaching basically the same system in the same way, riders receive the same instruction no matter where they learn to ride, so there is little confusion during the learning process. The standards are the same across the country in that horse shows reward similar performances and punish similar mistakes. Why is this so?

- In Europe, partly due to each country's cultural and financial support, horse sports are quite popular, making them viable and respected professions.

- The training of future horse professionals is supported by the government, allowing the government to have considerable control over the rule and regulations of the system.

- Professional horse trainers are required to proceed through the system, and the availability of the many riding schools and well-educated instructors and horses makes this possible.

- Entrance to the horse training profession is closely monitored by the government, and is strongly linked to their formal system of education.

ALTERNATIVE ROUTE

In the United States there exists no systematic approach to rider development.

- In the United States, there is no "one system" that is adhered to by professionals in the horse training industry. While this allows for new ideas and creativity to flourish, it also can be a detriment if professionals are not grounded in correct, proven principles before developing their own "style" and taking on students, horses and riders. For this reason, try to find an instructor who has a system that coincides with what is classically correct. The stages in this book can be a guideline.

- Because the entrance to horse training and rider education is not regulated in this country, riders can turn professional by just stating that they are a professional! This is a serious flaw in our system. Before you make a decision about your future, investigate your options employing the sound practices of an educated consumer. (See Chapter—Finding the Right Instruction Plan—Discovery Insights.)

- The availability and costs associated with a classical education differ greatly from region to region, and from state to state. Therefore, some riders do not have access to quality professionals, or, if they do, the costs may be prohibitive. You can create a plan that is realistic for you based on all the factors in your life. Lots of options are available if you are innovative and realistic.

- Learning to become correctly educated in equestrian sport takes time and commitment. Americans are notorious for wanting something "yesterday," so there is much pressure on instructors, trainers, and coaches to push ahead too fast, leaving the rider and horse lacking in some of the core fundamentals (namely, an educated and independent seat). Give yourself and your instructor permission to take the time to learn correctly.

Do you know your destination?

Recreational Riding

This type of riding deals with personal recreational needs. Usually, riders enter into recreational sports as a supplement to life, a way to unwind, relax, and do something that provides pleasure. Given that riding is by definition a time-intensive activity because of the needs of the horse, recreational riding tends to be more a part-time activity, and is often low key and noncompetitive. Sometimes recreational riders only ride in the summer months. Examples of recreational riding include trail riding, fox hunting, weekly lessons, or involvement in a local horse club that goes on camp trips or overnights. For many riders the most important benefit of recreational riding is the reduction of stress by having fun.

Competitive Riding

This includes competing locally, regionally, or nationally in the discipline of your interest. Competitive riding can be low key and fun, but the impetus for riders who like to compete tends to be the thrill of mastering a challenge or going "head to head" against other competitors. The thrill of victory seems to motivate many riders to seek out the competitive arena. It also can provide a social outlet, as horse shows are often a great occasion for informal get-togethers. The big difference between recreational riding and competitive riding is that, even at a local level, competing requires a commitment of time and money beyond the basics of just riding for fun. In addition, there is an added stress component inherent in competition, under which many riders thrive.

Professional Options

A Stage 3 rider can choose to enter the horse world as a professional in the United States. As long as you teach at a level at least two levels below your skill level, this can be a viable career choice. Some Stage 3 riders choose to start a beginners' lesson program; others enter the rewarding world of therapeutic riding for the disabled. Some Stage 3 riders go on to have successful careers as stable managers, farriers, horse sport journalists, or breeding managers, to name a few. However, if training and/or intermediate and advanced teaching is a career goal, riders are strongly encouraged to continue their own riding education up through Stage 5 so that they can be qualified to produce correctly educated students and horses. Sometimes Stage 3 riders enter the profession as a working student, intern, or assistant instructor/trainer, and develop their skills under the tutelage of another professional. If the professional is correctly educated, this can be the best of both worlds—earning a living and continuing your education at the same time! Finally, in the United States, riders can choose to pursue their educations at an equine college or an academic college with equine courses. Unfortunately, at this time, few of these schools offer riding instruction at Stage 4 and 5 levels.

What is realistic for you?

To answer this question, it will help if you first take a good look at your riding skills, your horse's skills, your time, your talent, and your money. The following list of questions can help you begin this process.

Education to date

- What has been your riding background to date?
- Do you need to fill in any gaps in your education?
- Do you have a firm foundation in the skills of Stage 3?
- Are you naturally curious, such that you will seek out new learning experiences?
- Where do you stand in terms of natural talent? Drive? Dedication? Work ethic?

Your horse's education and skill

- What has been your horse's training to date?
- Are there holes in his education?
- What is your horse happy doing? Does this match what you are happy doing?
- Can your horse be competitive doing what you want to do? For how long?

- Do you have a backup plan if you horse becomes lame or gets sick?
- Is your horse able to help teach you what you need to learn at this stage of you riding?

Time and Money

- How much time do you *want* to devote to riding?
- How much time *can* you devote to horses?
- What kind of financial resources are needed to help you take your next step? Is this possible for you?
- Are there other sources of financial support available to you?
- How much money can you personally devote to training and horses?
- Moving through Stages 4 and 5 requires access to good horses and good instructors. Do you have a clear picture of the realistic costs involved in pursuing such an education?

Goals

- How do you want to live your life? Do you want to make a living with horses, or do you want to make a living that allows you to enjoy horses as a hobby?
- What is it that you want to do in terms of your riding career?
- What are the next steps you need to take to get there? Are they possible?
- Are there alternative paths you can take to get there if the direct route is not an option?

 Evaluate your skill, time, money, aptitude, talent and goals to create a plan that insures a future filled with satisfaction, quality and growth.

Consider your goals and interests.

Let's take a look at all the information you have collected:

- Are you clear on your goals?
- What are the positive factors so far in your background regarding your goals?
- What are the obstacles you face?
- What are your riding strengths at this stage of your education?
- What are your weaknesses?
- Where do your passions lie?

- What do you need immediately?

- What needs will you have in the next year?

- What is a realistic role for your current horse at this stage in your education?

- Do your interests match your horse's talent? It is at this point that riders often need to make a choice of moving on to another horse or adapting their next step to one that is appropriate for their horse.

- What are your resources at this time in your life (financial, social, emotional, and horse-related)?

- Are there any limitations and constraints in your life that need to be entered into the equation?

- Who are your supporters? Mentors? Are your riding instructors, parents, and friends supportive of your goals?

Make a plan.

What do you need to do to put your decision into action? At this point, it helps if you can make a written list that lays out in black and white the plan you have been developing. This can be hard to do, as many people don't really want to see the actual roadblocks that are in front of them—it is so much nicer to keep the dream a dream and not bring it down into reality. This step is where most riders fail to act. Where there is no plan, often there is no progress. Don't let this happen to you! Think of your plan as giving you important knowledge, and knowledge is *gold*. Stick to what you know you can deal with. It is the unexpected or unknown that might take you off your path. So write your plan down—in any way or any format you can think of. Just write!

Investigate your plan.

Ask for an evaluation from two or more professionals. Based on what you have collected from your questions, arrange a time to talk with your instructor, and perhaps an educational consultant, or both, to discuss putting your plan into effect. This can be one of the most important things you do; they will give you solid advice based on their years of experience. Take advantage of all they have learned; it can save you from making common mistakes.

Put your plan into action.

Here is where you begin to *act*. The first step can be the scariest of all, or it can be the most exciting, with later steps being more effort and work. Remember that no plan is set in stone. Once begun, you may find that you want to change your plan, alter it, or scrap it altogether. But starting with a plan is the best way to go, as it guides you in clear directions. It does not force you to do what you don't want to do; it is meant to help you move toward whatever you want to do in life that will bring meaning, contentment, and happiness most of the time!

 It is very important to become aware of your assets as well as your limitations, so you will be able to make a choice that leads to success.

Tales From the Trip
Mary

I am Mary, and I started riding again when my daughter was ten. She loves horses, and I wanted her to enjoy her love of horses as I did as a junior rider. I decided this was a good time for me to rekindle my love of riding, and so we found a hunter seat instructor. I worked hard for two years to reestablish my skills that had been dormant for fourteen years. I discovered that I was bored and wanted to move back into the show ring. I met with my instructor to discuss purchasing a horse, and to my surprise she suggested that I explore some different options before I decided to buy a show hunter. My instructor suggested that I explore endurance riding and foxhunting. Surprised, but intrigued by the suggestions, I followed her advice. After considerable investigation I decided to take up foxhunting. I was able to enjoy hunting two days a week and go to shows with my daughter on the weekends. I had the best of both worlds.

Sandy

I am Sandy. I will graduate from high school in a year and I am torn by a difficult decision to have to make. I love horses and I am a Pony Club "C-3" and have dedicated most of my non-school time to riding; I think that I want to go to college and also explore social activities that I missed in high school. My parents have invested a lot of their time and money in my riding, and want me to continue to pursue riding when I am in college. I am not certain I will have time to do well with my college courses, ride, and have a social life. I don't want to miss out on any of these areas. Ms. Bailey spent time with my family and me and helped us find a solution. Ms. Bailey suggested an appropriate lease for my horse, just in case I changed my mind. During my second year in college, I realized that I missed my horse, but I did not want to continue with lessons and competition. Instead, I decided to trail ride and enjoy the time with my horse for fun when I visited home. Luckily, my parents were willing to take care of Rose.

John

My name is John. I love horses, and when I finished high school I was a Pony Club "B." I had the good luck of working with several of the "natural horsemanship professionals" and discovered that I loved to back and start young horses. With my parents and instructor I discussed the physical and financial dangers in choosing this career direction. Once it was clear that I was not to be deterred in following this love, my instructor put me in touch with several farms that had young horses. I contacted the farms and found the ideal intern position. I knew that if this did not work out, I could always go to college. I started out as an apprentice to the head trainer, and over the next two years I gained knowledge and experience. Today I am a well-respected handler and backer for young horses.

Ann

My name is Ann. I am a successful hunter/jumper rider and I love teaching at summer camp. My instructors thought that I had the skill to become either a trainer or an instructor. Without a doubt, after discussing options with my instructor, I was certain that I wanted to teach. Since I have ridden almost every day since I was six years old, I wanted to keep more avenues open. I decided to enter a college with an equine science program so that I could get my college degree, continue my competitive riding, and learn more about teaching. When I graduated I got a job that included some training and some teaching. I love my job and still have it today, twenty years later!

If you want to pursue a career as a trainer, instructor or in competition to levels higher than low hunters, novice eventing, or training level dressage, Crossroad 2 following Stage 4, is the time to decide if you have the time, talent, money and aptitude to continue on to Stage 5 which is an important part of the education you will need to achieve that goal.

STAGE 4—WHERE RIDER EDUCATION
And HORSE EDUCATION MEET

Big Picture

OVERVIEW

The first three stages of the Rider Education System helped you develop three important fundamental classical riding skills: 1) the establishment of a correct, basic balanced position, 2) a following, independent seat, and 3) a knowledgeable sense of feel acquired from the sensitive and correct application of the aids. At this point, you are now riding well enough to begin the process of shifting from a team to a true partnership.

In Stage 4, the emphasis shifts to the *quality* of the rider and horse partnership. The quality of your horse's performance is now even more dependent on the circular nature of influence between you and your horse. That is, how you ride affects your horse, which in turn affects how you ride. The concepts of looseness, throughness, and contact take center stage in your learning, with your riding abilities playing an active role in the quality of your horse's performance. Moving into this stage will be appropriate for the English disciplines as it is based on The German System of Education.

 Stage 4 demands an independent seat on the part of the rider, because there is more advanced coordination required.

 **ROAD MAP**

The German System of Education

What is the German System of Education?

What can Americans learn from the German System?

Why is an independent seat important at this stage of riding?

Rhythm

What is rhythm?

Looseness

What is "looseness"?

Throughness and Contact

What is "contact"?

What is "throughness"?

Putting It All Together

THE IDEAL ROUTE

As is the case in each previous stage, the ideal situation is one in which riders enter Stage 4 having established solid skills from the previous three stages. In this wonderful, ideal world you have developed a keen sense of "feel" for a rhythmic, round, and balanced horse, learned the proper coordination and application of aids, and developed correct muscle memory so that your mind is free to attend to the horse and not their position or use of aids. By this stage your timing is good, as is your body control and awareness. The result is that you now can confidently help fix horse problems that arise when riding trained horses. At this stage, you are now entering the "elite" levels of riding, which requires that you have an even keener and subtler sense of feel and coordination than in Stage 3. The focus of Stage 4 is on learning how to ride horses *consistently* "through" by maintaining rhythm, looseness, and a steady and quality contact. It is a necessity at this level that you have an independent seat because of the high degree of leg, seat, and hand coordination required to accomplish this task.

ALTERNATIVE ROUTE

Although the "ideal" learning experience would keep Stage 4 riders on well-schooled, educated horses that will teach them the "feel" of being really "through," the reality in the United States is that few riders get to experience this luxury. This is due to the constraints of equestrian sport in the United States. Many riders cannot find either an instructor or a horse that is educated enough to teach the skills at this level. Or, if they do have access

> *In the United States there is much freedom in the equestrian world, and thus anyone can call themselves a "trainer." However, common sense tells us that the fastest and most effective way to train young, or green, horses is to have them first ridden by riders who are well educated.*

to such training opportunities, the financial expense of doing so is prohibitive for most. The end result is that many American riders at Stage 4 take on "a project," which is usually a young, or green, horse to train. This is often the first time the rider has had access to a quality horse, and after all the years of riding and learning, these Stage 4 riders are anxious to "try it on their own" and use the skills that they have developed. This scenario, while not the "ideal" situation—or what one would find in Germany—can work out quite well if the Stage 4 rider works under the supervision of an educated trainer who can help guide them through the normal developmental difficulties that are common to the training process.

 In the German System of Education, riders would not begin to train horses until they have acquired the skills from Stage 5.

℗ POINTS OF INTEREST

- Horse training is in some ways a lot like human education. It proceeds most quickly and comfortably (for both rider and horse) when one member of the team is wiser and more educated than the other. For young, green horses, the ideal situation requires you, the rider, to be the teacher. Then you guide the horse through the learning process with tact and sensitivity.

- Horses are fairly simple creatures in terms of how they respond to their environments. A horse's brain is wired *to remember*. When a horse is first exposed to a new situation, results that produce pain will teach the horse to avoid this experience in the future, while results that are free from pain, or are pleasurable, will be approached willingly in the future. So, if a well-schooled rider is riding a horse and asks the horse clearly for a certain response, and then rewards the horse promptly for the correct response, learning is in progress. The same situation in the hands of a less experienced rider produces inconsistency in the asking, the rewarding, or both—causing the horse's brain to either record the wrong response or to become confused, recording many different responses. This results in frustration, anxiety, and possibly pain and fear for both the horse and the rider.

 It is *normal* to have periods of time in your training when you will have to go back and review or even reintroduce certain skills from earlier stages. This is true for both you and your horse throughout the learning process. Acknowledging the missing step, returning to it, and solidifying that step will help you (and your horse) stay positive and confident as you both progress in your training.

- The correct *basics* of horse training are a lot of work, but the correct foundation is the same whether you are training your horse to be a hunter, jumper, eventer or dressage horse. These basic principles must be mastered to have a confident partnership able to perform to maximum capacity.

- The theory behind Stage 4 of the Rider Education System is based on the successful German system, specifically the first phase in the Scale of Education for the horse. In order to successfully acquire the complex and demanding skills required in Stage 4, you will need to understand the order and foundation of the German System.

 # The German School of Education
A proven system of education

GOAL/DESTINATION

This chapter is designed to understand the German School of Education, what we can learn from it and why an independent seat is so important.

 ## ROAD MAP
What is the German system of education?

The German riding system as it exists today is not simply a manual on how to ride a horse, but rather it is a program of systematic education to develop the horse physically and mentally, with the goal of bringing each horse to its full potential, given its natural physical and mental aptitudes. The soul of this system is the Scale of Education, which is divided into two sections that have different goals. The first section includes the three requirements of rhythm, looseness, and contact, which develop a horse's ability to move forward with thrust. The second section includes the three requirements of impulsion, straightness, and collection, which develop a horse's ability to carry himself and the rider in balance. In our American system of education, Stage 4 focuses on the first three stages of the German system—rhythm, looseness, and contact—while Stage 5 emphasizes the last three stages. In actual practice, none of the six steps in the Scale of Education can really be considered separately as they are intimately related to each other. However, in order to be effective, they must be developed in a certain

Short History of the German System
by Stephan Kiesewetter

The German Equestrian Education System is a wholistic system. The system involves all aspects of the horse and the rider; this includes the physical aspects as well as psychological aspects.

The German system developed over more than 2000 years. The first roots of it are found in the work of the Greek philosopher Xenophon, called "Peri Hippekes," which means "About Horses." This work can be considered as the starting point of a systematic education of horses.

During the next eighteen centuries this system continued to develop, with lots of good as well as with a lot of curious and wrong developments. For example, the Duke of Newcastle, who was the inventor of the draw reins and the most popular horse trainer of his time, was able to educate a horse from a very beginner to an advanced horse within three month. Unfortunately, most of his horses suffered ataxia when the education was finished.

Löhneisen edited the first written version of the German Riding system in the eighteenth century. Nearly in the same time Francois de la Gueriniere, one of the most successful horse trainer of all Europe, invented the "coat feeling lower leg." This has had an incredible positive influence on the development of riding. These two masters can be considered the founding fathers of our training system today.

For a long time there did not exist any written version of the system; the knowledge was passed from generation to generation only by the spoken word.

In the beginning of the twentieth century two important books built the basis for our modern riding system: 1) The Gymnasium of the Horse, and 2) The Heeresdienstvorschrift Nr. 12 (Military Manual for Using and Educating Horses)

The first one can be considered the bible of the German horse trainers and professional riders. The problem is that it is very difficult to read and to understand, the reader needs a very exact knowledge about anatomy and physiology of the horse. The second is the basic version of the "Principals of Riding" and the "Advanced Techniques of Riding."

The result of this two-thousand-year process of development is an educational system which cares and is based on the rider/trainer listening to the natural abilities—physical and psychological prerequisites—of a horse.

order. This applies both to the use of the scale for daily training as well as to the long-term view of training the horse. In Germany, the Scale of Education is interwoven through every part of the horse's education. It is not only a long-term educational plan for bringing a horse from its initial backing to becoming a schoolmaster; the Scale of Education is also used as a daily training plan. With a solid understanding of the Scale of Education, riders are able to routinely test and check the quality of the horse's daily training.

What can Americans learn from the German system?

Most American riders do not have a system of riding and training available to them, as do the Germans and most other European countries. For many of you, progressing up the stages is a bit of a hit-or-miss proposition, filled with lessons and clinics from many different people holding many different viewpoints. The good news is that there is much in the German system that can be incorporated into your riding program that will help you develop you and your horse's true potential. Two main points stand out as being the most helpful and easiest to address:

1. The German emphasis on the development of a correct and educated seat. Riders here in the United States can follow this part of the system fairly easily by holding themselves to this standard. It is never too late to take lunge line lessons, no matter what stage you are in. All riders can learn how to sit on a horse properly and develop a seat that can follow the horse's movements freely, without grip or tension. *No single skill in classical riding is more important than the development of an independent, educated seat.* It is the foundation from which all good riders and horse trainers develop.

2. The German systems insistence on having a horse travel round and "through" before proceeding on toward the upper levels.

Riding horses truly correctly at the lower levels is one of the core reasons why the Germans are so successful in training horses; their training system does not allow horses to progress until they have the proper muscle development and physical strength to do so. This is only achieved by the horse being consistently and correctly ridden at the lower levels for whatever time it takes to develop that particular horse. Since each horse is unique, some need more time than others. Many times, Americans have become so enamoured with the "fun" of doing upper-level movements that the horse is pushed through the levels before the horse is physically or mentally ready, which automatically decreases the quality of the horse's performance. In other words, you need to avoid doing half passes, flying changes, and extensions on horses who are not demonstrating the basic fundamentals of being round and "through." So by simply adopting these two tenets of the German system, American riders can greatly enhance their riding and training abilities as well as their horse's performance.

"The goal of the Scale of Education is the "letting the aids through," which results in a horse that is a pleasure to ride because it is reacting to the "whistling" aids of the rider. This goal can only be achieved by a systematic, daily training process."
—Excerpted from Stephan Kiesewetter's lecture series.

Why is an independent seat so important at this stage of riding?

Independence in riders at Stage 4 is critical because you are being asked to work on the higher skills associated with riding horses consistently "through." This is a difficult task, and requires a high degree of tact, sensitivity, and timing in the use of the aids, *and a seat that is capable of following the movement of the horse*—all of

GERMAN SCALE OF EDUCATION CHART

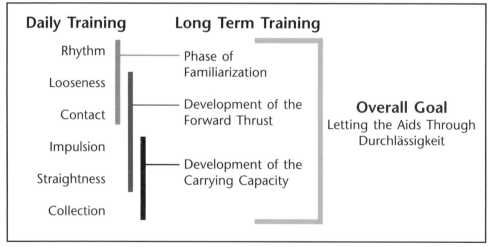

The Basics of Training for ALL horses

which is impossible if you are not independent in your seat. As well, in the United States, many Stage 4 riders take on a training project. Therefore, being independent is especially important for these riders as they need to have their bodies under their control in order to be of service to these young or green horses that they are beginning to train.

 In Stage 4, because your role in the partnership is to ride a horse through the training scale, you want to be independent so that your influence is fair, consistent, and positive.

O OBSERVATION POINTS

- Watch riders who have trained in Europe and who are successfully competing. Can you pick up the feeling and look of those riders who are truly independent, so that they are effectively communicating with the horse, no matter what the horse is doing?

- Watch videotapes of the European competitions and then compare that with the riders you see in your local shows. Pay particular attention to the quality of "throughness." Can you see the horses continuing to use their backs as they perform the more demanding movements such as half-pass, flying changes, and extensions?

- Watch a video of your own riding and try to pick out where you have a positive influence on your horse, and where you might be interfering with your horse's ability to move freely forward and with his back up and round. Does this knowledge match what you know and feel about your riding? What is your instructor suggesting you work on? Does this match what you see on your video?

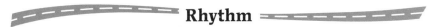

Rhythm

The foundation of the horse's training program

GOAL/DESTINATION

Rate and speed were discussed in the earlier stages. In Stage 4 they are taken to the next level, which focuses on the importance of developing a consistent, steady rhythm when riding. This is especially true when training a young horse through the first three stages of education of the German training system.

(RM) ROAD MAP
What is rhythm?

The definition of rhythm from the *Principles of Riding*[1] is: "The Regularity of steps and strides in each gait."

In other words, rhythm deals with the regularity of the footfall, how much ground each step covers, and the timing between the steps. Rhythm should be maintained while riding gaits, all lines, and during exercises. It is the basis for all further education.

"Why ride in rhythm?" You find the answer, when you consider two points; 1) the horse's use of his body and 2) your application of the aids.

Horses Use of Body

You want your horse to be able to work with maximum efficiency in using his body for performance and to avoid tiring the muscles. An exhausted horse can hurt himself during work sessions and be dangerous for himself and his rider. Muscles are responsible for the movement of your horse. You want the muscles in the horse's body working in rhythm so they don't get tired or exhausted during work. Muscles are built to contract and extend (stretch). The more rhythmically muscles are contracting and stretching the longer they can work without becoming tired. Under these circumstances the blood circulation and the metabolism works the best. The best example for this fact is your heart! It is a muscle and it works our entire lifetime (hopefully in rhythm!).

The more rhythmically you ride your horse, the longer your horse works without getting tired. Only muscles which are working in the physiological correct way are maintained by training. If muscles are not working in the right way they may develop incorrectly, causing stiffness or even atrophy, which prevents the whole body from working efficiently.

Application of Aids

The second important meaning of the rhythm lays in the application of aids. Every horse and rider has his won rhythm. For example a long legged, tall horse has a longer and quieter rhythm than a smaller horse; or a tall person makes bigger steps than a small person. The first step for you is to find the natural rhythm of your horse, and second is to synchronise your own movements (aids) to the horse's rhythm. Only if you find the horse's natural rhythm, will you be able to create looseness and relaxation. If you go too fast, you will receive only short and fast strides with less covering of ground and tightness in the back. If you choose a rhythm that is too slow, the hindquarters of the horse won't stay underneath the horse's body and the horse will fall on the forehand.

Rhythm is one of the main criteria of the quality of the education and training of the horse. If an on-going problem in the rhythm appears, there will be something basically wrong in the education and training of the horse. Directing your horse's energy by maintaining and improving the rhythm is the scale and mirror for the correctness of your horse's education.

—contributed by Stephan Kiesewetter

O OBSERVATION POINTS

Watch educated horses and riders as often as you can and consider the following questions:

- Are horse and rider working together in the same rhythm?
- Is the rider following the horse's rhythm or is he or she forcing the horse into the rider's rhythm?
- Can you see a difference in the way horses in rhythm carry their tails compared to those not in rhythm? The rhythmic horses are relaxed and swing their tails, while the horses lacking rhythm tend to either swish their tails back and forth, or hold them tight to their bodies.

Have as many of your rides videotaped as possible. When watching, look for the following:

- Are you matching your horse's rhythm at all three gaits? If not, are you too fast or too slow?
- Are you driving your horse all the time instead of having the horse bring to the ride the energy for you to direct and control?
- Are you giving your horse the opportunity to enjoy his own rhythm?

 **Looseness**

Looseness improves rhythm, and rhythm improves looseness!

GOAL/DESTINATION

To help you to understand the role of looseness in the process of training.

 **ROAD MAP**

What is looseness?

Looseness, often referred to as relaxation or suppleness, is a concept that is a bit elusive to grasp, as it does not simply mean relaxation or suppleness per se. Rather, the term looseness refers to the way a horse's whole circle of muscles works when he is traveling under saddle. Horses are considered to be moving with the quality of "looseness" when they travel forward with energy while maintaining some degree of straightness and rhythm. Most importantly, a loose horse will move with muscles that are free of tension and with joints that bend and straighten equally on each side of the body with each step. For a horse to be loose in the body, he needs to be focused on his rider. Distracted horses tighten their muscles. Riders of horses traveling with looseness describe the feeling as one in which the horse is traveling "across the ground" smoothly and with little effort. Every horse has a capacity to travel with looseness, but the degree and quality of their looseness will depend on many factors, such as age, training, natural freedom of movement, length of step, degree of stiffness, and individual conformation/muscular traits. A tight rider can reduce a horse's looseness. Stretching is essential to the concept of looseness, both as an exercise and as a test. As an exercise, horses that are asked to stretch become more longitudinally supple. As a test, once moving with looseness, horses will want to stretch.

🄾 OBSERVATION POINTS

Watch different combinations of horse and rider teams and consider the following questions:

- Does the horse look loose and elastic, or tense and uptight?
- Can you see the muscles of the horse's back swinging rhythmically in motion at all gaits and through all movements?

> **INDICATIONS OF LOOSENESS**
> - Content, happy expression in eyes, ears and movements
> - A rhythmically swinging back
> - A closed but not immobile mouth
> - Tail lifted slightly and swinging with movement

- Does the horse easily stretch out and down when asked?
- Does the horse seem to be covering ground with long steps and with ease?

- Can you see a difference in the horse's expressions (relaxed and happy versus tense and uptight)?

Watch videotapes of your rides, and consider the following questions:

- Does your horse look loose and elastic?
- Does your horse look like he is covering ground with ease?
- Is your horse using his back muscles properly, so that he is traveling "round"?
- Is your horse willing to stretch out and down when asked?
- Is your horse covering the ground with long steps and with ease?
- What does your horse's expression indicate about his emotional state?

 ## Throughness and Contact

Having a horse come "through" is the end result of the rider establishing rhythm, looseness and contact—in that order.

GOAL/DESTINATION

To understand the contact and its relationship to rhythm and looseness, resulting in throughness.

 ### ROAD MAP

What is contact?

Contact is one of the main forms of communication between rider and horse. The way contact is supposed to work is that the physical energy coming from the hindquarters (the engine) of the horse is captured, and then directed by the rider through the connection with the horse's mouth. The quality of this connection, or contact, depends on two factors: the rider's level of education, and the level of training of the horse. New riders are understandably a bit awkward and thus tense in their contact. Also, green horses often resist early attempts to take up contact. Therefore, the quality of a rider's contact tends to increase as both horse and rider become more educated. It is often said that riders spend their whole riding careers improving their contact; this is because contact has a direct relationship to the amount of engagement of the hindquarters.

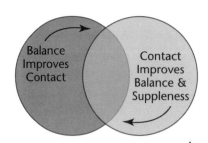

Once on contact, you work hard to keep your hands relatively quiet, and thus you are no longer able to move your hands wherever you want for balance. Instead, the hand is used for very clear communications and must stay steady, in front of the saddle (with a straight line from the elbow to the bit), quiet, and above all, must not "bounce." Over time you develop soft and relaxed shoulders, arms, hands, and fingers to create a steady, elastic-like feel in the reins.

Contact through the Stages	
Stage 1	Practice without interfering with hands
Stage 2	Develop light, following hands
Stage 3	Develop reference feel, light contact with some energy
Stage 4	Develop consistent contact, using reference feel, receiving energy from horse's hind legs ("on the bit")
Stage 5	Reference feel contact is elastic and powerful

The term "light contact" means picking up the rein with minimal weight in the rein, following the motion of the head and neck, much like what is required in hunter classes at horse shows. As you progress in their education, you learn to take more weight in your rein while maintaining the elastic quality of the connection. You also develop the ability to use your contact in various ways, such as to "hold," "resist," "stretch," and "soften," all which require a great degree of tact, timing, and feel. Over the course of your education, your hands become trained to be independent from your seat. Only then are you truly able to receive the energy of the horse.

In the stages of Rider Education System, the order of progression of contact goes from light contact,

"Balance and contact are complementary to each other: the better the balance, the better the contact. On the other hand correct contact will improve the balance and suppleness of the horse."

—Alois Podhajsky[2]

to light contact with the horse being round, to contact with a horse being truly "on the bit." "On the bit" is an expression that refers to a horse that is becoming balanced, and is engaged from back to front with his hind legs stepping well under his belly.

> *Over the course of your education, your hands become trained to be independent from your seat—only then are they able to receive the energy of the horse*

When the horse has an established forward rhythm and basic straightness, he will seek contact with your hand, and you provide it. Contact continues to develop as training progresses. Just as looseness improves the quality and consistency of rhythm, contact improves the quality of both rhythm and looseness. Indeed, the more steady and consistent the contact, the more the horse will travel in rhythm and with looseness; and the more in rhythm and loose a horse becomes, the easier it is to carry a quality contact!

> *Just as looseness improves the quality and consistency of rhythm, contact improves the quality of both rhythm and looseness.*

It is important to note that the quality of the contact does not happen only as a result of the rider. Similar to new riders, green or inexperienced horses tend to respond to their early experiences with contact with some anxiety. That is, these horses tend to get a bit tense and nervous when a rider first picks up the rein, leading them to stiffen up in their back, neck, and jaw. This response does not tend to produce a soft, elastic-like feel of the rein. With proper training, horses learn to respond correctly to a rider's hand by relaxing and softening in their back, neck, poll, and jaw, which then allows the rider to offer a relaxed and soft hand in return. The real gift of a trained rider on a green horse is that the trained rider can offer a quality contact even when the horse is being stiff, resistant, and tense. So the rider with educated hands can help a green horse accept the contact faster than an inexperienced rider can.

It is important for riders to learn the feel of contact on horses that accept the bit, and for horses to learn to accept contact by being ridden by riders who have learned the feel with "good" hands.

What is throughness?

Throughness is a word that attempts to capture a German phrase that describes the goal of all training sessions with a horse— "letting the aids through." In translation, this basically describes a horse: 1) who has a desire to move forward, 2) whose energy appears to move from the push of the hind leg through the horse's back and into the bridle, 3) whose muscles and joints are fully engaged, with the horse arching his neck using the "telescoping gesture" (which means that the middle neck muscles bulge, not the top neck muscles (*See Chapter—Biomechanics of the Horse Made Simple—Horse Insights*) and, 4) whose rider appears to be part of this flowing energy, in that they are simultaneously moving with and directing the energy flow. When all four of these qualities are present, a horse is said to be traveling "through." In order to create "throughness," a rider needs to be able to ride the horse in rhythm, develop a degree of looseness, and maintain a clear, consistent, elastic-like contact—in that order.

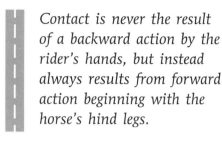

Contact is never the result of a backward action by the rider's hands, but instead always results from forward action beginning with the horse's hind legs.

⊙ OBSERVATION POINTS

Go to a dressage show and watch riders at the training and first levels and compare those rides that place first to those that place in the middle and last. See if you can recognize the horses that are correctly coming "through."

- Can you see the horse moving forward, in rhythm, with relaxation, moving his back, engaging his hind end, and gently arching his neck?
- Is the horse taking long, swinging, rhythmic strides, or are they short, fast, and choppy?

Watch the upper-level tests and notice which rides place first and which place last.

- Can you identify which horses are performing the difficult movements while "through" and which ones are just doing the "tricks" with stiff, flat, or hollow backs and lack of forward and rhythm?
- Can you see the middle muscles of the neck bulging, or are only the very top or bottom muscles of the neck the ones standing out?
- How freely forward does the horse move?

Watch a video of your own riding.

- Can you see your horse's muscles moving with looseness and swing?
- Does your horse look like he is freely moving forward?
- Is his back swinging?
- Is his neck gently arched, with his poll being the highest point on his neck? Or, is he "falsely" arching his neck by breaking at one of the lower vertebrae behind his poll?

Putting It All Together
Trip Review & Planning

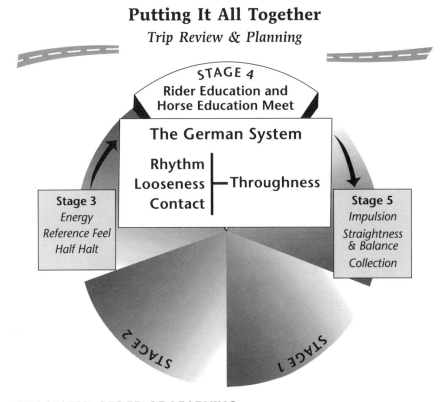

SUGGESTED ORDER OF LEARNING

In actual practice, none of the six steps in the Scale of Education can really be considered separately, as all of them are intimately related to each other. However, in order to be effective, they must be developed in a certain order. This applies both to the use of the scale for daily training as well as to the long-term view of training the horse. In Germany, the Scale of Education is interwoven through every part of the horse's education. Different exercises will develop a horse's coordination, balance, muscle strength (and mass), and responsiveness. Throughout all exercises, keep in mind the following qualities of a horse's performance:

-Rhythm
-Looseness
-Contact and throughness

• Exercises to benefit horse and rider in terms of rhythm, looseness and contact

EXERCISE BENEFITS FOR HORSE and RIDER		
Circle	Rider	Stay "on route" with horse following directions without aid of wall
	Horse	Balance, by carrying more weight on inside hind leg
Corners	Rider	Coordination, use of inside leg, release on inside rein, feeling of energy of inside hind leg going under seat with energy going to outside hand.
	Horse	Balancing and stretching body, engaging inside hind leg
Neck bending	Rider	Use of reins independently
	Horse	Supples stiff horse, acceptance of bit
Transitions "on route" with Bend	Rider	Feel straightness vs. resistance Coordination of inside leg to outside hand
	Horse	Supples and separates shoulder from hind leg
Riding cross-country	Rider	Improves balance, coordination, and timing
	Horse	Supples, builds muscle, encourages forward energy
Stretching long & low	Rider	Feeling of energy going forward, elastically through back
	Horse	Stretching and relaxing back muscles
Leg yield	Rider	Coordination of aids
	Horse	Supples horse via response to sideways, pushing aids
Turn on forehand	Rider	Coordination, one aid at a time
	Horse	Suppleness, response to aids
Shoulder-in	Rider	Coordination of aids
	Horse	Engagement and strengthening of inside hind leg Stretching of outside muscles
Grids and jumps	Rider	Increases feel, confidence in forward movement, speeds up reactions
	Horse	Forward, supple and having FUN

ROADBLOCKS

If you identify a lack of correct response from the horse, examine it to see whether it is due to a problem with your riding skills, the horse's training, or a combination of both. In all cases, go back, step by step, and reestablish the missing pieces in either your education or your horse's education.

Thought process for problem solving your roadblocks

1. Check your position; alignment, spring in joints and relaxation
   If you find a problem work on it and continue
   If you feel fine…

2. Check your horse's response to your leg and rein aids and relaxation
   If you find a problem work on it and continue
   If you feel fine…

3. Return to the previous step you learned successfully, confirm that you feel good in it
   If you have not solved your problem…

4. It is time to turn to your instructor to help you identify the cause (s) of the roadblock so that you can progress with your learning experience.

No matter whether it is the horse or the rider that has a problem, returning quickly to a step that you and your horse understand ensures progress. Sometimes this means jumping back and sometimes ahead, but the important piece is to always return to a successful experience for horse and rider. This keeps the learning process fun and encouraging so riders and horses stay open and receptive to new challenges.

Tales From the Trip

Pat, John, and Windjammer

I am Pat, an aspiring event rider. I have competed successfully through training level. My instructor, John, is the reason I am not going Preliminary. I respect John, but I am having a very hard time agreeing with him about this point. He insists that even though Windjammer can jump anything, he is not between the aids to safely ride Preliminary cross-country.

I finally asked John, "What is the problem, I don't understand?" because I know that Windjammer loves to jump and that my dressage is weak, but I love to jump and I hate dressage. After a few minutes of careful thought, John answered, "I don't believe it is safe to ride the obstacles with this degree of difficulty if your horse is not through and between your aids." Great answer, but I asked myself, "What does he mean?" Finally I got the courage to ask, and his answer was, "Let me show you."

He invited me to review some videos with him. The first video was a horse riding cross-country at one of the large events, getting over the fences but looking very uncomfortable. Suddenly there was a complex combination, and both horse and rider fell. This made a very big impression on me. Next he showed me the same series of jumps ridden with a controlled horse and rider who both looked so comfortable and confident. I could clearly see the difference. Last he showed me a clip of me jumping cross-country at my last event. The light went on, "Oh, I see, I need more contact and I need to ride my horse in a steady gallop rhythm." "Yes," was all he said. "What do I need to do to get to this point?" I asked.

Together we created a plan to work towards this goal. The competition we scheduled to make my Preliminary debut was in six months. In three months we would do a training event to see if I had made the improvement needed. John wanted me to strengthen my seat, so I worked every day without stirrups for 20 minutes. Windjammer and I worked on exercises to create contact with rhythm and looseness. My goal was to create a solid but sensitive connection where I could change the degree of contact but keep it elastic.

Three months later I did my training event. After the event John and I eagerly watched my video of cross-country on this course and my previous course. We also watched the dressage. I was *so excited,* I could see the change we made and was even more inspired to keep up the hard work for the next three months to prepare for my first Preliminary event.

The next three months passed quickly and I felt ready to go— my communications with Windjammer were so much better. We had a safe and *fun* event. I was tenth after dressage, the highest I had ever placed in dressage and I was clean in both cross-country and stadium jumping.

Thanks to John's strong beliefs, I am now enjoying the full program of training, including dressage, and I am looking forward to improving even more!

---

[1] Principles of Riding, Kenilworth Press, 2000, p.137

[2] Horse and Rider, Melvin Powers Wilshire Book Company, 1965, p.42

CROSSROAD 2—SELECTING A SPECIALTY AND MOVING ONWARD

OVERVIEW

Once you "graduate" from Stage 4 in the Rider Education System you enter another transition phase, where decisions are made about your equestrian goals and how you wish to pursue them. Riders desiring an advanced education, which can be equated to entering graduate school, will proceed onward to Stage 5. Other riders, for various reasons, will choose to stay at Stage 4 and enjoy the fruits of their labor. Regardless of your choice to stay at Stage 4 or move on to Stage 5, the partnership with your horse will continue to develop and grow. Reaching a Stage 4 level of riding competency and skill is an inspiring accomplishment. The dedication, effort, and time you have invested in reaching this goal is considerable.

ROAD MAP

Do you know your destination?

What is realistic for you?

Make a plan.

Investigate your plan.

Put your plan into action.

THE IDEAL ROUTE

Ideally, all riders who wish to pursue an advanced riding education would have the opportunity to do so. There would be no constraints or limitations based on external factors such as lack of financial support, quality horses, or time, or internal factors such as talent, attitude, and effort. For those who wish to pursue their classical training, the choices include a variety of options, such as traveling to Europe for training overseas, or staying in the United States, where they can seek out training privately or become an assistant trainer, intern, or apprentice with a qualified professional. No matter what option a rider chooses, the ideal situation would allow them access to highly trained horses, as well as quality young horses, so that their education is well-rounded

315

and thorough. And, ideally, time would not be an issue, so riders could pursue their training for as long as it takes for them to reach their potential. Now isn't this a fun dream?

 One of the harder things that you have to do is find a way to satisfy both your love of the sport and future educational desires within the limitations and constraints that "real life" imposes. You may find unexpected opportunities by being flexible and realistic enough to consider different approaches and avenues than you may have initially desired or expected.

 At this level it is essential to make an honest evaluation of both your and your horse's skills and talent.

ROAD MAP
Do you know your destination?

Staying at Stage 4

Stage 4 riding is considered advanced riding and requires a great deal of skill. At this point, you have logged serious hours in the saddle, and by anyone's standard, you ride very well. So now what? Stage 4 riders may choose to "park" at this stage for many reasons. For many, the reality of college or graduate school takes priority and riding has to take a back seat. For others, career and/or family demands preclude further intensive study at this time. And for still others, Stage 4 is a natural stopping point, as they don't wish to pursue the advanced education that Stage 5 entails. Being a Stage 4 rider offers many opportunities for horse lovers to enjoy their chosen sport:

- Riding for pleasure, improving your horse's talents in a gradual and progressive fashion

- Taking on the training of young horses, or reschooling older or spoiled horses

- Becoming a beginning or intermediate-level instructor

- Competing at the local level in lower-level competitions on horses you have trained or reschooled yourself

Advanced Competition

Many Stage 4 riders seek out more advanced competition. Being good at what you do is a great feeling, and testing this out in competition can be a real thrill. At this point, your riding skills are solid, and you are in a position to help your horse perform at his best. You are an active partner with your horse, and mastering the challenges of upper-level competition can be a wonderful source of inspiration, motivation, and confidence. However, with the demands of advanced competition come increased demands for rider and horse preparation. Some riders become spellbound by the thrill of competition and the glory of success. But the truth of it is that the day-to-day grind associated with the preparation is intense. Horses need to be kept in peak fitness and condition. This means an added investment of time and money. Riders also need to be in good shape—this means staying on top of your own fitness level *(See Chapter—Fitness for Riders—Fact Insights)*. Riders who compete at the upper levels often suggest the following to their students who think that they might like to follow in their instructors "big-time" competitive footsteps:

- Go to the schooling areas and stabling areas at the big shows and events to see the "less glamorous" sides to the sport. Talk to the coaches and competitors; ask what they like and don't like about their sport.

- Take the time to talk to top competitors to see what their daily lives are actually like.

- Offer to groom for instructors or other competitors you know, so you can get a well-rounded view of life at this level.

When talking about competing, there are issues you need to consider about your horse as well. To begin with, there is the issue of talent. Some riders fail to take their horse's talent (or lack of it) into consideration when choosing a sport or level of competition. Your desire to advance may be in direct conflict with the reality of your "best buddy's" limitations. This can be a trying and emotional time. The higher up you go in their education, the fewer the horses that can follow. Many times in your life as a rider you will come to a place where what is good for you is different than what is good for your partner. Deciding what to do in this situation is a personal decision, and the results may differ for different people.

There is also the issue of "career match." Does what you want to do match what your horse is good at? If you intend to advance through the levels of a particular sport, it helps to fully understand the physical abilities and mental demands your chosen sport will place on your horse. What are the most important qualities required? Each riding discipline favors slightly different talents. For example:

- Dressage—quality of the gaits, trainability of the mind.
- 3-day eventing—speed, boldness, and jumping ability.
- Hunters—jumping style and temperament.
- Jumpers—sheer jumping ability, agility and speed

So, what discipline is your horse most mentally and physically suited for? It might be helpful if you seek out different professionals' opinions, especially those that are successful in the sport of your choice. These people are in the best position to recognize your horse's future in the sport at the level of competition at which you desire to compete.

Professional Options

As a Stage 4 rider, you are well suited to consider a career in the teaching and training professions if you so desire. However, as we have stressed throughout this book, we strongly recommend that you teach and train two levels below your own training and skill level. This means that you are qualified to teach beginner and intermediate riders and to train young horses through the first few levels of dressage and jumping. As mentioned in Crossroad 1, there are many non-riding or teaching career opportunities as well. No matter what option you choose, it is important that you seek out continued training and support under the mentorship of a qualified professional. This may not be hard to do, as many instructors and trainers will be thrilled to find a correctly educated Stage 4 rider willing to work hard and learn, given that your skills can be quite valuable to them as an assistant trainer, intern, or working student. If you are serious about pursuing a professional career as an instructor and/or trainer, we strongly recommend that you continue through Stage 5, and that you seek out qualified trainers to provide you with an accurate and honest assessment of your skills and talent.

If you wish to proceed toward a Stage 5 education, honestly evaluate the demands, requirements, and resources that need to be available to you in order to pursue such an advanced education.

What is realistic for you?

Making choices can be stressful and fraught with many unknowns. Therefore, it is helpful to put down on paper what you do know, as this can help you see what you need to find out. This way, you can make your decisions based on factual information, not vague or wishful thinking. The following questions are designed to help you begin this process:

- What are your long-term riding (or teaching) goals?
- What are you current life circumstances? Do they help or hinder your long-term goals?
- How much of your life have you already devoted to your riding education? How much more do you want to devote to continuing your riding education?
- Do you have any "holes" in my riding education that need to be addressed before you move forward?
- What are your strengths as a rider? Do you have the talent, drive, and dedication to pursue advanced training?
- Do you have an appropriate horse (or horses) available to you?
- What is your current financial situation?
- Are you free to pursue your education at this time?
- Do you want to compete? At what levels? In what sport?
- What other demands and priorities do you have in life?

Choices are never easy. You may struggle with these important life decisions, such as choosing between continuing college education and riding (or doing both), or whether to live at college or become a working student and take college courses on the side. You may struggle with the choice between spending your money on a schoolmaster or continuing with your own horse while adding intensive training. You may find yourself asking the question, "How do I match my family's needs with my desire to ride?" or, "How can I balance my love of horses with the demands of my profession?" No matter what your choices are, it may be worthwhile to remind yourself that you are lucky to have choices! It is important that you are honest and realistic in your personal evaluations. Looking through the proverbial "rose-colored glasses" will only hurt you in the long run. There are many people out there who will tell you what you want to hear, if only because it serves them financially to do so. Seek out people who you feel will be direct, honest, and up front in their feedback as you perform your self-evaluation. Only by being honest with yourself can this process help you find success in your equestrian pursuits.

Make a plan.

Take a good look at the answers to the above questions. Now is the time to write up your plan. Your plan can be a rough draft, it can be short and to the point, or longer and very involved. No matter where you start, it helps to just write down that first draft. It then becomes easier to alter or modify your plan as you gather more information. Here are some ideas for writing up your plan:

- List your long-term goals, then step wise list the shorter-term goals it will take to get there, in the order in which you think you need to progress.
- List the positive factors in your background that you feel contribute to your goal.
- List the negative factors—things that may prevent you from reaching your goal.
- Write down a list of resources, including financial, social, emotional, and horse related.
- Identify alternative routes you might be able to take if your first choice route becomes impossible—think of it as an "option B" plan.

Investigate your plan.

Now that you have a written plan, it is time to share it with certain trusted people for feedback. This will be hard to do! But do it anyway . . . it can be truly amazing to see how much people will want to help you when they see that you are serious about planning for your future. Ask for an evaluation from two or more professionals, as each one may offer a valid but different viewpoint. Share this draft with your parents and friends as well, if appropriate. As you gather more information, adjust your plan accordingly.

Put your plan into action.

Taking the first steps of *action* can be the hardest. Remember, however, that no plan is written in stone, and that you can change your mind, go off in new directions, or go back and change routes along the way. The main point is that whatever your plan of action is, it provides you with meaning, a feeling of contentment, and happiness. Horses can be many things to many people, and at this stage of your riding career you are in a position to be in the driver's seat, and to work it out so that horses can be for you what you want them to be, even if you have to delay your gratification for awhile.

Tales From the Trip
Alex

I am Alex. During high school I rode several horses while working after school. I was a member of the Pony Club and attained my "B" rating, an achievement I was very proud of. I also competed in eventing quite successfully at the preliminary level. Although I have always been told I had "talent," and my instructors told me that I could pursue a riding career, I was committed to being a "normal" person and wanted to go away to college. Don't get me wrong! I *love* the horses, but I wanted them in my life as a supplement, not as the primary focus. I sold my horse, entered college, rode when I could, and entered the medical field. I am happy in my chosen profession, and I truly enjoy my horses as a hobby. No regrets.

Kate

I am Kate. I rode Western as a child and chose to take up a career in nursing. During my training I was unable to ride. Once I was working, I met a family which was very involved in dressage and they invited me to come to their stable. They treated me to a few lessons with their instructor on one of their well-trained Arabians. The lessons not only ignited my desire to ride again, I wanted to take up dressage. My husband and I agreed that I could take on a schoolmaster for my education, as I did not have access to regular instruction. T.R., the schoolmaster, served me well for two years until unsoundness took over. I struggled with what to do; my husband wanted to start a family and I wanted to get another horse. We could not afford a suitable horse, so we decided to find a good mare, and to lease and breed her in order to raise my own horse who would be ready to ride when my children were in school. This was a gamble, but it was what we could afford and we hoped it would work. We were lucky; our mare had a lovely foal, and when she was three we sent her to a trainer for two years. When I was ready to ride her, my children were in school and I had a wonderful time continuing my education with her. I am now competing her at local dressage shows and enjoying the challenge and the thrills.

Susan

I am Susan. All my life I have wanted to ride horses. As soon as I found out that it was possible to earn a living training horses, I knew that was for me. Unfortunately, my parents didn't agree! I went through Pony Club, achieved my "A" rating, and then took four years off to get my college degree (a deal I made with my parents). That time away from serious riding was difficult, although I did enjoy meeting "non-horsey" people and indulging my interests in political science and biology. After graduation, I sought out my old instructors and started riding again. I could not afford to ride full time without making money, so I looked into a working student program. I was able to find one with a top trainer, and for four years, I worked harder than I ever thought possible. I relearned much of what I thought I knew, had bad habits fixed, new habits confirmed, and after four years was invited to be an assistant trainer in another state. With the support and encouragement of my trainer, I accepted this position. I have never looked back, and am today competing at the upper levels on a variety of horses owned by my clients, and I hope someday to ride at the international level— who knows? Maybe someday the Olympics! Oh, I am *still* taking lessons, and I plan on traveling to Europe to study next year for three months.

Brian

I am Brian. I always wanted to ride and train for a living, but I became discouraged with the politics and hustle that seemed to accompany that life. After I reached Stage 4, I decided I wanted to use my skills and education to teach and train, but not at the higher levels. I went to work for a local teaching stable, and within 6 months had 60 students a week, was coaching and riding at horse shows, and was having a ball. I take in horses to train (I don't back them, but do start them once they are trained under saddle). I am learning all the time, and have recently been going to natural horsemanship clinics. I really enjoy this approach to horse training, and am beginning to incorporate it into my own program. My life is hard work, but I enjoy what I do, and my customers seem very pleased. I know I ride better than I did a few years ago, as I am riding and learning all the time. However, I have no desire to compete or show at the upper levels, or to train horses to that level. When my students get to the point where I can no longer teach them what they need to know, I refer them to a friend of mine down the road who deals with students at the more advanced levels. I guess you could say that I know my place—and I am fine with that. I am home at nights and most weekends with my family, and my two little boys are beginning to ride themselves! I really like my life.

STAGE 5—TRUE PARTNERSHIP DEVELOPMENT
Big Picture

OVERVIEW

In Stage 4 you were introduced to the first three phases of a horse's classical education—r ythm, looseness, and contact—which are designed to establish "forward thrust." In Stage 5 you are now introduced to the last three phases of the German Scale of Education—impulsion, straightness, and collection—which are designed to establish "carrying power." As in Stage 4, the quality of your skills as a rider has a direct influence on the quality of the horse's performance. At this level, you and your horse are working to develop a true partnership, one in which you both are working as one entity. In order to accomplish this, it helps if you have a thorough understanding of how straightness, balance, and collection are related.

 **ROAD MAP**

Impulsion

What is impulsion?

Advanced Straightness and Balance

What is the connection between balance and straightness?
What is advanced straightness?
What is balance?

Collection

What is collection?

Putting it All Together

THE IDEAL ROUTE

Again, as in the case in all the earlier stages, in the ideal world riders would have moved up through the first four stages of rider education on correctly educated horses under the guidance of a classically trained instructor. When this is the case, you will have developed correct habits and the "right" feel. Your "muscle memory" will be correct because of many repetitions of the "right" position and the "right" feel. You can now ride your horses "round" and "through" consistently by maintaining rhythm, relaxation, and a quality contact. Now in Stage 5, you learn how to ride with impulsion and straightness—again on a trained horse—which works to make their horse truly balanced. Finally, once your horse is really balanced, you will learn how to ride with collection.

ALTERNATIVE ROUTES

Two unique challenges for American riders deserve to be mentioned here. First, here in the United States, there exists the opportunity to purchase highly trained horses. Having trained horses readily available is a welcome development because it provides riders with the kind of horses that can help teach them to become classically educated riders. Unfortunately, this is not what always happens. Given our American tendency to want everything "fast" and "immediately," some riders are purchasing these well-trained horses and entering immediately into the upper levels of competition before they have developed the basics of a balanced position and an independent seat. The result of this premature entry into the upper levels is the development of "passenger riders" who can ride the movements, or stay on over big fences, but who are not able to help the horse in moments of difficulty, and in fact, often hinder their horse's ability to perform correctly. On the flat, this type of riding is at best not very attractive. Over fences, it is dangerous. While these riders may be asking their horses to carry impulsion and to collect, which are Stage 5 skills, these riders are actually struggling with Stage 1, 2, and 3 issues, such as the development of an aligned position, correct use and feel of the aids, proper timing of the aids, and most importantly, an independent seat. If you find yourself in this situation, seek out a qualified trainer who will help you fill in the gaps as you enjoy the education of your horse. This way your horse will be happier and remain sound for a longer period of time and you will be happier and safe.

The second challenge for American riders is the tendency for Stage 3 and 4 riders to take on a "project," and train a young horse (with the hope that this will someday be their 'good horse'). This is an ambitious undertaking, and is easily understandable from the rider's point of view- especially when one considers the cost of well-trained schoolmasters! However, as with any learning process, mistakes are made along the way. These riders, given that they are learning as their horses are learning, can often miss subtle but important training problems. As a result, these horse and rider combinations frequently exhibit training and position problems

To insure safety and soundness, riders need to be well grounded in the skills of Stage 1 through 3

stemming from a lack of solid basics. What is sometimes missing in the rider is a well-established basic, balanced position, or independent seat. What is often missing in these horses is a confirmed sense of "throughness," which can only come about as a consequence of habitual practice of the basics of rhythm, looseness, and elastic connection. When horses are not truly "through," they are tight and restricted in their bodies, especially through their backs. The problem with this (beyond the harm being done to the horse's muscles) is that riders have no choice but to struggle with position issues related to riding stiff horses. It is such a cycle! Rider influences horse—horse influences rider—rider then influences horse- and so on. As you can see, this circle can work both for the good and for the bad!

Fortunately for both of these situations, riders can, with proper instruction, fill in the missing gaps while progressing in their education. Once the basics are firmly in place, these riders find that all they have learned beforehand falls into place and they can proceed right along in their riding education. These riders tend to be eager students once they understand the need for going back and solidifying the basics. They are often wonderful and curious learners!

Impulsion

Rhythm, looseness, and contact lead to impulsion,
which is the development of forward thrust.

GOAL/DESTINATION

To help riders learn how to create energy in the horse that can be used to go forward with "thrust." This improved quality of forward movement can be used in all gaits and every aspect of movement to bring about the beauty that makes classically correct riding an art form.

(RM) ROAD MAP
What is impulsion?

Properly defined, impulsion is when a horse moves energetically from the hind end forward under his body with engagement and thrust. One way to visualize impulsion is to think of the difference between walking and skipping. When walking, there is energy expended to move you forward. When skipping, energy is still expended to move you forward, but additional energy is needed to move you forward and "up." This is similar to how impulsion works for horses. Not surprisingly, the word "impulsion," like "forward" and "engagement," is a source of much confusion. Instructors and riders alike have been heard to use these three terms interchangeably. You may hear, "You need more impulsion," when you are trotting lazily around on a training-level horse. The problem with this statement is that a training-level horse cannot yet work with true impulsion—but may indeed need more forward energy.

ⓟ POINTS OF INTEREST

- Working with impulsion is hard work. Think about how tired you would become if you skipped everywhere instead of walking. However, you would build up the muscles the human body needs to skip—mainly the leg and abdominal muscles. Horses also build up the muscles they need to maintain working with impulsion, mainly their stifles, gaskins, back, and hindquarter muscles.

- To move correctly with impulsion a horse needs a loose, swinging back.

- For a horse to move with impulsion you need to be able to ride with receiving contact, which your horse accepts willingly.

- Impulsion is directly related to suspension (suspension is a period within each stride where the horse is "in the air". There is *more* suspension when your horse is moving with impulsion because they are "lifting" their bodies higher up with each step.

- There can be no impulsion in the walk as there is no period of suspension in this natural gait.

- Impulsion is absorbed in the horse's back muscles (which *must* be round), allowing the rider to sit comfortably.

 If you push your horse too hard, even if rhythm is maintained, impulsion will be replaced with speed and suspension will be lost.

🅞 OBSERVATION POINTS

- Watch the amount of effort that working with impulsion requires of the horse by observing the degree of flexion in his stifles and hocks, and compare this to what you see when the horse is not working with impulsion.

- Watch other riders, and see if you can see the circle of muscles working as the horse is asked to move with impulsion. The horse's back (behind the saddle) should be swinging, the tail should be hanging down in a relaxed fashion, and the abdominal muscles should be seen contracting with the effort.

Through the stages, energy increasingly is used to create more engagement of the horse's hind end. When you combine engagement with straightness you get impulsion, and when you combine impulsion and straightness you will get increased levels of balance, until you finally have equal weight distribution on all four legs, which is collection.

- Observe other riders, and see if you can tell if the horses are being asked to work with impulsion without the prerequisites of rhythm, relaxation, and forward contact. Typically, such a horse shows a lot of tension, the tail swishes without rhythm, ears are back, and the rider appears to be working very hard, possibly even forcing the issue through aggressive movements of their seat or use of whip and/or spur. The contact will appear to be backward in nature, possibly even holding, or rigid.

Advanced Straightness & Balance

Straightness and impulsion create balance.

GOAL/DESTINATION

To understand how straightness and balance are interconnected.

🅡🅜 ROAD MAP

What is the connection between straightness and balance?

In general, straightness deals with the position of the horse's body, while balance deals with how a horse distributes his weight. How are these two concepts related? Simply put, the straighter a horse travels, the more balanced he becomes. And, the more balanced a horse becomes, the straighter you can ask the horse to be.

To better understand this concept, let's look at what a horse needs to do when first asked to travel straight. He is first encouraged to keep his body in line so that his hind hoof prints follow in the same track of his front hoof prints. When the horse succeeds in traveling with basic straightness, he will find that he needs to bring his hind legs up under his stomach, towards the girth area, to stay upright, especially in turns and on circles. These are the early steps of balance, and you usually feel a lightness and flow to the horse's movements that wasn't there before. As training develops, you begin to ask horses to perform movements on three tracks, such as shoulder-in. Horses who lose their balance will attempt to perform these movements by carrying more weight on one shoulder or another, which weights the opposite hind leg as well. To ask a horse to travel straight in these three-track movements is considered more "advanced," as the horse is being asked to keep equal weight on both shoulders and hind legs, much like the person carrying two water buckets down the aisle with equal weight on both sides of their body. When carrying one water bucket, you are forced to lean more on one side. You do not have equal weight on both sides of your body. When you carry two equal sized water buckets, you can walk a little easier, as you know you are "balanced" with equal weight on both sides of your body. Therefore, asking a horse to travel straight during the more difficult movements is actually asking the horse to become better balanced because the horse is being asked to distribute his weight more equally across his body. So, by riding a horse straight, you improve his balance. And, the more a horse's balance improves, the straighter the horse can be. Ultimately, you can ride a horse so straight (and engaged) that the horse actually distributes his weight *equally* on all four legs. This is called collection, and is the ultimate degree of balance a horse can obtain (not including airs above ground, like the levade and capriole).

What is advanced straightness?

After reading the above section on the connection between straightness and balance, you can probably answer this question yourself. But in case you are still a bit confused, let us clarify further. Earlier in this section we talked about straightness in basic terms: keeping a horse's body parts lined up so that both the hind and front hoof prints follow the route that the horse is on. For example,

Advanced straightness is when the horse maintains equal weight on both sides of his body, even when the line of the horse's movement differs from the line of the route.

if a horse is making a 20-meter circle, being "straight on the circle" means that the horse's hoof prints follow the bend of the 20-meter circle. Therefore, basic straightness can be described as when *the line of the horse's movement is the same as the line of the route.* In Stage 5, you are now ready to expand your perception of the term "riding straight." When talking about the more advanced concept of straightness, we must take into consideration those movements where the horse's line of travel (or route) is not straight in and of itself. For example, movements like the leg yield, shoulder-in, travers, renvers, and half-pass require the horse to be moving in one direction but positioning his body in another. The focus of straightness with these more advanced movements is now on how well the horse can distribute his weight equally on both sides of an imaginary line that dissects the horse down the middle, no matter what position his body is in. In reality, what we are talking about here is balance. When a horse is successful in carrying equal weight on both sides of his body, he is better balanced than if he was carrying too much weight on only one side (usually a shoulder and corresponding diagonal hind leg). Take for example the shoulder-in. The inside hind foot is in line with the outside front foot, and the route is being determined by the inside hind leg. Straightness in this movement is when the horse's weight is equally

Advanced straightness is concerned with how the horse carries his weight while performing the more difficult three-track movements, such as shoulder-in and half-pass. The "straighter" the horse travels, the more he carries his weight equally on both sides of an imaginary line that dissects him down the middle. When a horse distributes his weight equally, he is said to be in better balance. So, in effect, advanced straightness is balance.

distributed on both the left and right sides of his body. This can be determined by watching to see that the horse's hind and front hoofprints are falling *equally* on either side of that imaginary line that dissects the horse straight down the middle. So, if we could

> ## Straightness and Balance through the Stages
>
> Basic straightness (through 1st level dressage) – The line of the movement is the same as the line of the route. The horse begins to travel with early stages of balance.
>
> Advanced straightness (2nd level dressage and above) – The line of the movement may differ from the line of the route – the horse is considered straight when his weight is equally distributed on both sides of the imaginary line that goes from tail to poll. The horse can now travel with increased balance, as he is shifting more and more weight to the hindquarters as he distributes his weight equally side to side.
>
> Balance – the goal of all training, beginning with a horse equally distributing his weight on each side of the line he is traveling, to collection, where the horse is carrying equal weight on all four legs.
>
> Whether one is talking about basic or advanced straightness, the horse must remain balanced on the line of the movement while remaining on the line of route.

define advanced straightness in simple terms, it would be: *Advanced straightness is when the horse maintains equal weight on both sides of his body, even when the line of the horse's movement differs from the line of the route.*

What is balance?

What exactly we mean by "balance"? The confusion many equestrians feel about this topic is easy to under-stand. Just go into any riding ring around the country, and

Balance can be defined as a horse's ever-changing attempts to move most efficiently for the work being required.

ask the horse people there to define balance. Most likely you will hear as many definitions as the number of people asked! To make matters worse, there are many factors that can influence a horse's balance. To help clear up the misunderstandings and confusion surrounding the concept of balance, we provide the following definition, and then discuss that definition in terms of all four types of balance.

There are four distinct types of balance:

- Natural Balance
- Ridden Balance
- Lateral Balance
- Longitudinal Balance

Natural Balance

Natural balance can refer to two different scenarios.

- The way horses travel naturally "in the wild" or out in the pasture
- The way horses travel naturally within their gaits

In the wild

As described in the concept of the circle of muscles, a horse "naturally" balances when running around in the pasture by using his head, neck, and hindquarters as counterbalance measures. Keeping his back fairly straight, the head and neck swings in one direction, while the hindquarters swing in the opposite direction.

Factors Influencing Balance
• Conformation
• Terrain and footing
• Discipline or Activity
• Degree of difficulty of movement being performed
• Level of training
• Rider's position, seat & aids
• Amount of forward energy

This method is quite effective for the horse under many circumstances. He can wheel quickly (as we probably all have personally experienced), run fast, and stop on a dime! The only problem with this method is that is does not work very well when you climb on board. Your weight and center of gravity changes the horse's center of gravity, making it difficult for the horse to use the counterbalance measures of the forehand and hindquarters; thus the horse's efficiency when moving is lost.

Within gaits

Horses that are described as "naturally balanced" are those whose conformation traits make it easy for them to travel "level," in that they naturally want to travel with their weight fairly equally distributed on all four legs. This is often seen in the canter, during which the horse seems to maintain a regular rhythm and pace—not rushing, falling back to the trot or cross cantering. There are many different conformation traits that contribute to a "naturally balanced" individual. In general, these horses tend to be level across the croup to the withers, with middle to high set on necks. No one part of the horse tends to be grossly out of proportion. These horses usually move softly and lightly across the ground, and make the gifted athletes that can be trained most easily.

Ridden balance

Once you mount a horse, his balance must change to adapt to the additional weight. This is because the horse's typical methods of balancing himself are not very efficient with a rider on board. You also change the horse's center of gravity by sitting on top of the horse, making the horse, in effect, top heavy. Given that the horse does not want to fall down or lose his balance when under saddle, he must adjust how he moves. This adjustment is mainly one of body movement. Whereas the horse may feel free to swing his shoulders and haunches when running free, this way of moving is uncomfortable for both you and your horse under saddle. Therefore, you need to teach your horse to travel "straight" when being ridden, so that his hind legs step up underneath him, more towards the girth area. This is where the horse's natural center of gravity is located. If the horse can move his hind legs forward and inward towards the center of his stomach, he will find that he is now in a better position to balance himself with you on board. You will find that this method of balancing is much easier to ride than when the horse is shifting his weight in different directions! A horse's ability to balance himself under saddle is directly affected by the rider in many ways, such as the degree of balance, suppleness, elasticity, and education of the seat. So, the less educated the rider, the more the horse needs to know how to balance! This is one of the important reasons beginners learn best on trained horses, so that the horse stays balanced, which helps the rider develop balance faster!

Lateral Balance

Lateral balance is what we are referring to when we talk about advanced straightness. Lateral means "side," so a horse is considered to be balanced laterally when he carries equal weight on both sides of his body. In order to do this, the horse needs to carry an equal weight distribution on both sides of that imaginary line that dissects the middle of the horse from poll to tail. One way to bring this concept home is to think about carrying water buckets *(See Chapter—Stage 2—What is basic straightness and why is it important in Stage 2)*

Longitudinal Balance

Longitudinal balance refers to the horse's ability to shift his weight from *back to front.*

The horse can only shift his weight from front to back when his back is round.

That is, a longitudinally balanced horse attempts to redistribute the weight from his front end (where most horses "naturally" carry about 60% of their weight) to his hind end. In the early stages of balance, horses initially make very small adjustments to their longitudinal weight distribution. Most of their weight stays on their forehand, just a little bit less as the horse is asked to travel straight. As training progresses, horses begin to really shift weight off their front end, and to carry more of it behind. When the horse succeeds in shifting enough weight off the front end so as to have all four legs carrying equal amounts of weight, the horse is said to be collected. It is important to realize that this weight distribution *seldom* reaches a fifty-fifty split. At most, such as during the piaffe, the horse achieves a weight distribution of 55% to 45%, front to back. This is because the forehand carries more of the heavy bones and musculature of the horse than does the hind end.

Horses often go off route because they have lost their lateral or longitudinal balance.

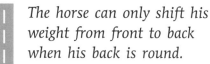 **Collection**

Collection is the result of riding with rhythm, looseness, contact, impulsion and straightness

GOAL/DESTINATION

To understand what collection is, and how it is related to straightness and balance.

 ROAD MAP
What is collection?

Collection is the *equal distribution* of the horse and your body weight on all four legs. This is difficult for a horse to achieve as a horse's center of gravity is under his girth area and thus he naturally has more weight on his forehand. Collection then, is the result of a straight, balanced horse now shifting his weight back while maintaining forward thrust and impulsion. Your hand receives the energy created from this process, making the horse more elastic, ready, and willing to perform with minimal aids from you. The hocks and stifle joints bend more and carry more weight. While the steps become shorter, they maintain energy, show more expression, and feel more powerful.

For example, think about jogging down a hill with the same speed and tempo as on a flat surface. In order to accomplish this you will find your weight shifting back, and your strides becoming shorter yet having more energy (thrust). You will feel this in your thighs, which are acting in a way similar to how a horse uses his gaskins.

🅟 POINTS OF INTEREST

- It takes a lot of energy and muscle building for a horse to work in collection. Not surprisingly, horses get tired easily when working with collection, which is why you do not want to work them for long hours at this level. Twenty minutes of doing exercises that demand increased impulsion may be all that is asked, followed by a cool down that allows the horse to finish with exercises that he can do easily, which maintains his self-confidence and enjoyment of his work.

- In collection the horse's steps become shorter without loosing energy.

- Working in collection requires regular training with appropriate exercises to develop the horse's muscles in the hind legs and back, so that the horse is *able* to carry more weight.

- The horse's poll rises as a result of increased impulsion or carrying capacity. It is important to note that the rider does not "lift" or force a horse's poll to rise. This happens naturally when the horse begins to carry more weight on his hind end.

OBSERVATION POINTS

- You can see the amount of effort impulsion requires of the horse by watching the degree of flexion in his stifles and hocks and compare this to when the horse is not working with impulsion.

- While watching horses in collection, do they look more uphill?

- While riding collection do you feel your horse more uphill and "ready to go"?

Putting It All Together

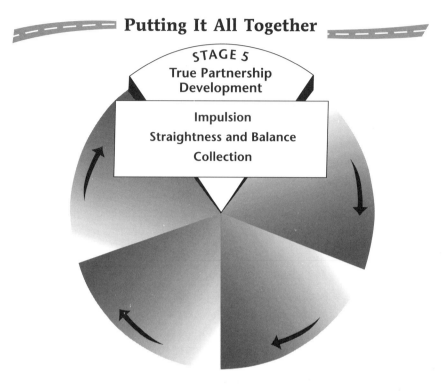

SUGGESTED ORDER OF LEARNING

As we stated in Stage 4, the six steps in the Scale of Education are closely linked, and are not as linear in practice as they appear in print. Each step builds on the previous, as well as improves the step ahead. Therefore, we suggest you think of these six steps as "in order," but allow yourself to move back and forth between them as needed:

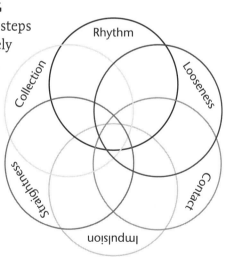

- Rhythm
- Looseness
- Contact
- Impulsion
- Straightness
- Collection

ROADBLOCKS

Roadblocks at this stage tend to include a combination of rider and horse problems that are interconnected at many levels. The demands placed on both members of the team are high, and require training and skill to execute. Both parties need each other to be successful. What tends to happen at this level is that the focus gets put on the horse, mainly because the horse is the one that is easiest to watch and observe, and also because it is the horse's performance that is ultimately being judged. In addition, because the training of the horse is so exciting, riders (and instructors) are tempted to focus singularly on the horse's performance as evidence of progress. It is important that the diagnosis of a problem and its correction takes into account *both* rider and horse issues. That is, it helps to remember that few problems at this level are "one-sided," involving only the rider or the horse. The nature of equestrian sport is that we can rarely separate rider and horse—they move together as one unit, thereby constantly influencing one another. The following is a list of common roadblocks horses and riders face at this level:

- Horse is not "through": The horse may be missing basic straightness or forward energy. The rider may have some stiffness and/or lack independence.

- Horse loses forward energy, especially during movements: The horse may be missing straightness, forward energy or correct conditioning. The rider's seat and/or arms may lack flexibility or independence, or the thoughts in the rider's mind are not progressively forward enough(positive thinking about what you are doing and the route energy and feel you want.)

- Horse loses rhythm: The horse may be pushed past his level of confidence, conditioning, or education. The rider might not have an established sense of feel or awareness and may be asking for too much.

- Contact is too loose or too tight: The rider might lack independence, or is holding some stiffness in upper body.

Tales From the Trip

Kim and King

My name is Kim. I was constantly frustrated because my horse, King, was always in a hurry. He listened to adjustments only for a step or two at a time. Todd, my instructor, insisted that the problem was that King was stiff and not using his back, and thus was always running to keep up with his lack of longitudinal balance. It happened that his stiffness was in the shoulder area, and in particular his right shoulder was bearing more weight in each step then any other body part. The rest of his body was trying to keep up with his right shoulder. I could not "feel" this, so Todd experimented with King and I. I had been competing at Preliminary-level eventing, going clean jumping for two years, but my dressage was always close to the bottom percentage. The first thing Todd had me test was King's ability to flex equally to both sides. I quickly felt the difference in his two sides. Once I felt this, Todd gave me exercises using overbending. Since King was so nervous we kept the exercises simple so that we could both gain confidence by understanding the exercise results through feel. I was so excited, as King now stopped running and required about 50% fewer adjustments. Over the next few lessons I added more and more exercises to King's program, each one building up engagement with the flexion. King's gaits started to become more and more beautiful because his back came up, and he stopped running!

Cindy and High Water

My name is Cindy, and my partner of ten years is High Water. We compete at Prix St. George, and are working toward Intermediaire. At a recent clinic, the instructor complimented me on the beauty of my horse's gaits but was disappointed in High Water's responsiveness in the upward transitions. For the past six months I had been working on developing more strength using exercises in collection. As the instructor described what she saw, I realized that I was thinking too much about collecting in a backward fashion, not in forward thoughts. In the process, I had not noticed High Water's slight delay in response to my leg. Sure enough, I was restricting the forward energy by not being supple enough with my seat and by locking my hips, which prevented High

Water from coming truly forward and "through" his back. I discovered that my body was restricting because I was thinking backward and not forward or as my instructor said, progressively. We practiced transitions with my seat being flexible and moving with my horse, keeping a receiving forward hand, and progressive mind. Within twenty minutes my collection was light, elastic, and forward and my upward transitions were prompt!

Supplemental Learning Insights

"The object of training for riders is to give them the physical and mental proficiency to be able to understand their partners, to execute with them all movements, to be able to follow them with skill and power and to be able to resist them if necessary." —Alois Podhajsky

Make your riding more comfortable for you and your horse by becoming a more efficient rider. Riders who explore this holistic approach to learning will discover that the learning process is much more enjoyable.

The supplemental learning section includes a collection of practices that increase your potential to learn both physically and mentally. Each of the practices endorsed has been time-tested and has proven to be very useful to riders. Perhaps one of the greatest gifts you can give yourself is spending time to research the "right" supplemental learning tool for you and putting it into regular practice.

Supplemental Training for Riders—by Sophie H. Pirie Clifton

The Relaxed Rider– by Russell H. Scoop

Pilates for Equestrians – by Janice Dulak

Yoga for Equestrians – by Linda Benedik

Tai Chi for Equestrians – by Jill K. Hassler-Scoop

SUPPLEMENTAL TRAINING FOR RIDERS
by Sophie H. Pirie Clifton

The following chapters will introduce you to a few exercise modalities that have proven to be effective for many riders seeking to improve their technical skills and their enjoyment of being on a horse. These chapters not only supplement what you do on a horse, but they also complement the ideas in the other chapters in this book on the mental aspects of riding. For example, riders who fear falling will find that working on their balance through T'ai Chi or exercises mentioned in the physical fitness chapter *(see Fact Insights—Fitness for Riders)* will have fewer moments when they are off balance and feel like they may fall; they will also have greater confidence that they can regain their balance and prevent a fall. Working on their flexibility will also give them confidence that, should they fall, they are more likely to be able to fall in such a way that they avoid injury. In other words, certain physical exercises can reduce their actual likelihood of falling or injury, which can then help the psychological work they are doing to reduce their fear; just as reducing their mental fear will reduce their physical tension and thus make them less likely to actually fall. Similarly, Relaxation Therapy complements the emphasis in the following and *Fitness for Riders* chapters on breathing techniques; if you can employ Relaxation Therapy when you are riding, you will find it easier to breathe with the movement of your horse and thereby deepen your seat and improve the timing of your aids.

The physical exercise supplements discussed in this book are only a few of the many that you might consider. One could consider all sports—indeed, all movement—as potentially beneficial to riders. The supplements that we have included are ones that we have seen produce substantial benefit to riders and whose basic tenets are in harmony with the basic physical needs of good riding: flexibility, balance, strength, alignment, breathing, reflexes, and heightened body awareness. The following chapters are designed as introductions to help you understand the ways in which different physical modalities can help your riding. To undertake any of these programs, we recommend that you seek out specialists, so that you learn correct form and which exercises will most benefit your riding. You may need to work with both the specialist and your riding

---

Finding the "right" instructor
A few important questions to ask

- What type of training has the instructor had?
- How many years of experience?
- What certification does the instructor have?
- Does the instructor continue to practice and learn?
- Does the instructor have experience with riders?

---

instructor to integrate the benefits of these programs into your riding. If the specialists you find for, say, T'ai Chi or Pilates, know nothing about riding, try taking them a video of elite riders in your discipline so that they can see what your sport demands of the human body. Or, if you are working on something particular like your fear of falling, show them pictures of people falling off horses to demonstrate exactly how demanding a fall can be on the body, and how legitimately scary to the psyche. People who are specialists in any form of physical exercise usually know a lot about anatomy, physiology, and motion dynamics and can see how these factors are involved in any sport just by looking at some pictures or video clips.

How then to choose among all the different exercise modalities that are available? Ultimately, more important than *which* program you choose is being conscious about *how* you learn that program and integrate it into your riding. Still, there are some programs that make more or less sense in certain situations. For example, many men are strong but lack flexibility, especially in their hips. I would probably not recommend more strength training to them, though I do recommend it to many women. But while I might like to encourage some men to take ballet classes to work on plies and turnout, many of the men I know who ride would dump me as their instructor if I suggested that! So, I might suggest they try yoga classes or ask a personal trainer at a local gym to give them a program of stretches to complement their weight training and target a few areas causing problems for their riding. Similarly, some riders whose

Supplements to riding need to be in harmony with the physical needs of good riding: flexibility, balance, strength, alignment, breathing, reflexes, and heightened body awareness.

Benefits of Supplementary Learning

Releases
- Tension

Increases both mental & physical
- Awareness
- Flexibility
- Strength

Builds
- Muscles

Improves
- Posture
- Balance and timing
- Coordination
- Performance
- Breathing

---

fearfulness and dynamic balance could benefit from martial arts training may not like the combat aspects of Tae Kwon Do and Karate; for them I might suggest they start with T'ai Chi and then try downhill skiing, river kayaking, or rock climbing to develop their boldness.

Speaking practically, though, the two most important things in choosing a supplemental exercise program are probably enjoyment and convenience. If we don't like it, we are not going to do it. And if we have to drive an hour to get there, we may well not make the commitment to integrate it into our already busy lives. Sometimes, though, it is worth taking a weekend workshop to give a program a try. Even one weekend of yoga can give you a number of exercises that you can do at home safely and effectively and can provide enough sense of the correct basics that you can then progress quite far by relying on books and videos. In contrast, Pilates and Gyrotonics, two machine-based exercise systems, are best done with the assistance of a trainer working one-on-one with you until you are quite advanced. Martial arts and dance are usually taught in groups and, for many people, their interactive nature is part of what makes these programs attractive.

Just as riding helps everything else you do in life, most everything else you do in life can help your riding. Even sitting in a chair in front of a computer *can* help your riding position, *IF* you sit correctly. As you learn more about riding, you will learn more about your body and its needs. And as you learn more about your body through experimenting with or studying non-equestrian disciplines, particularly those like T'ai Chi and yoga that emphasize body awareness, you will find it easier to determine what your riding needs in terms of supplemental physical exercise, learning, and fitness.

THE RELAXED RIDER
by Russell H. Scoop

Relaxation makes you more alert,
so you can focus on what's really important.
—Herbert Benson, *The Relaxation Response*

Relaxation is, ironically, both a natural state and a learned skill. You, like all riders and horses have your own natural state of relaxation in body and mind. Situational, environmental, or emotional stress interferes with your ability to relax. Achieving relaxation on a horse is essential for safety, learning, communication, performance, and enjoyment. Relaxation on a horse is a trained response of alert, responsive, mutual attention to the art of movement between horse and rider. The keystone of your ability to progress is a refined sense of feel, and the mortar is relaxation. Relaxation does not mean being floppy or having no tension at all in your body; but it is a state of mind and body that provides the basis for both partners to develop the correct muscle tone that promotes efficient use of the body and accurate communications.

You have been reading chapter upon chapter about the importance of feel and how to learn it. At the root of feel is relaxation, so how do you learn to relax?

First you need to discern whether your tightness is physical or mental. If it is physical, does it begin in your mind because you are worried, or protecting an old injury or a tired muscle group, or you are simply stiff in a joint or two? If it is mental, is it because you are worried, anxious, fearful, lacking confidence, or are thinking too much about what you are doing?

Like many people, you might have considerable trouble relaxing your mind because of distracting thoughts. A relaxed mind increases your ability to empty it and get 'into the moment,' it allows you to feel, to focus appropriately, to respond quickly and accurately, and to establish a balanced and effective seat.

From the first time you mount a horse, relaxation is a vital ingredient for successful riding. Loss of control and/or losing your balance are natural fears for all new riders, and for many

345

Benefits of all forms of relaxation
■ Overrides stiffness
■ Corrects crookedness
■ Helps rider feel more and think less
■ Calms mind
■ Calms nerves
■ Increases optimum focus
■ Improves coordination
■ Speeds up reflexes

who have had bad experiences. If you have the "right" experiences you quickly learn that you gain more control through relaxation. As you advance, relaxation and correct muscle tone become essential, as you need to communicate with more finesse and quickness.

Physical and mental relaxation can be pursued in several different ways. Depending upon your circumstances you may find one method more appropriate than another. Combine what you know about yourself with an investigation of the different avenues that promote relaxation. Learning relaxation is one of the most difficult challenges a rider faces. Stick with it, no matter how many road blocks you encounter. The end result is well worth the effort.

Tales From the Trip

Lori and Sunshine

Lori and her horse Sunshine looked great until Lori asked Sunshine for a leg yield. As soon as she did, both got tense. Investigating it, Lori discovered that when she was doing the leg yield she was very busy thinking of exactly what to do with each part of her body. Lori was a thinker, so this process was normal for her. We discussed that her thinking process might be slowing down or stiffening her body responses. Lori could not imagine this possible, but decided to listen to the clinician. The first step was to do the leg yield and think only of staying on route and moving body over, without worrying about forward or Sunshine's head position. This was very hard to do as Lori hated Sunshine's head going up in the air. After three tries she was reluctantly able to focus on route alone. As soon as Lori felt this, she added forward at the same pace. Again, she discovered that it took her several tries as she thought about what to do. When Lori was able to think about the route and forward, she discovered that her body was more relaxed. Odd, she thought, but Sunshine was clearly going more forward and the leg yield was much better. Lori decided two things from this lesson experience: first, she needed to learn to empty her mind, and second, she needed to think less.

May

May had a very stressful job working for the government. She had the same trouble as Lori when asked to do leg yields—she and her horse got tense. However, she and her instructor discovered that her horse did not go forward because May's joints were too tight. May asked, "Why is the problem showing itself during leg yield when I can sit the gaits fine when going straight?" She learned that when she asked her body to communicate the aids and follow the motion, her seat lacked the flexibility to do this. May decided upon a few exercises to supple her body and a few massage sessions to work on the tension that had accumulated in her body.

The Roads to Relaxation Response

A book cannot teach you to relax, you cannot make yourself relax, you must learn to relax. Following are several suggestions to help you investigate the best method for you.

Relaxation therapy for riders

This form of autogenic relaxation is a skill that enables you to utilize your own capacity to relax. Designed especially for riders, it teaches you how to quickly and effectively perform a quick body scan, seeking out and releasing excess tension. It involves taking a mental trip through your body, something that riders need to do while riding.

Deep breathing

Taking a few minutes to empty your mind and breath deeply, following your own breath can be very helpful. Some riders enjoy going to their horse's stall for a few minutes and breathing with their horse.

Walking

Some people benefit from going for a walk mounted or off the horse, which can be meditative in a natural setting.

Meditation

There are a variety of mediations methods one can choose to learn.

Massage

While massage is designed to help you physically by releasing tensions in the muscles and joints, many people report that it relaxes them mentally as well. Taking care of your body through massage and fitness training will help you perform effectively.

PILATES FOR EQUESTRIANS
by Janice Dulak

"It is the mind that guides the body." —Joseph Pilates

WHAT IS THE *PILATES* METHOD?

In the early 1900's, Joseph Pilates developed the "Art of Contrology." Now called the "Pilates Method", this system of body conditioning integrates strength, stretch, and control in specialized exercises that are initiated from the center or "Powerhouse" of the body. The exercises are performed using the six principles of Pilates:

- Centering
- Concentration
- Control
- Precision
- Flow
- Breath

The goal of Pilates is for the body to attain symmetry, grace, ease, and efficiency of movement while connecting the mind to the body.

Starting with seemingly simple exercises, Pilates requires a qualified instructor to guide the student through the levels from basic to advanced workouts with the systematic use of Pilates mat and apparatus work. Pilates employs eight pieces of apparatus designed by Joseph Pilates: Reformer; Cadillac; High Chair; Wunda Chair; Large Barrel; Small Barrel; Spine Corrector; and the Pedipole. All exercises are designed to create balance in the body by working toward equal strength and stretch in the muscles and symmetry in the torso. Attention to detail, correct form, and the six Pilates principles are paramount in a Pilates workout. A qualified instructor tailors a Pilates session to the individual. This ensures that the work actually begins to change the shape of the body by improving posture, toning, and elongating muscles and increasing flexibility in the whole body.

WHO WAS JOSEPH PILATES?

German-born Joseph Pilates began his study of the body and exercise at a young age. A sickly child, Pilates wanted to find a way to improve his own physique. His search led him to the study of the body and movement through anatomy, eastern philosophies of movement such as yoga, and Chinese acrobatic training. He also observed how animals moved and stretched and became a believer in the ancient Greek philosophy of the classically sculpted body. Coming to the United States in the early 1920's, he opened a studio in New York City. Here, his mat work and experiments with resistance training came together, and he developed the eight apparatus to further expand his method. Joseph Pilates and his wife Clare ran his studio until he died at the age of 87.

PILATES THEORY AND THE RIDER

The perfect harmony seen in world-class horse and rider combinations is something toward which all riders strive. For the rider to communicate clearly with the horse, she needs ultimate control over her body. This control allows for the freedom of movement and expression of the horse. If riding can be considered an art and a discipline, then one can readily see how the six principles of Pilates applies to the rider in her quest for harmony with her mount.

Centering

Work in the Pilates Method requires that all movement initiate from the center or "Powerhouse" of the body outward to the extremities. The "Powerhouse", as Joseph Pilates called it, is literally the abdominal and the gluteal muscles. Their use and strengthening are the priority of any Pilates exercise. Along with this principle, attention to the symmetry of the "Pilates box", or torso, creates the principle of centering. Each exercise requires the student of Pilates to work from her center while being cognizant of working symmetrically so that the muscles are working and developing evenly. This can benefit the rider by increasing her strength and ability to use the center of the body to initiate aids. Working to even out any asymmetries in her "Pilates Box" will increase the rider's ability to sit evenly on the horse's back with improved posture.

Concentration

As Joseph Pilates stated, "It is the mind that guides the body." All Pilates exercises require participation of the body and mind. The student will use the strength and control of one set of muscles to perform a stretching exercise for another set of muscles, while being aware of initiating the movement from the center of the body. This requires full mental focus. The practice of moving with concentration can make riders become aware of how they use their whole body from their center while on a horse. The ability to stay focused on the center while working towards a goal is a discipline for all forms of riding.

Control

From the practice of centering and concentration comes control. This is why Joseph Pilates called his method "The Art of Contrology." For a rider to control a horse, she must be in control of her own body. It takes control over the body to develop independent seat, legs, and hands. The practice of Pilates develops the understanding of control by requiring that each exercise integrate the mind and the whole body. What may appear to be an exercise for the leg requires the control of the "Pilates Box" as well as studied use of the arms and head. With the help of a qualified instructor, the student of Pilates learns to use the muscles correctly to develop symmetry and a balance of strength and stretch within the body. Pilates also helps to expand the range of motion within the joint while strengthening the muscles around the joint to help prevent injuries.

Precision

Although every equestrian activity requires a certain degree of precision, precise aids result in clearer communication with a horse. Joseph Pilates believed the body can be fine-tuned by exercising with accurate form and fewer repetitions. Work in this way can lead to maximum effect with minimum effort. With the practice of Pilates, the body becomes more toned and aware, able to respond to minute directions or corrections. Devoting concentration to precision in Pilates can help a rider learn to "whisper" an aid to her horse so that the horse may respond in harmony.

Flow

Free flowing movement of the body with strength and dynamics within an exercise, and during transitions from exercise to exercise, is the goal of every Pilates workout. To watch advanced students perform a Pilates workout is a study in grace, ease, and beauty. Here, the student has learned to allow energy to emanate from the center of the body and flow to the extremities without blockage by muscular or mental tension. The Pilates Method helps the student to understand relaxation within movements that require strength. During a workout, the student is guided to flow from one exercise into the next with the awareness that the transitions between exercises are part of the workout. This training can be beneficial for the rider to understand how the flow of the body's energy can be directed with precision, concentration, control, and centering. This practice can serve the rider to feel strength within the free flowing movement required of most equestrian activities.

Breath

All Pilates exercises require rhythm and breath. Each exercise has a deep breathing pattern with emphasis on the exhalation. The use of breath helps create the dynamics and rhythm for each exercise. It also encourages relaxation in the muscles, which allows the body to elongate and move with ease and grace. To learn to use the breath during moments of physical exertion can help the rider to remain relaxed, which, in turn, can help relax a tense horse. Understanding the relationship of breath to rhythm is also complementary to riding. Awareness of how breathing patterns can help maintain a horse's gait can make a difference in how the horse goes.

PILATES PRACTICE AND THE RIDER

For riders to benefit from the Pilates Method, they should seek qualified instruction. A qualified instructor will meet with the student in one-on-one sessions generally lasting 50 minutes. During the sessions, the instructor will continually evaluate the student's posture, skeletal alignment, habitual movement patterns, and muscular imbalances. Utilizing the whole Pilates system, the instructor will design each session to help the student address these issues. Ideally, the student will study Pilates two to three times a week in the beginning to make the quickest progress. If and when the instructor allows, mat classes can augment private sessions. When taught correctly, a Pilates session provides a deep workout, leaving the student refreshed and energized.

HOW TO FIND QUALIFIED INSTRUCTION

Because Pilates has become so popular, a myriad of Pilates studios have sprung up all over the country. It is wise for the prospective student to inquire into the instructor's qualifications. Certification programs in Pilates range from weekend seminars to intensive training courses requiring 600-hour apprenticeships with stringent testing. The most extensive teacher certification course is offered by The Pilates Studio® Inc. Information on where to find their certified instructors can be found at www.pilates-studio.com.

Tales From the Trip
Alisha and Arriba

Alisha is an adult amateur rider who has competed up to second level dressage and has a small, family-owned riding stable. She rides two to three horses per day, as well as doing general barn work, and considers herself to be in fairly good shape. Alisha has some previous experience in yoga and uses some of the stretches daily to help her loosen her muscles and joints before riding. She has just returned from a two-week adult dressage camp, where she rode their schooled warmbloods. She says that riding two horses per day there absolutely wore her out, and she was surprised to feel that her aids were not as effective as she thought they would be given her experience and previous training. She is riding a five-year-old energetic Thoroughbred gelding, Arriba, who is beginning first-level work.

First Lesson
Pre-lesson observations:

As Alisha and Arriba warmed up together, Arriba was tense and alert, jigging rather than walking, and often trying to pull the reins out of Alisha's hands. Alisha looked like she was sitting on top of the horse rather than sitting deeply in the saddle, and when Arriba pulled, Alisha's whole body was pulled out of position for a moment as she determinedly kept the reins the same length. Alisha had a correct position, and she fit Arriba well. Neither seemed to be fearful at all.

Greetings and Introduction:

After our introduction, I asked Alisha about her background. She said that she has always loved horses and has been riding since she was a teenager. She started riding hunt seat and jumpers and then took a few years off from riding when she got married and had children. She started riding dressage about eight years ago, and has mostly ridden older, schooled horses. This is the first young horse that she has ridden. Her goal is to train this horse correctly as far as he can go in the levels of dressage.

I asked her what they usually work on, and if the horse has any special problems. "He is often tense and has a hard time concentrating, so I usually begin by trying to relax him while keeping his attention. We do lots of turns and circles and transitions to get his attention. The most frustrating thing about riding him is that he always tries to pull the reins out of my hands. I hold them tightly so that he can't, but he pulls me forward out of the saddle."

"What about you? Do you have any physical problems?"

"Nothing major. Just some tightness and stiffnesses. I do some yoga before I ride to loosen my hips and hamstrings."

"How often do you ride?"

"I usually ride six days per week. I thought I was in pretty good shape, but I just came back from an adult dressage camp riding experience where I found myself exhausted after the first ride on their schooled warmbloods. I try to be light and nice with my horses, but when I rode those horses I really had to use a lot of strength just to get the horse to go. It was frustrating."

"Ok, well, lets see you ride for a little while and we'll go from there."

Warm-up and lesson all in one:

I watched Alisha ride around for a few minutes, and saw that while she had a basically good position, she had a weakness in her abdominals and lower back that was allowing her to be pulled forward when Arriba jerked on the reins. She was counteracting this by having a tight hold on the reins, which was transmitting tension up her arms and into her upper back. Arriba felt the tension and transmitted it through his neck and back. Alisha was trying to sit very lightly on Arriba's back to help him "relax," but instead this was causing her to be perched on top of him, which allowed him to maintain his tension too. After watching Alisha ride a little longer, I asked her how her ride felt today compared with other days. She said this was about normal, although he was a little more tense. After telling her some of the good things I saw happening between her and Arriba, I asked her how effective she felt her position and aids were. She said it didn't feel very effective or secure, but she was trying to be light and nice so that he would relax. I asked how she managed at the dressage camp, and she said that after the first couple days of kicking and pulling and feeling discombobulated, she had really started to engage her seat, but that it was so tiring to her that she couldn't maintain it for very long. While that helped on the big warmbloods, she wasn't sure how to apply it to her "hot" Thoroughbred, especially because she didn't feel very strong in her seat.

I said that I thought doing some unmounted work in Pilates might help strengthen her "powerhouse" and also help her develop control so that she could be precise about how strongly she wanted to use her seat with this horse. We discussed how a slightly stronger seat might actually give Arriba a sense of security which would help him relax, and it would also help her stay in the saddle without having to grip so tightly on the reins, thus allowing her to relax her upper back.

We went back to work, with Alisha focusing on using her abdominals to sit a bit more deeply in the saddle for short periods of time at the walk and trot. Arriba did begin to relax some more.

Review:

We discussed further what Pilates was (as Alisha had never heard of it before) and the role it would play in helping her communication with Arriba and her other horses. She was reluctant to commit as she had already been involved with yoga, but agreed to look for a qualified instructor and give it a try for six months.

Initial Pilates Sessions

In her first few Pilates sessions, Alisha's instructor taught her about her center, or as it is called in Pilates, "the powerhouse."

Alisha learned and felt how the abdominals can work to draw her energy toward her center, and she learned to use her gluteus in conjunction when needed to perform a certain exercise or find correct skeletal alignment.

Her Pilates instructor used the image of pulling the abdominals "in and up." At first this seemed contradictory to riding, as if this might take her farther away from the saddle, but as she tried it she felt that pulling the abs in and up actually lengthened the spine, so that the energy can flow *up and down* the spine, and also helped hold the alignment of the spine. In order to find these muscles, her instructor took Alisha through a series of exercises designed by Joseph Pilates. One of the first exercises Alisha learned is the "100's." This exercise entails lying on one's back, using deep inhalations and exhalations, a vigorous pumping of the arms for circulation, and maximum contractions of the abs and gluts while keeping one's lower limbs, head, and neck loose and relaxed. Other exercises that Alicia learned built on this concept, and she additionally incorporated stretching and control.

Second riding lesson (One month later)
Pre-lesson observations

Arriba is less tense and Alisha is more securely seated in the saddle. There is not as much tension in her upper body.

Greetings and update:

Alisha tells me enthusiastically about her Pilates sessions, and the difference they have already made. She said she was really tired after her first session, and that it had helped her realize how weak her abdominals were, which surprised her. Just having attention called to that area allowed her to make use of them more, especially to help her sit more deeply in the saddle. Arriba seemed to like her deeper seat too, and he was not pulling on the reins as much. I asked her what she wanted to do today and she said she wanted to continue to work on a deeper seat and a steadier connection with Arriba.

Lesson:

Alisha and Arriba began in the walk, and Alisha focused her attention on her "powerhouse," engaging those muscles to pull her deeper into the saddle. As she did this, she was more able to control Arriba's stride and to help it lengthen and become rhythmical. She was also following the motion with her hands, and Arriba began to stretch into the contact. Every now and then he would tense up a little or jerk the reins, and Alisha was able to maintain her seat deeper and stronger in the saddle, encouraging him to relax again and maintaining his walk strides with her seat. As they moved into the trot, she continued this kind of work. Her muscles were still not very strong, so sometimes she would lose the deepness in her seat, and Arriba's strides would get shorter and tense again. We would return to walk and regain the rhythm and relaxation in a gait that did not require quite as much strength from Alisha's developing abdominals.

Review:

I asked Alisha how she felt today. She said she felt much more in control, both of her own body and of Arriba's body. The combination of awareness of her weakness and the Pilates exercises to help develop the weak muscles gave her hope and a goal to strive for. We agreed that she would continue the Pilates lessons with her instructor weekly for the next six months.

Instructor's insights:

Alisha's open mindedness to trying something new in Pilates and her willingness to commit to the time it would take to develop these new muscles assured her success. Because she could feel the difference after just a few Pilates sessions, Alisha would be patient with herself and Arriba, realizing that the end of this particular problem was in sight, but would take a little time.

Six Months Later

Pilates:

After several months of individual sessions, Alisha's instructor had her begin coming to group Pilates sessions, and these classes gave her ideas for exercises she could practice daily at home in a relatively short amount of time to maintain the muscle tone she had developed. She felt much stronger and more stable, and a lot of her overall stiffness had disappeared. She felt that her whole life had a better quality, not just her riding.

Lesson:

When Alisha came for a lesson after six months of Pilates work, she and Arriba moved rhythmically and in harmony. Arriba showed no tension and stretched consistently into Alisha's hand. He responded to her seat during transitions between gaits and within gaits, and she remained balanced and secure throughout all their movements. Her leg yields were smooth and steady, as the aids originated from her seat rather than just from the lower leg, and her upper body was quietly following his motion with no residual tension in her upper back and shoulders.

Instructor's Insights:

Alisha was open minded and dedicated to following through on what she tried. She had already had experience in yoga and found it helpful in loosening tension in her lower body, but it had not helped her develop muscle tone. She was almost too relaxed in the beginning. Learning that tone is different from tension, and that the proper muscle tone in the rider's body can help lower tension in the horse's body, was an important insight for her. The Pilates program worked with her lifestyle and goals.

YOGA FOR EQUESTRIANS
by Linda Benedik

*Yoga is a timeless practice that provides a path toward
self-discovery, health, well-being, balance,
and inner harmony*

WHAT IS YOGA?

Union

Yoga, a word that means "union" or "to make whole," is as classical as horsemanship itself. By far, my favorite answer to the common question, "What is yoga?" is a quote from A.G. Mohan, author of *Yoga for Body, Breath, and Mind*. The author explains, *"The unification of two things, whatever their nature, is called yoga."* In considering this concept, equestrians can even think of riding— itself the unification of two beings, human and horse—as a very special form of yoga.

An Ancient Practice for our Modern World

Yoga is a timeless practice that provides a path toward self-discovery, health, well-being, balance, and inner harmony. Yogic teachings have been passed down for thousands of years and are still practiced to achieve the integration of body, mind, and spirit. In light of the stress-filled, fast-paced, technologically-altered lifestyles that many of us lead and the resulting disconnection that people often feel toward their physical bodies, as well as others and the natural world around them, it is no wonder that yoga is enjoying an explosion in popularity. Perhaps the rising interest in yoga shown by our society is symbolic of a widespread sense of separation from such elemental experiences as breathing, rhythm, movement, equilibrium, and the need for caring, nurturing, and centering in our lives. A diminishment in those areas may account for our extensive efforts to gain a healthy balance between body, mind, and spirit, and to feel at peace with our world.

East Meets West

An Eastern tradition, yoga has been adapted in many ways to suit our Western culture. Medical professionals, therapists, fitness trainers, and large companies often recommend yoga as a stress-management tool, and yoga classes are commonly offered at hospitals, health clubs, and corporate gyms. Yoga has also become an effective cross-training practice for athletes, helping to improve the performance of runners, skiers, tennis players, golfers and, now, equestrians. There are several distinct branches of yoga that all guide the practitioner toward wholeness, but the most practiced form of yoga in the West, and the ideal yoga form for rider cross-training is hatha yoga.

Hatha Yoga: Harmonizing Polarities

"Hatha yoga practice harmonizes the body, breath, and mind. This is an exhilarating, holistic experience, one mirrored in moments of intense physical pleasure, in playing sports or music, or in deep absorption in a mental task. A consistent, thoughtful practice of hatha can make that experience of integration available to us consistently."
—Kevin Hoffman, "Hatha Yoga,"
Yoga International Magazine (Reprint Series)

Hatha yoga is the most familiar path of yoga. It directs attention to the physical body through postures called *asanas* and breath control exercises known as *pranayama*. Hatha yoga enhances awareness, improves health and posture, strengthens, supples, and tones the body, and provides relaxed energy, focus, and vitality to the practitioner—qualities that are of great value to equestrians and enhance a rider's ability to cultivate the same general qualities in the horse. Through the integration of body, mind, and breath, hatha yoga teaches us to harmonize the *polarities*, or positive and negative energies, within ourselves. Concepts such as "give and take," "active and passive," and "punishment and reward" are examples of polarities recognized in riding and horse training.

Because we must learn to orchestrate the driving and yielding aids to communicate effectively with the horse, it is helpful to equalize these opposing forces in our own body first, through yoga. Equalizing abilities such as these can be enhanced by hatha yoga, which guides you to still your mind and *listen* to your body, to recognize limitations and accept where you are without judgment. As a result, your awareness will increase through your practice of the asanas, and you will know when to push and when to yield with your body, an important quality to bring to your riding. Harmonizing your polarities and building awareness through yoga teaches you to use your body more consciously and effectively in riding. This allows you to better influence the horse and ride with a balanced, intuitive feel, knowing when to be active and when to be receptive with your equine partner. It is also important for integrated riding instructors to consciously balance the driving and yielding techniques used in teaching to develop a feel for when it is appropriate to challenge a student or when a less impelling approach is best during a lesson.

Body Language & Awareness

Simply put, riding is a study in body language, both equine and human. To communicate fluently in both of these languages, we need to develop an understanding of the horse's language and learn to use our body as a communication tool. Horses communicate with one another through a nonverbal language of postures, expressions, gestures, and movements. We must do the same when working with them on the ground and on their backs. Through yoga practice, riders can learn to heighten their self-awareness first in an unmounted setting, without the distraction of being on an unpredictable flight animal. This supplemental bodywork is extremely beneficial for developing the physical coordination and subtle body language necessary for effective riding. Yoga teaches us to understand our body and identify our strengths and weaknesses, our asymmetries, and our energy blocks. With patience, dedication, and the guidance of integrated teachers, we can learn how our body functions on the ground and on the horse, where it is tight and where it is limber, and we can improve the body's ability to receive and respond to the horse's movement. And, with practice, we can learn to use our body to communicate with the horse in a silent, kinesthetic language of balance, alignment, posture, weight shift, and feel.

Breathing in Rhythm with Movement

The common denominator underlying all riding activities, and the most fundamental acquired skill in a rider's repertoire, is the ability to breathe in rhythm with movement. Although breathing is an involuntary physical function (we are all breathing all the time), it can also become *conscious* and, as such, is an invaluable rider tool for producing rhythm, focus, and inner calm within ourselves and our horse. Yoga is instrumental in teaching conscious, rhythmical breathing to riders and pranayama, the breathing exercises key to hatha yoga, are invaluable tools for building awareness and control of the breath. Learning to center the breath in the lower abdominal region and breathe diaphragmatically and rhythmically has far-reaching benefits for the rider. Through conscious breathing, a rider's center of gravity is located and maintained deep within the body's core. With deliberate, focused control over the breath, a rider can realize an enhanced rhythmical awareness that allows the movements of their own body to blend with those of the horse. Breathing deeply and consistently also instills a sense of calm through the rider's mind and body, which transmits to the horse. One of the most valuable gifts that yoga practice can offer equestrians is the deliberate focusing on breath work during unmounted yoga practice. Working with integrated riding teachers who can teach correct breathing techniques in a riding lesson expands the value of this gift, as nothing is more vital to riding than learning and teaching how to breathe in rhythm with movement.

Prepare for Riding

In practicing the asanas and pranayama, riders will realize how accessible yoga practice is and how easily it can be integrated into their riding repertoire. The breath work and postures, involving gentle stretch and slow movement, provide an ideal rider warm-up. Even a brief session of hatha yoga can help limber your joints, align your spine, and help you de-stress before riding. And the convenience of yoga is appealing for riders who have limited time to spend with their horses. Many of the standing and seated asanas, as well as the pranayama, can be practiced almost anywhere, at the stables in riding clothes, at a show or competition, and at home, school, or work to prepare in mind and body for riding. Just as we concern ourselves with properly warming up the horse, it is important to give the same consideration to our own body, and yoga works wonders!

Evolution in the Horse World

When conventional equestrians open their minds to new possibilities, there will be a greater appreciation among riders and trainers for the current changes being introduced in the horse world. As riders seek out holistic learning systems and alternative cross-training techniques, yoga jumps to the forefront. Although some riders and trainers may have preconceived notions about what yoga is and may shy away from it, with the increase in popularity of yoga in our culture today, it is becoming easier for equestrians to welcome yoga as a practical, beneficial form of exercise. The unmounted practice of asanas and pranayama will facilitate a rider's body-mind awareness, resulting in more rapid learning on the horse. Cultural misconceptions will be replaced as integrated riding teachers and trainers spread the news that conscious breathing and a centered body can benefit a rider's ability to remain in balance on the horse through all gaits and transitions. Stretching or holding a yoga posture is far less mysterious than one may have thought. More than ever, equestrians are rejecting rigid, forceful training systems and taking responsibility for their own learning experiences and enjoyment with horses. Yoga integrated with riding provides a path that many have been seeking: a fresh, gentle approach that encourages the gradual, sequential progression of riding skills. In reflecting on the ongoing evolution in the horse world, we see that, while our integrated techniques may be innovative, the desired results are not new at all. We have simply returned to our roots and continue in pursuit of the essence of horsemanship described by Xenophon thousands of years ago, asserting our fair leadership and cultivating unity with the horse in the spirit of kindness, knowledge, and compassion.

Conclusion

Despite the pronounced differences in riding theories and techniques that exist in the horse world, we riders and teachers, amateurs and professionals, artists and athletes comprise a global community of equestrians and horse lovers. What bonds us together is our deep, soul-level desire to connect with the horse in synchronous, rhythmical movement on the path to achieving union. The responsibility of riding instructors is to serve as guides for equestrians seeking union, as it is a complex, although thoroughly rewarding journey. Regardless of technical style or discipline, teachers who blend yoga and riding instruction will contribute ease to the equestrian education process, allowing union with the horse to become more accessible and attainable for riders. Just as yoga fosters union between rider and horse, it also enhances the connection between teacher and student as, by it's very nature, yoga helps to diminish our separateness.

Getting Started

It is possible to embark on a self-study of yoga, using books and videotapes for guidance, but it is even more beneficial to practice in the company of others, guided by a qualified yoga teacher. Yoga studios abound throughout the country, and many provide an atmosphere that fosters relaxation and tranquility. Others slant toward a more powerful yoga and an intense physical workout that causes the body to generate heat during practice. Whatever your preference, there are ways to creatively integrate yoga into your daily life, your riding, and your lesson plans. Short, frequent practices, upon rising in the morning, during short breaks throughout your day for stretching and conscious breathing, before and after you ride, and before bed at night, are invaluable tools for riders. Nothing will inspire riders and instructors more than the greater pleasure achieved from riding with increased consciousness that encourages a deeper connection with the horse who will appreciate the positive changes that yoga brings to your riding as much as you do!

Tales From the Trip
Why I Chose Yoga

For over two decades, I have been teaching riders to effectively use their bodies to communicate with horses. In my observation of the mainstream horse industry, I've seen far too many trainers advancing riders without first providing them with a secure foundation in riding basics. In contrast, I chose to specialize in developing a rider's seat and position, working with those new to riding as well as with long-time riders who may have significant gaps in their learning. I noticed similar traits among the majority of amateur riders: lack of correct breathing techniques, an unstable center of gravity, muscular tensions, joint inflexibility, and an underlying disconnection typically generated by fear, anxiety, and lack of balance. To address these issues and facilitate the learning process of my students, I initiated unmounted programs for equestrians in the mid-1990's. *Yoga for Equestrians* became a popular feature of the Harmony With Horses Balanced Riding Program, and the book of the same name was written and published internationally not long afterward.

Both my own study of hatha yoga and my training as a singer taught me the benefits of relaxing and centering through conscious, abdominal breathing and demonstrated the fundamental importance of flexibility, alignment, and balance. I knew yoga in an unmounted setting would help my riding students more easily acquire this awareness. At the same time, I consistently integrated breath and body work into their riding lessons. Blending yoga with riding instruction has augmented my work as a riding teacher, and I am continuously amazed by my students' easy, steady progress.

Yoga has also benefited me as a rider by helping me attain new levels of awareness and symmetry, and a stronger body-mind connection. While personally incorporating yoga practice, I have moved up to the FEI levels of dressage, combining a more fine-tuned physical mastery with an increased ability to balance, supple, and influence the horses I ride. All of the horses in my program communicate consistently how happy and content they are and continuously show their gratitude with their willingness to take part in the education of riders. This is a huge reward in itself! As an integrated riding teacher and student of the horse, my journey has been incredible, and my experience of union continues to expand every day.

Tales From the Trip

Virginia and Buddy

Virginia sought to fulfill her childhood dream of riding horses and someday having a horse of her own. As an adult, she began taking lessons at a traditional riding school but realized that their competitive training methods did not resonate with her. Virginia intuitively sensed that riding could be a holistic experience, and this prompted her to find a new teacher and a new path. When Virginia integrated yoga with her riding, it not only facilitated her equestrian learning, it benefited her entire life.

Background

After raising her son and establishing successful careers in both the entertainment and graphics fields, Virginia had reached a point in life where she felt it was time to honor her Self on a deeper level by fulfilling a childhood dream. This impulse led her into the horse world, where she embarked on an exciting journey. Her case study spans a period of four years and illustrates how the synergy of yoga and riding combine in an extraordinary package.

Prior Riding Experience

Before I met Virginia, she had been riding for six months and was a working student at a prominent riding school. She believed the instruction she would receive there in English riding would be top-notch. She started taking group lessons and remembers her early trainers as having "a dictatorial, masculine approach." Virginia was dissatisfied by their unsympathetic, forceful manner of teaching as she and the other adult beginners in her class were presented with tasks they weren't ready for, such as jumping. Although she never fell off, Virginia often felt anxious, especially after witnessing riding accidents. She was disheartened at times, particularly when some of the adults in her group were driven to tears of frustration and humiliated in their lessons. Virginia didn't want to quit riding, but she knew there had to be another way to learn. She began researching and reading all she could that pertained to riding and horsemanship. The first book she read was *Centered Riding,* by Sally Swift. This gave her encouragement and confirmed that her intuition was right; there were, in fact, trainers who advocated a gentler, more holistic, even spiritual approach to riding.

Lesson

Greeting & Introduction

Virginia discovered the Harmony With Horses Balanced Riding Program and our unmounted workshops in Yoga for Equestrians, the Alexander Technique, and Guided Visualization through local advertising. She contacted me and described her current riding situation, as well as the supportive path she sought with horses and her long-term goal of owning her own horse. I shared my riding and teaching philosophies with her and outlined the integrated programs I offered, both mounted and unmounted. I invited her to schedule a private lesson with me, to experience balanced riding blended with yogic practice and principles, which she was eager to do. Although she mentioned she had been practicing yoga on and off since college, I surmised that she had not yet realized how truly beneficial yoga was for equestrians.

Pre-Lesson Observations

When Virginia arrived for her first private lesson, I observed she was slim, petite, and in good physical condition. She had just turned fifty and, in addition to riding and taking occasional yoga classes, Virginia did Pilates. In her work as a graphic artist, she sat throughout her workday in front of a computer. When asked about physical restrictions, she identified chronic tension in her lower back, hips, neck, and shoulders. I commended her for choosing an integrated path to riding, and I suggested that our unmounted program of Yoga for Equestrians would be ideal to help alleviate the stiffness in her body. Then, Virginia was introduced to "Buddy," the Arabian gelding she was to ride, and I explained how he and I would work together to teach her on the lunge line. Although she had been riding for six months previously, Virginia had never been lunged and was understandably nervous.

Yoga and Riding—First Lunge Line Lesson

I felt it necessary to start Virginia on the lunge line to give her the opportunity to relax, center, balance, and align her position in the saddle before taking up the reins. Holding the reins would have added a complicated element at this early stage, contributing to upper body tension and interfering with Virginia's ability to feel, listen to her body, focus, and center. Without reins, she was free to move her hands about while modifying and improving her posture and balance in the saddle and experiencing new sensations in her body as it connected more closely with the horse. I knew that the tightness she had described in her body would certainly influence her riding and, because she was still rather new to equestrian activities, she had the underlying anxiety and fear typical of beginners. Lungeing would provide the most direct path to enable Virginia to release tension through the breath work and gentle stretches that would encourage awareness, release, and relaxation in her body. It was also a great way for Virginia to integrate yoga with riding in a more specific manner, allowing her to listen and pay more attention to her own body, as well as increase her awareness of the horse's body.

The Halt: Center, Relax, Breathe

Beginning at the halt, without reins or stirrups, I asked Virginia to take a deep breath. As she inhaled, she lifted her shoulders toward her ears and drew her breath into her chest, common symptoms of a novice rider's tension. Her shallow chest breathing alerted me to the probability that her aerobic endurance would be low and her breath irregular when the horse was moving. I mentally noted that it was likely she habitually held her breath when concentrating on riding, which would cause her to lean forward over her center of gravity while in motion on the horse. To help her breathe more fully, reawaken her awareness of her center, and relax her body-mind, I led Virginia through some fundamental breath work. While practicing pranayama, or breathing exercises at the halt, with her eyes closed, I attended to Buddy so that she could center herself completely and establish a conscious feeling of being grounded to the horse. I observed Virginia's breath become deeper, fuller, and more rhythmical. She exhibited increased levels of relaxation in her body as her tension dissipated, and she began to feel more comfortable and safe, sitting on a horse with her eyes closed, without reins or stirrups, for the first time.

The Walk: Stretch, Align, Freedom of Movement

Virginia was now centered, focused, and sitting beautifully at the halt. She then moved Buddy into walk, and her legs started to grip the saddle. I discussed the importance of not interfering with the horse's freedom of movement and asked her to release her legs to gravity, letting them dangle passively. I then presented Virginia with Yoga in the Saddle warm-up stretches, first for her legs, then her upper body, to open joints, increase range of motion, improve vertical alignment, and to promote relaxation. Scissors Stretch, Frog Legs, Arm Raise with Breath, Seated Side Stretch, and Twist were some of the mounted exercises introduced to Virginia at the walk. I periodically asked her to quiet her thoughts and focus on her breath and to consciously match her breathing pattern to the movements of both her body and the horse's. Virginia affirmed that she was feeling more connected and "in sync" with the horse.

The Trot: Release, Absorb, Move in Rhythm

Using stirrups, Virginia next proceeded at the rising trot. While posting, I observed her pushing off her toes and tightening her knee grip. To help release her knees and improve the shock absorbing qualities of the joints, I asked her to ride in a two-point position. As she adjusted her legs so that they were supporting her, I encouraged Virginia to maintain an awareness of her breath to keep her center of gravity deep in her abdomen, her movements rhythmical, and her body relaxed and soft. I could see tension dissolve as her joints softened in this position and, although she started to tire after awhile, I watched as Virginia's body became softer and more united with the horse in rhythmical movement. She was pleased at the new sense of balance she felt in her riding.

Final Relaxation: Centering Breath, Reflection

As is also customary in an unmounted yoga practice, at the end of her lesson, I led Virginia through a final relaxation at the halt. With her eyes closed and stirrups dropped, I asked her to take a few deep, abdominal breaths. I guided her awareness sequentially through her body, as she released even more, reaffirming her centeredness and connection to the horse. I then asked Virginia to open her eyes and reflect on her lesson. She shared her excitement for this gentle, integrated approach to riding, as it was exactly what she had been seeking. She was amazed at how much she had learned about her own body . . . and she had fallen in love with Buddy.

Instructor's Impressions

Virginia initially rode with a narrow fork. Like a clothespin, she sat stiffly at the walk and trot, her knees unconsciously gripping the horse's sides, pushing her seat further away from the horse's back. She also tended to draw her legs up, closing her hip angles and creating a chair-like seat. In prior group lessons, her body undoubtedly had resorted to this "survival technique" to stay secure in the saddle. In the rising trot, her knee grip intensified as she pushed off her toes and braced her ankles. She was shocked to learn that she had been riding this way for six months, and that her previous trainers had never brought this to her attention. This tightness in her inner thighs and hip joints began to diminish with the mounted warm-up stretches, and Virginia realized that her legs had never stretched this way before! Throughout her lesson, I encouraged her to work slowly and gradually, not forcing her body in any way. I assured her that all riders are faced with physical challenges when learning to ride, and each rider improves at their own pace. I reminded her that this was a non-competitive environment and to simply enjoy her journey as a rider.

My initial evaluation of her seat indicated that Virginia was not yet secure enough to canter, even though she had cantered before in her group lessons. I assessed that Buddy's canter would have been more active than any canter she had experienced previously. Therefore, her mounted work focused on the halt, walk, and trot to deepen her seat, keep her safe, and build her confidence.

Yoga and Riding: Unmounted Programs

Although Virginia had never before heard of "unmounted programs for riders," the idea struck a chord with her and attracted her to Harmony With Horses. Shortly after enrolling in private riding lessons, she began attending weekly Yoga for Equestrians classes and HWH Monthly Clinics. She quickly realized that a dedicated cross-training practice off the horse supplemented her lessons and enhanced the body-mind awareness, balance, flexibility, and suppleness needed for riding. Virginia found that weekly yoga classes helped her to achieve short-term riding goals such as releasing her lower back tension and limbering up her stiff right side to sit more evenly on the horse and provided a great way to prepare and warm up for her lessons. Clinics featured unmounted workshops in Yoga for Equestrians, the Alexander Technique, guided visualization, relaxation techniques, and rhythmical training followed by small group riding lessons. This format enabled Virginia to practice what she had learned in an unmounted setting on the horse and brought increased levels of relaxation, flexibility, and awareness to her riding. Group lessons were fun and gave her the opportunity to interact with other riders, sharpen her observation skills, and learn visually by example. She enjoyed all of the HWH unmounted programs but was particularly drawn to Yoga for Equestrians.

Yoga and Riding: Virginia's Progression
Year One

Virginia began an integrated program at Harmony With Horses. This included private riding lessons and unmounted programs, monthly workshops, and weekly Yoga for Equestrians classes. Her mounted work consisted primarily of lunge-line lessons, paying particular attention to her seat and position at the halt, walk, and trot.

- Five months: In addition to lunge lessons, she added a semi-private lesson and was riding 2x weekly.

- Nine months: She began leasing the lesson horse, Buddy, and riding 3x weekly. She continued her lunge lessons, added more arena practice riding, and occasionally enjoyed the mountain trails on Buddy.

Year Two: Virginia entered her first English horse show on Buddy in walk/trot equitation and pleasure classes and took home a ribbon! She continued to improve her seat, balance, alignment, and security on the horse and started enjoying bareback riding and cantering. Her unmounted yoga practice continued to enhance her body awareness, facilitating her equestrian learning and advancing her riding abilities.

- Six Months: Virginia purchased Buddy and fulfilled her childhood dream!

Year Three: As a teacher's assistant, Virginia began warming up riders on the lunge line with Yoga in the Saddle exercises. She started teaching unmounted Yoga for Equestrians at HWH and intensified her study of Hatha yoga at a Los Angeles area yoga studio. Her riding evolved to include additional canter work and dressage fundamentals.

Year Four: Virginia's integration of yoga and riding has become a lifestyle. Yoga practice has provided her with pronounced health benefits, such as increased strength, flexibility, relaxation, body-mind awareness, higher energy levels, and stamina, all resulting in a more balanced life and better performance in the saddle. She continues to teach unmounted Yoga for Equestrians classes at HWH and is now assisting with workshops, demos, and presentations at out-of-town clinics and trade shows. Her relationship with Buddy has grown deeper and more fulfilling, and she rides 5x a week. She has become a competent horsewoman and has expanded her knowledge of horse keeping, training, equine health, nutrition, holistic horse care, and equine bodywork. Her riding abilities continue to evolve, and Virginia enjoys a variety of mounted activities including trail riding, vaulting, and introductory level dressage.

Instructor's Conclusions

Virginia was highly motivated to succeed at riding. Like many novice equestrians who begin riding in their adult years, she brought with her a lifetime of habitual behaviors, expectations, and dreams in addition to the understandable anxieties and fears that novices experience when sitting on a large, unpredictable flight animal who speaks a language they don't understand yet. By integrating the patient, nurturing, compassionate nature of yoga into my teaching, I was able to help Virginia safely work through her fears and develop technical skills in an atmosphere of encouragement and self-acceptance. Her riding has steadily progressed throughout the brief time she has spent in the saddle, and integrating yoga with both my teaching and her riding has helped Virginia become a safe, conscious, capable rider. Virginia states that yoga and riding are so blended together in her life that they influence everything she does in a holistic, positive way. Now that she's realized her dream of owning a horse, Virginia continues to learn and grow, setting new goals for herself and her equine partner as they expand their partnership on their journey together.

T'AI CHI

by Jill K. Hassler-Scoop

When performing, you should be centered, balanced, stable, and comfortable. —Master Wu Yu-hsiang

Traditional forms of t'ai chi date back at least 600 years. There are many styles, but all can be traced back to China.

T'ai Chi has a lot in common with riding. Both require a flexible working arrangement with gravity. Successful performance demands similar mechanics of movement, postural alignment, and energy management. Both disciplines train people to move economically with precision. One of the best ways for a rider to become more in tune with movement and balance is by practicing t'ai chi. Like riding, t'ai chi is about engaging and directing energy. T'ai chi's smooth, flowing, circular movements integrate muscle and mind connections. T'ai chi and riding share many of the same complex, precise, deliberate actions. These actions, when practiced effectively, become second nature to riders.

> *Even a human being needs gymnastic training for smooth and supple athletic action.... balance is the basic requirement for pure and impulsive paces . . . It is the rider's art to balance the centers of gravity of horse and rider so that the former is not disturbed in its movements.*
>
> —Alois Podhajsky

Tales From the Trip

Angie and Wildrose

Angie attended a clinic that included exercise off the horse as well as lessons. During the first exercise class, which was taught by a T'ai Chi instructor, Angie realized that she could not do the simplest exercise with the group. Embarrassed, she gradually made her way to the back of the group, trying very hard to keep up. The discussion after the class proved very interesting for Angie: several of the riders asked questions about similar difficulties they were having while doing the exercises and their challenges while riding. Angie listened intently but was too embarrassed to speak up. The next day in her lesson she decided to ask the instructor about a possible connection between Wildrose, her horse, not moving freely forward, and t'ai chi. With the instructor's help she began to understand the connection between the two and asked for a private session. During the session Angie experienced feeling energy for the first time in her life. She was so excited! She got on her horse after the lesson to see if she could "feel" his movement. She could feel a little more but nothing remarkable. So on the third day of the clinic, Angie and her instructor created some exercises that would help her feel the energy that she could practice at home. Angie went home with two exercises to do on her horse and three unmounted exercises. Angie practiced three days a week, and within a month both she and her regular instructor agreed that Wildrose was moving forward beautifully.

Suggested Reading & Biblioraphy

PERSONAL INSIGHTS

Ackerman, Sherry L., *Dressage in the Fourth Dimension*, Xenophon Press, Cleveland Heights, OH,1997.

Belasik, Paul, *The Songs of Horses, Seven Stories for Riding Teachers and Students*, J.A. Allen, England, 1999.

Calais-Germain, Blandine. *Anatomy of Movement;* Eastland Press, Seattle, WA, 1993.

Carter-Scott, Ph.D., Cherie, If Life is a Game, These are the Rules, Broadway Books, New York, 1998.

Hassler, Jill K., *Beyond the Mirrors, A Study of the Mental and Spiritual Aspects of Horsemanship*, Goals Unlimited Press, Huson, MT, 1988.

Hassler, Jill K., In Search of Your Image: A Practical Guide to the Mental & Spiritual Aspects of Horsemanship, Goals Unlimited Press, Huson, MT, 1993.

Jenkins, David B. *Hollinshead's Functional Anatomy of the Limbs and Back* WB Saunders Co, 1998.

Maltz, Maxwell, *Psycho-cybernetics*, Pocket Books, New York, 1973.

Swift, Sally, Centered Riding, Trafalgar Square Press, 1985.

HORSE INSIGHTS

Smythe, R.H., The Mind of the Horse, The Stephen Greene Press, 1965.

Seunig, Waldemar, Horsemanship, Doubleday and Company, 1956.

Tellington-Jones, Linda and Bruns, Ursala, *The T.E.A.M. Approach to Problem Free Training,* Breakthrough Publishers, 1988.

FACT INSIGHTS

Bailey, Covert. *The Ultimate Fit or Fat: Get in Shape and Stay in Shape*, Houghton Mifflin, 2000.

Batmanghelidj, F. *Your Body's Many Cries for Water: You Are Not Sick, You Are Thirsty!* Global Health Solutions, 1997.

Belasik, Paul. *Dressage for the 21st Century* ,Trafalgar Square, North Pomfret, VT, 2001.

Davis, Adelle. *Let's Eat Right to Keep Fit* ,Harcourt Brace Jovanovich 1988.

Egoscue, Pete. *The Egoscue Method of Health Through Motion,* Harper Collins, 1992.

Holmes, Tom. *The New Total Rider: Health & Fitness for the Equestrian,* Half Halt Press, Boonsboro, MD, 2001.

Meyners, Eckhart. *Fit for Riding,* trans. Elke Hermann, Half Halt Press, Boonsboro, MD, 1992.

LEARNING INSIGHTS

Savoie, Jane, *That Winning Feeling! A New Approach to Riding Using Psychocybernetics,* Trafalgar Press, North Pomfret, VT, 1992.

TECHNICAL INSIGHTS

Hassler-Scoop, Jill K., Equestrian Education, Professional Development for Instructors, Goals Unlimited Press, Huson, MT, 2002.

Klimke, Ingrid, Cavaletti, The Schooling of Horse and Rider Over Ground Poles, Lyons Press, 2000.

Kursinski, Anne, Riding and Jumping Clinic, Doubleday, 1995.

Lindgren, Major Anders, Major Anders Lingren's Teaching Exercises: A Manual for Instructors and Riders, Half Halt Press, Boonsboro, MD, 1998.

Lock, Sylvia, The Classical Rider: Being at One with Your Horse, Trafalgar Square Publishing, North Pomfret, VT, 1997.

Lock, Sylvia, The Classical Seat: A Guide for the Everyday Rider, Trafalgar Square Publishing, North Pomfret, VT, 1988.

Lunging: The German Riding and Driving System: Book 6, Kenworth Press, England, 1990.

Morris, George, Hunt Seat Equitation, Doubleday, 1990.

Podhajsky, Alois, The Complete Training of Horse and Rider in the Principles of Classical Horsemanship, Melvin Powers Wilshire Book Company, North Hollywood, CA, 1965.

Podhajsky, Alois, My Horses, My Teachers, Trafalgar Square Publishing, North Pomfret, VT, 1997.

Suenig, Waldemar, Horsemanship, Doubleday and Company, New York, 1956.

The Principles of Riding: The Official Instruction Handbook of the German National Equestrian Federation, Kenworth Press, England, 1997.

Von Dietz, Susanne, Balance in Movement: the Seat of the Rider, Trafalgar Square Publishing, North Pomfret, VT 1999.

Zettle, Walter, *Dressage in Harmony,* Half Halt Press, Boonsboro, MD 1998.

Wofford, James, Training the Three Day Event Horse and Rider, Derrydale Press, 2000.

SUPPLEMENTARY LEARNING INSIGHTS

Relaxation for Riders

Kabat-Zinn, Jon, Wherever You Go There You Are: Mindfulness Meditation for Everyday Life. Hyperion, New York; 1994.

Pilates for Equestrians

Pilates, Joseph, compiled by Romana Kryzanowska and Sean Gallagher, PT Return to Life- The Complete Writings of Joseph Pilates, Philadelphia: Bainbridge Books, 2000.

Siler, Brooke The Pilates Body, New York: Broadway Books, 2000.

Yoga for Equestrians

Benedik, Linda and Veronica Wirth, *Yoga for Equestrians, A New Path for Achieving Union with the Horse*, North Pomfret, Vermont: Trafalgar Square Publishing, 2000.

Carrico, Mara, *Yoga Journal's Yoga Basics, The Essential Beginner's Guide to Yoga for a Lifetime of Health and Fitness*, New York: Henry Holt & Company, Inc., 1997.

Couch, Jean, *The Runner's Yoga Book, A Balanced Approach to Fitness*, Berkeley, California: Rodmell Press, 1990.

Farhi, Donna, *The Breathing Book, Good Health and Vitality Through Essential Breath Work*, New York: Henry Holt & Company Inc., 1996

Hoffman, Kevin "Hatha Yoga," *Yoga International Magazine, Reprint Series*, Honesdale, PA: The Himalayan Institute Press, 1997

Mohan, A.G, *Yoga for Body, Breath, and Mind, A Guide to Personal Reintegration*, Cambridge, MA: Rudra Press, 1993

Pierce, Margaret D. and Martin G., *Yoga for Your Life, A Practice Manual of Breath and Movement for Every Body*, Portland, Oregon: Rudra Press, 1996.

Schiffmann, Erich, *Yoga: The Spirit and Practice of Moving Into Stillness*, New York: Pocket Books, a division of Simon & Schuster, 1996.

Walton, Todd, *Open Body, Creating Your Own Yoga*, New York: Avon Books, a division of the Hearst Corporation, 1998.

Xenophon, *The Art of Horsemanship*, translated by Morris H. Morgan, Ph.D., London: J.A. Allen & Company, Ltd., 1962

Index